This collection of more than 100 bright, bold recipes, influenced by the vibrant flavors and convivial culture of the Arab world, is filled with moving personal essays on food, family, and identity mixed with a pinch of California cool from chef and activist Reem Assil

Arabiyya celebrates the alluring aromas and flavors of Arab food and the welcoming spirit with which they are shared. Written from her point of view as an Arab in diaspora, Reem takes readers on a journey through her Palestinian and Syrian roots, showing how her heritage has inspired her recipes for flatbreads, dips, snacks, platters to share, and more. With a section specializing in breads of the Arab bakery, plus recipes for favorites such as Salatet Fattoush, Falafel Mahshi, Mujaddarra, and Hummus Bil Awarma, *Arabiyya* showcases the origins and evolution of Arab cuisine and opens up a whole new world of flavor.

Alongside the tempting recipes, Reem shares stories of the power of Arab communities to turn hardship into brilliant, nourishing meals and any occasion into a celebratory feast. Reem then translates this spirit into her own work in California, creating restaurants that define hospitality at all levels. Yes, there are tender lamb dishes, piles of fresh breads, and perfectly cooked rice, but there is also food for thought about what it takes to create a more equitable society, where workers and people often at the margins are brought to the center. Reem's glorious dishes draw in readers and customers, but it is her infectious warmth that keeps them at the table.

With gorgeous photography, original artwork, and transporting writing, Reem helps readers better understand the Arab diaspora and its global influence on food and culture. She then invites everyone to sit at a table where all are welcome.

Arabiyya

Reem Assil

with Emily Katz

Foreword by Alicia Garza · Photographs by Alanna Hale · Illustrations by Cece Carpio

Arabiyya

Recipes from the Life of an Arab in Diaspora

TEN SPEED PRESS
California | New York

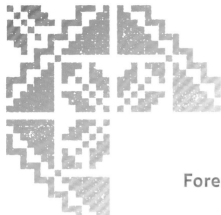

Foreword by Alicia Garza

EVERYTHING IS POLITICAL—including food.

The recipes that get handed down to us, from generation to generation, are like treasure maps and time capsules all at once. They are treasure maps because they help us find our way through roadblocks (can I substitute butter for lard?), crossroads (what happens if I put this appetizer with this main course?), and obstacle courses (can I get this done before my guests arrive?). When the food is on the table, we celebrate a sense of accomplishment for having navigated our way to the treasure, which is (hopefully) a delicious meal that puts a smile on everyone's face.

Recipes are also time capsules—they show us the ways in which those before us navigated the conditions of their lives and persevered. In my own cultural traditions, our recipes consist of the foods that were available to us, due to our social and economic status. Racism often meant that foods that were available to those in power were not available to those of us who were not. Still, we learned how to navigate these roadblocks both because of and in spite of them.

The traditional staples of my family were not as widely celebrated as they are now. Sometimes, the food you eat is a telltale sign of your social, economic, and political standing. The kale and collard greens that are so popular today were once rations that were given to enslaved people. My people learned to make these tough, leafy greens tender and delicious. Yams, sweet potatoes, and other starches were also a part of this basic diet, mostly formed from rations under enslavement. We have taken devastating times and found ways to persist, and that struggle is reflected in our food.

My best friend and I met over food—she, native Hawaiian, Japanese, Chinese, and white, and me, Black, in a mixed family, in a high school that was predominantly white. We shared a class—geometry—which neither one of us was particularly good at. Our teacher was an aging hippie with an excellent mustache who didn't believe that rows of desks provided the best learning environment, and so we sat at round tables. She and I found each other at one of those round tables, alongside another friend who was also a student of color. Every week we sat together, sharing food from our homes. I would bring fried chicken, creamed corn, greens with ham hocks, and cornbread. She would bring kalua pig and taro, or that delicious blackberry peach cobbler that her mama made that involved hours of picking blackberries across the street from their home. Our other seatmate brought food from the school cafeteria where he worked—french fries, nachos, pizza, and any candy we wanted—and we would put everything in the middle and share equally.

I looked forward to our gatherings each week. Our little round table was defiant—we were definitely more interested in what we were eating than what we were learning about shapes in space, but more than that, we'd found commonality in our differences. Through those meals, we shared our differences as well as the things we had in common. And we learned about each other through our weekly geometry banquets, which showed me the power of food to connect.

I met Reem more than a decade ago, through our organizing work. She did work specializing in building strategic partnerships between labor organizations and community-based organizations. I was working in San Francisco, at an organization fighting gentrification and displacement. Where I saw Reem really find her voice, however, was at the intersection of food and community. When she opened a bakery just a few blocks from my home, I marveled at the way in which she matched community values in front of and behind the counter. I knew that Reem employed local residents, many of whom were systems impacted or formerly incarcerated, and of color. Around her kitchen buzzed women, Black people, and people of color; immigrants, gender-non-conforming people, and queer people. I knew that Reem paid a living wage and offered generous benefits, and that she aimed to interrupt the ways in which our food industries dehumanize people. That's how I know that like everything, food is also political.

It was also political when Reem's restaurant was attacked for a mural displaying a Palestinian activist, Rasmea Odeh. I hadn't seen Reem in years, my own life having changed dramatically with the emergence of a resurgence of the Black freedom movement led by Black Lives Matter. But on one of my few days not spent on an airplane, my partner and I went to visit. There was Reem, bouncing a new baby on her hip, visiting tables in a beautifully vibrant location with bright colors. A few weeks after visiting, I heard that the bakery was being attacked in an attempt to put it at the center of conservative political rhetoric about Palestine and Palestinians—all because of the mural that greeted you when you arrived at the bakery. A mural of a Palestinian woman, who had been attacked, tortured, and demeaned for daring to be free, for daring to even assert that Palestine *exists*. I knew that Reem was Syrian and Palestinian, that her family had fled war. I knew that Reem herself and her family had endured slurs of "terrorist" and things much worse than that, simply because of the region that she hailed from. I showed up then for Reem because she is my friend, because I know her work, and I know her heart. I showed up for Reem to support her business and keep her in business—and in the process I learned more about her culture, her history, and her story.

With food, we find one another again. We learn our stories, get a window into our history and our present, and learn about how we have been resilient together in the face of unequal power. Perhaps these discoveries come from the few kids of color meeting over a round table in geometry class, or a Syrian Palestinian woman finding herself and home in food. The politics inherent to food can not only divide us, but also bring us together.

An Arab Tells Her Story

I WAS BORN in Waltham, a little town twenty minutes outside of Boston, in the hottest month of the year. Forty-eight hours had gone by since labor pains had interrupted my mother's birthday picnic beside the cooling breezes of the Charles River, where she had spread a blanket to behold the July Fourth light show. She often pointed out the irony of a birthday greeted each year by the haunting sound of pyrotechnics. A child of war, my mother had fled Gaza, Palestine, in 1967 only to land in the crossfire of an oncoming civil war in Lebanon that would fully erupt several years later. Fire-filled skies were nothing new to her.

Growing up, whenever I put up a fight, she was quick to remind me of her long, hard labor, and that from my very birth, I insisted on doing things on my own terms. Crossing the street as a toddler, she'd tell me I needed to hold her hand. "I'll hold my own hand," I would reply, clasping my hands in front of me.

From the time I could sing, I picked up refrains from Tina Turner's "What's Love Got to Do with It" and Madonna's "Papa Don't Preach," sending ripples of discomfort through my Syrian father and Palestinian mother. From their telling, I never chose the easy way. When I was upset, our entire apartment complex would hear about it. Neighbors reported that my cries could be heard from the McDonald's parking lot across the street. Sympathetic to the struggles of new parents, they laughingly called me the neighborhood terrorist. It never occurred to my parents to take offense.

My parents started me on toasted pita for teething and garlicky hummus as my first solids. However, my own earliest food memory was not of these Arab staples but rather of eating chocolate cake with my first crush, my neighbor and best friend David. Dressed only in Pampers, we dove into that cake headfirst, bathing ourselves in frosting, sucking fistfuls of the sweet goo from our hands.

One day, after learning that David's family had moved away, I escaped from our apartment to sob at the foot of his door, where I'd so often gone to find him. Soon after, we, too, would move.

My parents chose Sudbury, a woodsy suburb known for its outstanding schools and its role in the American Revolutionary War. Our home was nestled in the historical footpaths of American legends such as Babe Ruth, Ralph Waldo Emerson, and Henry David Thoreau and served as a perfect staging ground for my magic shows and theatrical performances. In elementary school, I won a starring role as Mary Poppins in the first-grade play and tested my parents' patience, practicing the songs from the moment I woke in the morning until lights-out at night. It was my dream to broadcast into people's living rooms like Julie Andrews.

Inside our home, my parents established a strong foundation of Arab culture. But outside, the customs of our well-to-do, largely white town inevitably won out. I learned to code-switch at an early age. While we spoke Arabic at home, we were encouraged to speak only English in school. Early on, my teachers pushed my parents to switch to English, worrying that my reading and writing would fall behind. My sister often joked I switched into my "white voice" on the phone or in the store, when I wanted to blend in: upbeat and high-pitched, demonstrating good vocabulary, and offering a disarming smile, especially when someone pointed out I had a "slight accent." I learned American idioms such as "the cat's out of the bag" and tried to use them correctly. Every once in a while, I would mix them up, as in "I can read him like the back of my book."

I planted a foot in both worlds. One weekend, I'd slip into my Girl Scout vest to sell cookies door-to-door, followed by memorizing verses of the Quran with my father on the way to Sunday school. The next weekend, I'd sneak into parental controls to watch Salt-N-Pepa's "Let's Talk about Sex" on MTV and later ride along with my uncles to live orchestral concerts to hear iconic Lebanese musician Marcel Khalife's brilliant political ballads saluting Palestine.

My food memories are etched with morning bowls of Kix cereal and afternoon snacks of Chips Ahoy! cookies dipped in milk; the only time you'd find me over a stovetop was to boil instant ramen packets and to make Kraft macaroni and cheese from a box. These memories also include long pot-luck dining tables, extended with desks and folding tables dragged in from other rooms, stacked with olive oil–drenched mezze dips, mountains of rice, cardamom-scented ground meat casseroles, herbed salads, and, inevitably, a box of supermarket cookies added by a family that had run out of time.

By high school, identity began to weigh large. My Arab features and olive skin tone were mistaken for every imaginable ethnic identity—from Indian to Puerto Rican. Though I didn't develop race consciousness until college, my awareness of racial injustice was born at Lincoln-Sudbury Regional High School. We were but a handful of Brown kids. While I felt uncomfortable being misidentified, I was even more fearful of saying where my family came from. I had few friends and spent lunch, book in hand, nestled into a corner of the cafeteria, lost in a world created by George Orwell and other grimly imagined futures that matched my mood.

My distress was lifted by teachers of color, few though they were, and one lefty Jewish teacher from the Bronx, whose obsession with Jack Kerouac inspired field trips to New York to hit the highlights of the Beat Generation. Taking his lead, I helped organize a trip to the Deep South, visiting places that had changed the course of American history—from Philadelphia, Mississippi, where three civil rights workers had been murdered, to Birmingham, Alabama, where a church bombing by the Ku Klux Klan had killed four young Black girls. Meeting with civil rights activists and hearing their stories helped channel my angst. I learned to question the world and imagine how I, too, might help make another, better world possible.

In each place, I became more enraged at America's legacy of white supremacy and more inspired by people who put their bodies on the line for nonviolent resistance. I began to make connections between the conditions in Mississippi and Gaza, the Montgomery bus boycott and the Palestinian intifada, and the forced migration of Black folks from the South and my own parents' migration from Palestine and Syria. I wanted to be like the change-makers who inspired me on that trip.

I set off for college, hoping to solve the issue of "peace in the Middle East." I felt a new sense of possibility, and I even told my professors that I would become the first Palestinian Muslim woman president. But soon, I recognized a familiar discomfort. Diplomacy, I learned, mostly meant maintaining US influence over the fate of countries like the ones I came from. With anti-Arab fervor erupting following the September 11 attacks my first week of college and with war looming, I fell into a deep despair. I feared for the safety of Arabs both in America and in our homelands. I couldn't imagine how it might feel to experience justice in the midst of such darkness (and cold Boston winters). I dropped out of school and found my way to sunny California. Like many before me, I fell in love with the Bay Area for its diversity and rich history of social movements. I discovered that you could actually get paid to knock on a door, walk inside, drink some tea, and inspire someone to stand up to a local corporate landlord to lower the rent. To be a part of that transformation was life-changing.

When I was not at work, I was helping transform a decades-old Arab political nonprofit into an organizing hub for working-class Arabs. Through it, I built my own Arab community. We made the streets of Oakland and San Francisco our second home, amplifying our power through bullhorns, calling for an end to the US-backed war and occupation of Iraq and building deep alliances with like-minded Black and Brown activist groups. My mother has often jokingly reminded me that when she used to visit, her itinerary often involved locating me at the intersection of a protest march route.

While I honed my skills as an organizer, I also built the kind of community I had always yearned for on a soccer team that proudly called itself anti-imperialist. On the field, I met my husband, an impassioned literacy educator, along with other teachers, artists, cultural workers, and activists, each contributing to social change in their own way. We built up our running skills to evade the police in the city's anti-war street protests and countered burnout with laughter, dance parties, and mountains of home-cooked food.

For self-care, I built an aptitude for mental calculus and straight-faced trash talk through playing poker. I represented my league at the World Series of Poker in Las Vegas and dreamed of going pro. And, at the very same time, I fell into Buddhism at Oakland's first people of color–led Buddhist center.

Yet none of these things, even when put together, fully satisfied me. Throughout my ups and downs, between episodes of burnout and heartache, I gradually recognized that working with food had become a source of emotional, even spiritual, comfort. The sense that food might provide a vehicle to connect me with my life's purpose grew, and I recognized I needed to find ways to explore it.

So, I left my job as an organizer to see whether life as a baker might nourish my spirit and connect me to my ancestors. I arrived at my first interview at Arizmendi Bakery & Pizzeria—a renowned worker-owned cooperative in the Bay Area—determined to wow them with freshly baked chocolate chip banana muffins and blueberry scones, made just the way I remembered having first tasted them years before at the Cheese Board Collective, their sister bakery in Berkeley. Going to that interview overprepared paid off, and I landed my first bakery job.

On the journey to build the bakery of my dreams, I began the same way many women do in the food business: by taking classes and hustling jobs in catering, bakeries, coffee shops, and bars. Next came pop-ups, which earned me a spot in a women's restaurant incubator program, La Cocina, an organization that provides low-cost kitchen space, business training, and sisterhood to budding entrepreneurs.

I spent hours in that kitchen working alongside women from every corner of the world: Cambodia, Senegal, Nepal, and Mexico—each day learning a bit more about the resilience that had brought them to this launching pad for women's food business ownership. I watched in awe as they established ventures that not only expressed their lineage through food but also built wealth for their people. I had an epiphany: my future bakery, Reem's California, would do more than just tell my peoples' stories. It would also create good jobs and build community, wherever it found a home.

From La Cocina's shared commercial kitchen, I opened farmers' market stalls, where I hauled a saj, a traditional dome-shaped griddle custom-welded for me in the mountains of Lebanon, from market to market. I set out to master mana'eesh, the za'atar-topped bread that was a quintessential street food of my parents' childhood. Word of our mana'eesh spread, and soon we were selling out at the markets. Long lines and happy eaters attracted media buzz, and a few years later, La Cocina scouted a corner spot for me on a major

transit line in Oakland's Fruitvale neighborhood, far from the rapidly gentrifying food and yoga clusters farther north. This area was Oakland's most racially diverse neighborhood. I knew, instantly, I had found the first home for my Arab street corner bakery.

Man'oushe, the Arabic word for a single serving of this bread, derives from the Arabic verb *naqasha* (*na'asha* in colloquial Arabic), meaning "to shape, engrave, chisel, indent" or more literally, to stretch out and dimple the dough with your fingertips, creating wells for the spice mix and olive oil to seep into the bread. That act of kneading, rounding, stretching, and shaping dough has brought me joy over the last decade, and that joy is a key part of this cookbook. This book is about not just food but also about the communities and culture that inform it.

I have titled this cookbook *Arabiyya*, which translates to "Arab woman," as a declaration of who I am. Claiming my Arab identity in a country where being Arab can get you jailed or, in my experience, make you a magnet for death threats, is a form of resistance. The recipes in this book are recipes for resilience. Many of them center on bread, a longstanding obsession of mine, as the lifeline of Arab history. Eating bread is a sacred communal act. The bread I offer in my recipes is a living thing, borne of yeasts and shaped by our own hands. Reaching into a basket for a warm round pita, ripping off bite-size pieces, and eating with our hands from the same shared plate, we feed our hearts along with our bodies.

This book is an homage to Arab hospitality. In my research, one story emerges again and again: when we encounter strangers, we welcome them into our homes, establish bonds, and even learn from the food practices of our guests. Arab hospitality is how my people have survived desert travel, wars, and invasions, and it inspires the dishes I create. That lineage is a beautiful thing, worth tracing and celebrating.

In this book, I refer to my parents' homeland as the Arab world, which means primarily Arabic-speaking countries, but I also refer to it as Southwest Asia and North Africa (SWANA) rather than the colonial construct of Middle East (middle of whose east? one might ask). SWANA is inclusive of the region's many ethnic groups who influence the cuisine. Practically speaking, that means the food I serve at my restaurant and the recipes in this book aren't identifiable as solely Lebanese, Palestinian, or Syrian. So many of our dishes have North African, Armenian, or Ottoman lineage, because all of these countries once made up a single region before colonial forces came in and broke it up. To distinguish the specific region my parents are from, I use Belad al Sham-Arabic for Greater Syria interchangeably with the Levant, a term bestowed by the French when they and the British determined our borders. I admit there are some contradictions and limitations in this language that I've not yet solved.

Despite our deep-rooted hospitality, there is friendly competition among Arabs in the region, over whose rendition of a dish is superior, as with the green spice mix za'atar (the name for both the herb and the mix). Some people call the herb that makes it wild thyme; others call it oregano. Jordanians, Lebanese, Syrians, and Palestinians each claim their za'atar spice mix sets the standard and that others are only imitations. In the end, everyone is right; it's their truth.

I am not as concerned with the ownership of dishes the way some food writers are but more with sharing the context in which they are eaten and served. Jockeying for ownership, I feel, disconnects the food from its many influences and the

people who make it. However, in some circumstances, as in our case as Palestinians, claiming (or reclaiming, as I like to call it) ownership of food becomes a tool of resistance. Communities like ours have been invisibilized by the takeover of our foods as a way to cut us off from our lineage. This process is called food theft and is a form of conquest and ethnic cleansing. Where I see it, I always name it.

And finally, this book is a celebration of place; in my case, California. Cooking and sharing food are ways to make a place our home, wherever we may be. In these recipes, I celebrate the resourcefulness and healthful nourishment of Arab cooking, bringing flavors of the homeland to life with the bounty of ingredients available to me. These are proudly "Arab" recipes because they reflect us: vibrant in color and taste, made with fresh local ingredients, and unafraid of bold flavors.

Take this book as an invitation to experience the joy Arab food has brought me. I hope that in sharing my story and my struggles, you will find here inspiration for your own pursuits and nourishment to carry you on your own path. At the very least, every dish can be savored alone, shared with family, or offered as connection with others, as you find your own rhythm in the dance of hospitality.

Part One

HOW TO
Host Like an Arab

There came a moment each summer, during visits to my grandparents' Los Angeles home, when my grandmother would declare the time had come for a mountain picnic. The trip meant leaving the heat of the San Fernando Valley for the San Gabriel Mountains to the north. After she finished her morning fenjan 'ahwah, a tiny tapered ceramic cup of bitter morning coffee, my grandmother would fill not one, but two thermoses with Arabic coffee and another with maramiyah, Ceylon tea brewed with dried sage leaves from Palestine.

Out came the coolers and ice packs to stow hunks of cheese wrapped in wax paper along with tomatoes protected in perfectly fitted plastic boxes. Fruits and cucumbers would be washed and packed into more boxes. She'd transfer her stash of roasted pumpkin and watermelon seeds into smaller bags and decant a pint or two from her gallon jug of home-spiced olives into travel-size containers. When everything was set, she'd ask if I wanted sweets, and a final tin of syrupy namoura semolina bars and nut-filled baklava would be nestled into the cooler.

In the fresh air and expansive view from the mountains, my grandmother's joy was infectious. It was impossible not to get swept away by her enthusiasm. Hospitality, for her, was not restricted to the walls of her home. She could create the feeling of abundance wherever she was.

I wonder now if my grandmother's outdoor rituals reminded her of the summers she had spent escaping Beirut's heat for the mountains of Lebanon. Where my grandmother was over-the-top opulent (if two dessert options are good, three is surely better), my own disposition is fairly practical. For someone who has staked a claim in the food world on the principle of Arab hospitality, I'm not, actually, all that domestic. It's not in my nature to scrub my house for you and lavish you with sweets, until you drag yourself away, a hand in the air, bursting at the seams. That person was my grandmother.

My grandmother Nabigha Anani, the fifth child of nine, was born in Jaffa (Yaffa in Arabic), Palestine, to an orange-growing family. At age ten, she and her siblings climbed aboard a raft, fleeing militia from pre-state Israel, who took over her uncle's farm. Her family had refused to leave their land during forced land evacuations and were met with settlers, who extracted, at gunpoint, the cultivation techniques for producing the family's Jaffa oranges, the product that had made the region famous. Her uncle was brought to the field and forced to watch his workers and foreman lined up before a trench and killed execution style. He was released to tell the story of the impossible brutality as a message to others: you will not be returning.

My grandmother and her siblings were among the 700,000 Palestinians who were expelled in the spring of 1948 to create Israel. Many, like the workers on their farm, did not make it out alive. We call this time the *Nakba*, Arabic for "the great catastrophe."

The next seven years would find my grandmother recovering the bounce in her step and her sense of assuredness, even as she adjusted to life forty miles south of her family's estate—as a refugee in Gaza. Her optimism and beauty made her hard to miss, and at age seventeen, she found herself trading glances with the handsome boy at the local Mercedes-Volkswagen dealership, as she passed by on her daily errands. The boy knew immediately that he was in love and made what would be the first of many stands on behalf of my grandmother, refusing his family's matchmaking efforts and courting the girl who had won his heart.

That boy was my grandfather, Tahsin Kishawi, a teenager with an uncanny knack for numbers and hard-driving instincts, honed on the Palestinian National Football Team (what we call soccer here). My grandfather came from a prominent Gazan family with far-flung enterprises that included car dealerships, textiles, and citrus farms.

In the search for an heir to take over the family's business interests, my grandfather, at age seventeen, was pulled from school for the role. Soon, his wholesale textile business picked up, and he bet big, expanding into an abandoned three-story Barclays Bank building in Gaza City. The gamble paid off, as the trickle of Egyptians arriving on charter buses from across the border turned into a flood. Late-night shoppers kept him open until 3 o'clock in the morning, as they pored over his selection of European fabrics that were no longer available in shops nationalized by Egypt's new revolutionary president, Gamal Abdel Nasser.

My grandparents married soon after, and my grandfather's businesses flourished. By the time my mother, their eldest, turned four, they had moved to a waterfront villa on the Mediterranean Sea. But in the summer of 1967, they were tipped off by a neighbor, a senior officer in the Egyptian military, about a pending invasion from Israel. They prepared a hasty trip to Lebanon, hoping to flee for a short while to avoid the same kind of violence that had made my grandmother a refugee. It was hard to imagine they wouldn't be returning soon, so my grandparents packed a few personal items, withdrew twenty-five thousand liras, and rented a summer home in the Lebanese mountains. Over the course of the war, Israeli forces confiscated their Gaza home and all of the family businesses.

Summer turned to winter, and everyone remembers the chill in that home, equipped only for use during the warmer months. My grandfather recognized that Lebanon would now be his family's new home, but he worried for their safety since the Lebanese government viewed Muslim Palestinian refugees as a demographic threat to the ruling Christian minority. Calling on a family connection, my grandfather secured Jordanian citizenship papers to conceal their Palestinian identity and signed the lease on an apartment in West Beirut, before heading to Kuwait to start a wholesale textile business to generate income for his family. There, he lived and slept in his shop for three years, saving up to rejoin the family and relaunch his business in Lebanon.

I'd like to think that I've inherited something of my grandfather's entrepreneurial resilience. Over the course of his life, he built and rebuilt his businesses too many times to count, as the family bounced among seven countries. His second great loss came in the 1980s, when Lebanon's civil war was five years underway. Shelling and bombing wiped out the textiles my grandfather stored in the port, and the retailers holding fabrics on commission defaulted. Once again, he lost nearly everything.

As they adjusted to the war, my grandmother and grandfather each assumed a role to secure the family's safety and survival. He was the financial provider and she was determined to gird her family with thrift, and bread. The bakeries became a bombing target; she made sure my grandfather never stood in the bakery lines for bread and often baked her own, repurposing dry scraps into chips and puddings.

At gatherings, my family loves to tell the story of a time my grandmother, short on supplies, dashed out for lemons during a lull in the bombing. A local fisherman had supplied his fresh catch, and, as everyone knows, it's impossible to serve fish without lemon. She made it down to the pier and found a lone vendor, trying to get out of the crossfire. Lemons in hand, she asked him whether rockets were coming from the east or the west. "Ma'am," he replied in dry Lebanese fashion, "I didn't ask them."

On her way home, a rocket swept her down the street in its undertow, knocking her unconscious. When she awoke, she asked the person who'd pulled her to safety, "Am I in heaven?" And then, just as quickly, "Where are my lemons?"

One of the things that stands out to me, as the injustice of my grandparents' stories rattles around in my bones, is my grandmother's ebullience in the face of adversity. Despite seeing the worst of what people could do to each other, she brought an open heart to each place she landed.

The lifelong friendship she forged with her neighbor Rougie, a refugee like her, helped her feel more at home in Lebanon. Rougie had escaped to Palestine in 1944, when German Nazis invaded Hungary, her homeland. She was taken in by a Palestinian family and eventually met her husband,

Simone, who was part of the resistance. They fled to Beirut after 1948, when Zionist militia invaded Simone's home and killed his family.

Rougie and my grandmother sat together for coffee each morning, over Rougie's sfoof, a lovely turmeric-infused cake that my grandmother would later add to her own baking repertoire. After they had shopped for groceries, she and Rougie would often spend afternoons in a salon, their hair set in curlers and nails painted to perfection. They had already seen the worst of two wars and were determined to preserve some sense of normalcy. The two shared a sisterly companionship against the backdrop of war. Later, when sectarian war endangered my grandmother's family, Rougie would offer to house-sit the family's apartment to secure it from Christian militia, who targeted Muslim homes.

The year 1982 was a turning point in the Lebanese Civil War. Israel bombarded Beirut by air, land, and sea in a scorched-earth campaign, cutting off food, water, and electricity in Palestinian refugee camps and neighborhoods. Under Israel's military occupation, Lebanese militia entered the Sabra and Shatila Palestinian refugee camps right outside of Beirut, and brutally massacred thousands of Palestinians and anyone thought to be supporting the Palestinian resistance. My grandparents knew they had to leave, once again, to keep the family safe.

My grandmother flew to the United States to help my newly immigrated mother settle in her new life, while the rest of the family found a way to escape through a Christian caravan, on the safest and shortest route out of East Beirut. The story goes that my grandfather, in a standoff at the checkpoint, turned the car around and left the caravan of travelers for a longer, but safer, road to Damascus. Later they found out the caravan had been bombed.

A year later, the family returned to Lebanon, hoping to resume their lives. Instead, things had gotten even harder. While they had been gone, Harakat Amal, a Shiite Lebanese political party, had turned the family home into a staging area for fighters. The family received word that Harakat Amal was demanding a bounty for my grandfather on the pretext that objectionable political propaganda had been found in the home. They had uncovered a pamphlet in a stack of one of the kid's school papers that promoted one of the opposition parties. It was not uncommon to target middle-class businessmen in order to raise funds for political parties.

While my grandfather was lying low at the home of one of his regular customers, my grandmother, back from the United States, resolved to clear my grandfather's name and reclaim their apartment. She pushed her way past the militia into the commander's office and convinced him to evict his team from the apartment. That night, to secure the home, she slept there alone. However, some of the militia, unhappy with their leader's decision, placed a small deposit of dynamite sticks at the front door, in a jumble with family photos, souvenirs, and collectibles. The next morning, she opened her apartment door and gingerly stepped over the explosives to recover whatever memorabilia she could carry, then met up with my grandfather and declared, "We're done." The family climbed aboard a dinghy to Cyprus and from there, went on to Greece to start a new life.

Looking back, I sense my grandmother's grit, facing risk with fearless determination. When I hear family retell the story, I also hear the echoes of my grandfather's voice, shouting the words that trailed my grandmother, as she dashed out the screen door to the patio of their Los Angeles home, balancing a tray of Arabic coffee, or darting across the kitchen to lift a pot too heavy for her arthritic wrists: "*Istenny! Istenny shway!* (Wait! Wait a sec!)" I love the irony of his protective gestures toward a woman unafraid to confront armed militia. Perhaps protecting each other had become, over time, reflexive.

I remember waking on family visits to find my grandmother in her lacy nightgown, smelling of face creams and tonics, her hair loosely curled, sitting at the kitchen table, a glass of tea in its saucer, peeling a head of garlic for the afternoon feast. I appreciated her enduring elegance; she never allowed her status as a refugee to define her. Her Palestinian identity was seen as a threat first in Lebanon and then again in the United States, and yet, she moved with grace and brought her gift for creating the warmth of Arab hospitality with her to each new home.

Upheaval, beginning with the rheumatic fever she had contracted when she fled to Gaza, left my grandmother with health issues, eventually leading to a heart condition and triple bypass surgery. A lifetime of medications and surgeries further weakened her system and resulted in dementia.

I barely knew my grandmother's story. I only pieced it together after her death, learning versions of it from aunts and uncles and from my mother. My grandmother rarely spoke of the past, and as her memories faded, I lost my chance to ask. I didn't link my own journey to hers at first. I just knew I longed for something that was missing. As I have built a business and a life of purpose, rooted in our Arab food ways, I've come to realize that my grandmother, who loaded the table to its edges with tasty morsels of my favorite foods, lives through me. I'm determined to tell the story of our family and of our people with the fire that ignited my grandmother and to live my life with joy, dignity, and maybe just a touch of her fashion sensibility.

Setting Up Your Kitchen

YOU COULD SMELL roasting meats from my grandmother's oven before you even opened the front door. As we made our way toward the kitchen, the aroma of spices and herbs intensified. Her kitchen was the summer landing pad for our large extended family: all five of my mother's siblings, along with their spouses and kids. We'd laugh and talk over each other, while my grandmother dashed around the kitchen, jamming snacks onto the middle of the table.

No spontaneous guest ever caught my grandmother unprepared. When the Northridge earthquake brought the city of Los Angeles to a standstill, a family friend braved the broken freeways and bridges to check up on my grandparents, only to find the garage doors rolled up and my grandmother inside, boiling Arabic coffee on a camping stove and dishing out baklava.

Many staples of Arab cookery reside in the spice aisles and in the international sections of local grocery chains. In most major cities, Arab grocers carry every ingredient listed here. If no Arab grocer has set up shop in your neighborhood, all the items are a few clicks away at specialty purveyors, who source excellent single-origin products. See page 286 for my favorite spice and specialty ingredient suppliers. I recommend substitutes as well, so you can improvise with the ingredients you have on hand.

I've organized these lists to match my own kitchen. Through my restaurant experience and the years spent learning about my cuisine, I've become comfortable using the ingredients and tools I used to ignore in my childhood kitchen.

Stocking your kitchen with the ingredients in this section will ensure you'll be ready to cook from this cookbook and whip up Arab flavors at a moment's notice.

THE ESSENTIAL PANTRY

We always joked that my mother stocked her pantry as if we were preparing for the apocalypse. After the 2020 pandemic, that doesn't seem so farfetched. I like to bulk up on the following items since they are shelf stable.

Canned Tomatoes

Many veggie and meat recipes call for tomatoes stewed down to a sauce. Both fresh and canned work well. I keep canned San Marzano tomatoes on hand for their balance of sweetness and acidity.

Grains

Arabs mostly use long-grain basmati rice to accompany one-pot stews, but for stuffing, we go for medium-grained jasmine or short-grained Arborio rice that creates a nice absorbent filling. Stock up on fine bulgur for many of the dishes in this book; it's usually labeled bulgur #1. The darker it is, the less refined and the more nutritious. Other specialty grains included are freekeh, cracked green wheat with a smoky flavor, and maftool, a large

Palestinian couscous made from bulgur or from a wheat and bulgur mixture.

Flower Waters

Orange blossom water and rose water douse all manner of Arab sweets with blossomy springtime no matter the time of year. These floral essences are available at many chain grocery stores, but if you are unable to find them, make your own by submerging fresh orange blossoms or rose petals in a saucepan with water, just enough to cover, and bring to a simmer. Then cook at the lowest setting for 15 minutes; cool completely before straining and bottling. Store in an airtight container in the refrigerator for up to a month.

Legumes

I use both dried and canned beans. When I have time for a presoak, dried beans produce a better product, but let's face it, it can often be hard to think a day ahead. If you are blessed to have an Instant Pot, dried beans can go straight into it. I keep the basics on hand: chickpeas and a varietal of fava bean called ful madammas, which is also a mezze staple (see page 151). I also keep lentils, both brown and red, on hand; these are integral to Arab cuisine.

Molasses

Arabs use a variety of fruity molasses to sweeten drinks, swirl into tahini to scoop with bread on the mezze breakfast table, or even in meat marinades. I mostly use pomegranate molasses. It complements both bright flavors and darker warming spices beautifully. If you cannot find it at your Arab grocery store or on the specialty shelf in your local grocery store, it's simple to make. Just cook down any available pomegranate juice on a low simmer, until it's reduced to a quarter of its volume. It should be thick to the touch and heavily coat your spoon.

Nuts

I keep shelled pistachios, walnuts, almonds, and pine nuts on hand for both savory and sweet dishes. Pistachios from the Arab world are far different from the ones you will find at a conventional grocery store. They have a brighter green color and a slightly sweet, edible purplish cover with an earthy tone. If you have access to a local international store, it is worth the investment to buy from small-scale regional producers. You can also get pistachios roasted in the shells for snacking. All nuts will keep better in resealable bags in the refrigerator or freezer if you can spare the room.

Oils

For Arab cooking, I stock neutral oils such as canola, sunflower, or grapeseed for frying and roasting along with richer varieties of olive oils for mixing, drizzling, and everything else.

Oil used for frying can be strained back into a clean jar, cooled, and then refrigerated for several more uses. Once your oil is a deep dark golden color or acquires a bitter metallic aroma, it can be recycled or thrown away.

To make the recipes in this book, you'll need ample olive oil on hand. In Arab cooking, olive oil is an ingredient unto itself and is not simply a function of food preparation. A generous moat of olive oil tops hummus and most of the mezze dishes in our cuisine. My son slurps olive oil by the spoonful. It's one of the ways I know he's Palestinian. Never pass up locally pressed oil if it crosses your path. If it's pricey, it's probably worth it. When it comes to olive oil, cheaper is almost never better.

Tahini

Tahini translates to ground sesame; its seeds provide the most ancient source of cooking oil known to humanity, and its creamy nuttiness forms the

base for many of our dishes. I prefer a lighter-color tahini, made from hulled seeds, and brands that stir more easily since solids settle, making it harder to reincorporate them. A darker-color tahini, made from unrefined seeds, is a little more bitter. It's worth your time to sample a few small jars to discover the differences and to find your favorite.

Salt

I use two types of salt: kosher for cooking and flakes of coarser sea salt to top finished dishes. Diamond Crystal kosher salt comes in a three-pound box. I prefer it to Morton's, which is twice as salty. Yes, the same measure is actually double the salinity. If you're using anything other than Diamond Crystal for the recipes in this book, reduce the salt by half and adjust to taste from there. Kosher salts simply mean the crystals are larger. I like the way they rub onto meats. Kosher salts take a little longer to dissolve, so stir your dish between pinches when you're adding salt.

Shatta

THE hot sauce of the Arab world, this fermented red chile paste takes just about any savory dish to the next level. There are a variety of brands available at Arab groceries; I like mine with garlic. Homemade hot chile paste goes a long way, so if you feel inspired, see Shatta (page 44). Vietnamese chile garlic sauce makes a comparable substitute.

Vinegars

I keep vinegars on hand for pickling and salad dressings. My go-to staples are apple cider and white balsamic or champagne vinegars for a touch of sweetness.

SPICES

Nothing is more Arab than a kitchen with spice-scented cabinets. Over the years, layer upon layer of spices seep into the wood, leaving a scented trail to the kitchen's history. As a kid, the smell of our cabinets filled me with an embarrassment I couldn't name, but with three thousand miles between me and my mom's cooking, just a whiff of the pantry in the homes of Arab friends sends ripples of nostalgia through my body. You'll need a LOT of spices for Arab cooking. Buying spices whole, toasting them, and powdering them in a spice grinder or mortar and pestle is a game changer. They not only will taste richer but will also stay fresher a lot longer.

See pages 20–21 for a breakdown of spices I stock in my cupboard and some work-around suggestions in case you don't have these spices on hand. Two spice mixes, Saba'a Baharat (page 26) and Khalta Harra (page 27) scaffold most of my meats and stews with warm, earthy notes. Making small batches to have on hand accelerates the cooking process. Spice mixes will keep fresh for months in resealable bags or in airtight containers in the freezer.

VEGGIES AND HERBS

Having fresh herbs, chiles, and flavor builders on hand gives a dazzling bump to mezze, main dishes, stews, and salads—just about any savory dish in Arab cuisine. My grandmother used to wrap her herbs and chiles in paper towels and newspaper and then tuck the bundles in the vegetable drawer in the refrigerator to keep them fresh longer. When herbs start to wilt, you can also wrap and freeze them for later use.

Below is a list of my go-to veggies and herbs.

IN THE REFRIGERATOR	AT ROOM TEMPERATURE
Cilantro Cucumbers Dill Flat-leaf parsley Mint Serrano or jalapeño chiles	Garlic Onions (red and yellow) Lemons Tomatoes (Roma for cooking, Early Girl for salads, Toy Box cherry for flatbreads)

DAIRY

Arab cuisine, breakfasts and pastries in particular, is rich in fermented dairy, boosting microorganisms that aid digestion. These staples, which I've listed below, were always in the refrigerators of my mother and grandmother. They can be added to any breakfast or snack and will make possible numerous dishes in this book, without having to make an extra trip to the store.

Akkawi Cheese

A salty, brined cow's cheese from the eponymous coastal city of Akka (which appears on maps today as Acre). Akkawi is eaten fresh with fruits and vegetables, crumbled over Mana'eesh (page 77), and, most famously, desalinated in a water bath and melted into Knafeh (page 265), a phyllo-crusted sweet cheese dessert.

Feta Cheese

I take a page from my grandmother and go for the creamier Bulgarian or French sheep's milk feta cheese.

Halloum

A little harder than Akkawi, Halloum (Arabic for Halloumi cheese) keeps for months unopened and is great to have on hand to fry up for breakfast and serve with scrambled eggs or to sprinkle over salads.

Labneh

This was a go-to staple in my pantry while growing up. Thicker, tangier, and more complex than your average Greek yogurt, labneh results from the simple process of removing whey from yogurt. The more whey that is removed, the thicker and richer it gets. My grandmother used to strain it to the point of a goat cheese consistency, roll it into balls, and preserve them in oil. Many stores now sell labneh. You can either purchase it or make your own at home. To make at home: For every cup of whole milk yogurt, mix in ¼ teaspoon of kosher salt, then scrape the yogurt into a fine cheesecloth, tied tightly and suspended over a sink or bowl; drain overnight. My mom used to hang it outside for our neighbor's dog to lap up the whey drippings.

Samneh

Samneh is clarified butter. You can make your own (see page 96) or buy ghee (the two are interchangeable). Why bother to clarify butter? Without its milk solids, samneh's burn point is a hundred degrees higher, allowing your pastries to brown beautifully without burning.

Whole Milk Yogurt

Whole milk yogurt is essential for making labneh, to use as the base for savory hot dishes, and to serve as a cold accompaniment to rice dishes.

FREEZER

I love storing premade stocks, dough, and meats to get a head start on many of the recipes in this book. Freezing baked pita bread and pastries to revive at a moment's notice is also another crafty way to impress guests with little effort. The following additional items are the main ingredients I keep on hand for hosting.

Coffee Beans

Freezing coffee is the best way to preserve the flavor and integrity of the beans, and I grind mine right before brewing. However, I often get Arabic (or Turkish, as many places call it) coffee preground to the fineness it needs to be to execute a perfect boiled pot. I freeze those grounds as well. If your beans are whole, you'll need a very fine grind similar to that of an espresso to make Ahwa Arabi (page 275).

Nut and Seed Mixes

My grandmother packed her freezer to the brim with varied mixes of nuts and seeds. Her favorite was roasted watermelon seeds. Since nuts and seeds do go rancid, freezing is a surefire way to preserve the freshness of your snacks for hikes and day trips.

Phyllo Dough

Phyllo's thin sheets store easily in the freezer to use for beautifully layered sweets or savory wraps to impress family and guests alike. A good phyllo is the perfect balance between a strong dough and delicate texture.

Shredded Phyllo Dough

Shredded phyllo dough, sometimes named kataifi, is the key ingredient for Knafeh (page 265). If you are planning to wow guests with this quintessential Palestinian delicacy, make sure to have shredded phyllo on hand.

TOOLS AND EQUIPMENT

It won't break the bank to have the tools you need to cook like an Arab. These are eight tools I've come to rely on, especially for bread making, spice prep, and coffee.

Bench and Bowl Scrapers

These flat rectangular scrapers come in handy when making breads and sweet pastries in many of the recipes in this book. Mine are always within reach. Gripped across the top, they make scooping out batters and cutting dough easier, functioning like an extension of your hand. You can purchase these at any well-stocked kitchen store or online.

Digital Scale

Many of my recipes were converted to a volume suitable for home cooking. This took some doing, since it required that I shift from my professional cook mindset of precision and production to the right balance of deliciousness and ease for home cooking. Most of the baking recipes in this book include both volume and weight measurements, so there will be no doubt in your mind what I mean when I call for a cup of flour, which can vary in weight. Scales are affordable and can be purchased at most homeware stores or ordered online.

Ice Cream Scoops

When I took up baking, I found myself purchasing different-size scoops to evenly portion batters and cookie dough without getting my hands all sticky. I have suggested a scoop for many recipes in this book. I recommend a two-ounce scoop with a release mechanism for its rounded ball shape and its ease of use.

Pizza Tools

Technically, this cookbook has no pizzas. However, the flatbreads synonymous with Arab cuisine require a high-heat hearth just like a pizza oven, and that's where specialty tools can give home ovens an extra edge. Investing in a pizza peel (a shovel-like tool to slide large flatbreads in and out of the oven) and a flat pizza stone can replicate the effect of a professional oven. There is nothing like Mana'eesh (page 77) with beautifully browned crusts. I also invested in a wheel-shaped pizza cutter to divide my flatbreads into pieces for sharing without displacing the toppings.

Rakweh

A rakweh doesn't have a direct translation in English, but it refers to a distinctive copper pitcher used to make Arabic coffee. Growing up, the rakweh had a specially reserved spot on our stove, awaiting spoons of Arabic coffee that were then boiled into a rich espresso-like drink (see page 275). But the pot isn't used only for coffee. A stainless-steel version, called a Turkish warmer, available at Bed Bath and Beyond, costs less than $10. It's a perfect no-spill, dishwasher-friendly pot for whipping up small batches of sauce, reducing gravy,

melting chocolate, making Attar (page 97), toasting seeds, or steeping tea. Its tapered shape helps brings a small volume of liquid to a boil, minimizing the splatter that causes burns. I believe my mother would approve of this hack.

Rolling Pin and Dowel

In the bread chapter, you will be rolling out a lot of dough. I prefer a French rolling pin with its tapered edges for easier control. To make the turnovers, a dowel comes in handy for rolling those smaller pieces of dough. These dowels can be found, for just a few dollars, in Asian specialty stores, since they are an essential tool for making dumplings.

Spice or Coffee Grinder

In Arab cooking, you nail the flavors by preserving their quality. For as little as $15 or $20, a little electric grinder will maximize the flavors of the food you cook. Buying spices whole and then roasting and grinding them a little at a time preserves their pungency. I offer a few key spice recipes you can premix to have on hand, but it takes less than three minutes to warm a pan and dry-roast single spices. This releases the aromatic oils before grinding and increases their intensity. A spice grinder can also double as a coffee bean grinder. If you're using one device for both purposes, grind and discard a tablespoon of rice between uses.

Instant-Read Thermometer

You can take out some of the guesswork in the baking and sweets recipes by using a $15 instant-read thermometer online or at a kitchen supply store.

SPICE	WHY IT'S SO MAGICAL	WHAT IT'S USED FOR	A GOOD SUBSTITUTE
Aleppo pepper FILFIL HALABI فلفل حلبي	This fruity, mild chile mix comes from the food mecca of Aleppo, Syria. Semi-dried and coarsely ground, sweet and tart notes temper its mild kick. The ongoing civil war has made Aleppo pepper scarce and has opened a market for imitations. It's worth the extra effort to hunt down this deeply aromatic pepper.	Meat rubs, garnishes, sauces, marinades, vinaigrettes	Cayenne and sweet paprika mix or crushed red pepper flakes
Allspice BAHARAT بهارات	Warming and powerfully intense, this aromatic spice serves as the dominant flavor in many savory Arab spice mixes. Baharat translates to the universal word for "spices," the same name we use for our seven-spice mix (see opposite).	Stews and braises, meat rubs, marinades, rice	Equal parts cinnamon, nutmeg, and cloves
Anise YANSOON يانسون	Its licorice flavor speckles sweets across the Arab world, and it's no wonder, since it's among the oldest spices in the region. It's stocked in Arab kitchens for its medicinal qualities, aiding digestion and relieving stress, and it's added to babies' bottles to help them sleep. It's also distilled with grapes to make the ubiquitous Arab spirit arak.	Cakes, cookies, sweet breads, candies, medicinal drinks, arak	Fennel or caraway, anise liquor like ouzo, Pernod, or arak
Black pepper FILFIL ASWAD فلفل اسود	Whole, freshly ground peppercorns really do make a difference. Pepper that's oxidized loses its bright flavor and some of its digestive health properties.	Most savory dishes, both fresh and cooked	A pinch of hot pepper, ground or flakes
Caraway KARAWYA كراوية	Spicy and sweet seeds essential to Meghli (page 255), a special rice pudding served at births.	Breads, puddings	Fennel or anise
Cardamom HUB AL-HAIL حب الهال	Among the most ancient spices in the world, this pungent spice delivers a fruity, piney, menthol flavor. I use it in both sweet and savory dishes, but my first love for it is brewing whole pods in Arabic coffee (see page 275).	Grains, stocks, sweets, desserts, coffee, tea	No close substitute, but mix cinnamon and nutmeg, if you must!
Cinnamon QIRFEH قرفة	Cinnamon is a workhorse of the American pantry and for good reason! This sweet bark will lend a warm Arab flair to meat, grain, and dessert dishes if you don't have other options on hand.	Meat rubs, grains, desserts	Nutmeg or allspice
Cloves QURUNFUL قرنفل	A powerful warming medicinal spice. A little goes a long way; it can be slightly astringent if used to excess.	Stews and braises, teas; can be applied whole to soothe toothaches!	Nutmeg
Coriander KUZBIRAH كزبرة	Perfect balance of nutty, spicy, warm flavor with citrus undertones. When toasted and ground, these flavors release maximum intensity.	Stews, sauces, meat rubs, marinades, pickling	Cumin or garam masala
Cumin KAMMOON كمون	Perhaps the most widely used spice for its complex warm, earthy, sweetness, tempered by subtle bitter undertones. Appreciated for myriad health benefits including serving as an anti-inflammatory, controlling blood sugar, fighting parasites, and adding iron.	Stews, sauces, meats, beans	Coriander or garam masala
Dillseed AIN JARADEH عين الجرادة	Grassy yet licorice taste; a milder version of caraway. *Ain jaradeh* translates to "grasshopper's eye."	Salads, pickles	Caraway

SPICE	WHY IT'S SO MAGICAL	WHAT IT'S USED FOR	A GOOD SUBSTITUTE
Dried lemon or lime LAYMOON JAF ليمون جاف	Sun-dried with a bitter, citrusy, fermented flavor.	Rubs, marinades	Lemon or lime zest
Dried mint NA'NA' YABIS نعناع يابس	Strong, sweet, and cooling.	Meats, marinades, yogurt dishes, salad dressings, fruits, tea	Fresh mint
Fenugreek HILBEH حلبة	Sweet, nutty cross between maple and celery; said to aid a woman's milk production.	Sweets, tea	Anise or fennel
Mahlab MAHLAB محلب	A kernel extracted from the pit of St. Lucie cherries. Combines subtle bitter almond and traces of cherry.	Sweet breads, cookies, holiday desserts	Almond extract or amaretto
Mastic MISTIKA مستكة	Granules of tree resin. Makes ice cream and pudding stretchy. Adds a subtle fresh cedar scent unique to Arab cooking.	Breads and pastries, ice cream, puddings, chewing gum	Cornstarch or sorghum
Nigella seeds HABBAT AL BARAKEH حبة البركة	Floral, peppery, slightly bitter.	Breads, cheeses, seed mixes	Black caraway seeds or black sesame seeds
Saffron ZA'FERAAN زعفران	Adds a vibrant color and distinct musty sweetness to dishes.	Sauces, soups, rice, desserts	Turmeric
Seven-Spice Mix SABA'A BAHARAT سبع بهارات	My version of this seven-spice mix is warm, earthy, nutty, and sweet. Keep a batch on hand, and you'll be ready to make most of the mains and sides.	Meats, grains	Allspice; any element of Seven-Spice Mix (page 26)
Sumac SOUMMAA' سماق	Ground berry from the sumac shrub. Sour, fruity, bright. It's a perfect alternative to citrus and adds acidity and a beautiful crimson color. Doubles as a meat tenderizer.	Meats, salads, garnishes	Lemon zest with a pinch of Maldon sea salt
Turmeric KURKUM كركم	Strong, mustard-like flavor. Comes from a root in the ginger family and adds a vibrant yellow color. Not all turmeric is created equally, so cheaper isn't always better here.	Stocks, rice, desserts	Ginger or saffron
Za'atar زعتر	I could write a whole ode to za'atar (see page 24); some people refer to it as hyssop or wild thyme, while others say Syrian oregano. I recommend substitutes reluctantly. See my list of purveyors (page 286) for how to source yours. The spice mix is special when you customize it to your taste at home, but there are plenty of great premixes. Check for ingredients listing wild thyme, sumac, sesame seeds, salt . . . there shouldn't be anything else added.	Meats, dressings, breads, condiments, yogurt dishes, a balm for a broken heart—EVERYTHING!	It's irreplaceable but in a pinch, oregano, marjoram, or thyme

Chapter One

Spice Mixes and Pantry Snacks

ZA'ATAR · زعتر

Wild Thyme, Sumac, and Sesame Mix

Makes 1 cup

NUTTY, TART, HERBACEOUS za'atar is a beloved spice mix of my childhood. No Arab household from the Levant is complete without it. Activated by heat, za'atar in olive oil emits an irresistible savory scent. When I was building my bakery, I joked about creating a fan system to blow the za'atar scent into the street to lure people in, just as with Mrs. Field's Cookies. That ploy turned out to be unnecessary, however, since curiosity quickly turns to delight after people taste za'atar for the first time. I'm often asked if the taste can be bottled up to take home. Luckily, since this is a spice mix, it can!

Za'atar is the ultimate superfood of Greater Syria, or Bilad al Sham. It has antiseptic qualities, helping to strengthen immunity and prevent foodborne illnesses, and it contains iron, supporting bone strength and blood circulation. Many Arabs I know say their mothers used to feed them za'atar before a big test to improve memory; enthusiasts insist the medical research backs them up. It doesn't take a scientist to affirm that the power of this flavor combo lights up the frontal lobe and leaves happy bellies in its wake.

Many breakfasts start with a small plate, filled half with za'atar and half with good-quality olive oil. Eaten the Arab way, we dip our bread into the oil to create an adhesive and then dip it into the spice mix. The combo of grassy, fruity oil with the complex flavors in this spice mix make it comforting and craveable enough to eat daily over a lifetime. Mix yours with olive oil or sprinkle on meat, salad, or anything else your heart desires.

Za'atar refers both to the spice mix and the plant that is the main ingredient, which translates to Syrian oregano or hyssop and can be found in specialty stores. If you cannot find it, you can substitute dried oregano or marjoram (or a combination of the two!).

¼ cup dried hyssop or Syrian oregano
2 teaspoons sumac
½ teaspoon kosher salt
2 tablespoons toasted sesame seeds

In a spice grinder or blender, pulse the hyssop to a fine powder. Sift to remove any stems. Mix with the sumac, salt, and sesame seeds.

Za'atar can be stored in an airtight container at room temperature for up to 1 month.

Terroir and Territory

Like any plant, za'atar takes on the flavor of the soil in which it is grown, so no two za'atar plants taste exactly the same. Resilient, drought-resistant za'atar takes root even on the most arid hilltops and between rocks, not unlike our people. In an unwinnable bid for control, Israel, using the pretense of conservation, now prohibits foraging za'atar in the wild.

Outlawed za'atar grows all over the world in the greenhouses, farms, and backyards of diasporic Arabs, who have smuggled the precious seeds from their visits home. In Palestine and Lebanon, entrepreneurs in the slow food movement are helping small farmers scale their za'atar production and sell directly to consumers. I dream of saving the best seeds to set up a za'atar farm one day in California, where I could demonstrate our symbolic rootedness, creating home and connection to the land in our adopted countries.

Don't get discouraged in your search for this elusive plant. If you ask a grocer in Palestine for za'atar, you might get thyme, while in Jordan or Lebanon, you might get a variety of oregano, hyssop, or marjoram. The plants produce a similar earthy profile, and recipes often use them interchangeably.

Try out whatever varietals you're able to find and adjust the proportions and combinations to suit your taste. I like mine on the earthier side and go easy on the sumac. Too much of the sour berry can cause heartburn. As herbs in the Arab World become harder to access, some manufacturers add wheat to stretch their mix: a vibrant green mix indicates the purity of the herbs; a dull, dusty color means it's been diluted. Most importantly, have fun testing and tasting until you have a mix that makes your heart sing.

SABA'A BAHARAT · سبع بهارات
Seven-Spice Mix

Makes ¼ cup

THE MIXTURE IN baharat, which literally means "spices" in Arabic, varies from region to region and family to family in the Arab world. In the Levant, baharat is most commonly prepared as a seven-spice mix that relies on warming spices tempered by woody flavors like cumin and coriander. The spice is so foundational to stews, meats, and rice dishes that, while every family has its own recipe, it seldom needs to be written down. If you equip yourself with only one spice mix to make the recipes in this book, this would be it. I use this spice mix as a base for much of my cooking and layer on other spices as needed.

This recipe can easily be doubled or tripled and stays fresh for a month when stored in an airtight container. If you multiply the recipe, it's better to toast the spices one at a time to ensure each has sufficient access to the surface of the pan.

TIP • If you don't have all the spices in your pantry to make the seven-spice mix, you can omit the cloves and cardamom to make a five-spice mix for recipes that call for seven-spice.

1 tablespoon whole allspice
1 tablespoon whole cumin seeds
1 tablespoon whole coriander seeds
9 cardamom pods
1-inch piece cinnamon stick
½ tablespoon whole cloves
½-inch piece nutmeg, crushed

Combine all of the spices in a small pan and toast over medium heat until warm and fragrant. The spices should start to gain the slightest color, have a noticeable fragrance, and begin to make a faint crackling sound. I gently touch the spices with the palm of my hand. They should be hot but not burn you. Do not let them smoke. If that happens, you've gone too far, and you'll need to toss them and start fresh. The whole process should take 2 to 3 minutes.

The spices can go straight from the pan to the bowl of a spice grinder, but be sure to allow a minute or two for them to cool, uncovered, before grinding to avoid condensation. Then pulse in a grinder or high-powered blender until coarsely ground. A coffee grinder works well, too. Just make sure to wipe or run a spoonful of rice through it afterward to clean the cup.

KHALTA HARRA · خلطة حرة

Chile-Spice Mix

Makes ⅔ cup

THIS CHILE MIX packs a perfect balance of earthy, sour, and salty flavors with just enough heat from the sweet Aleppo pepper to let you know you're alive but keep you from losing the other flavors. It's equally at home as a rub for the grill, a garnish for mezze spreads, or a seasoning for roasted vegetables and sauces.

This recipe could easily be doubled or tripled and stay good for about a month in a dry, tightly sealed container. A larger batch can be stored in the freezer in a tightly sealed container indefinitely. It's great to keep on hand for those nights when you need a quick dinner. Rubbed on ground meat or vegetables with a little olive oil, it can go from fridge to grill to table in about 10 minutes.

TIP • If you can't find dried lime, sumac makes an excellent substitute.

1 tablespoon plus 1 teaspoon whole coriander seeds
2 teaspoons whole cardamom seeds (about 17 pods)
2 teaspoons whole cumin seeds
6 tablespoons Aleppo pepper
2 teaspoons kosher salt
2 teaspoons dried lime, ground
½ teaspoon ground cinnamon

Toast the coriander, cardamom, and cumin in a dry pan over medium heat until fragrant, 2 to 3 minutes. The spices will begin to dance around in the pan when they are close to being done. Be careful not to let them burn. Once they are slightly darker in color and fragrant, remove them from the pan and let cool completely. Then grind them to a coarse powder in a spice grinder or mortar and pestle. Mix with the Aleppo pepper, salt, dried lime, and cinnamon.

MUKASSARAT · مكسرات
Spiced Sweet and Salty Nut Mix

Makes about 3 cups

ARAB HOSPITALITY HAS its own rhythm, but essential to a beautifully orchestrated experience are roasted nuts. My nut mix marries my love of sweets with salty, savory, and spicy flavors, as well as an array of shapes and sizes. In Arab homes, we snack on nuts before, after, and between meals.

There's a special art to scooping up favorites while artfully disguising the selection process so it doesn't look like less desirable nuts are being left for others. I've combined almonds, walnuts, and pistachios here, but I often use pumpkin seeds or cashews as well. Blanching the nuts softens them so they absorb the sugar as they toast and cool into a crunchy shell.

I use Syrian Aleppo pepper in this and many of my spice mixes. It's been harder to find in the years since Syria has been at war; Marrakesh pepper from Turkey makes a good substitute.

This nut mix is great to make ahead when you are hosting and tastes even better the next day.

1 tablespoon extra-virgin olive oil,
plus 1 tablespoon for greasing the tray
1 tablespoon confectioners' sugar
2½ teaspoons Aleppo pepper
1¼ teaspoons ground coriander
1¼ teaspoons ground cardamom
1 teaspoon ground cumin
½ teaspoon ground cinnamon
½ teaspoon cayenne pepper
1½ teaspoons kosher salt
3 cups mixed nuts and seeds (walnuts, pistachios, almonds, hazelnuts, pumpkin seeds, or cashews)

Preheat the oven to 350°F. Place the oven rack in the center of the oven. Grease a 13 by 18-inch sheet tray with olive oil.

Fill a 3-quart pot two-thirds full of water and bring to a boil. While the water comes to a boil, mix the sugar, Aleppo pepper, coriander, cardamom, cumin, cinnamon, cayenne, salt, and the remaining 1 tablespoon oil in a large bowl.

Once the water is boiling, ease the nuts into the water to avoid getting splashed. Soften the nuts in the boiling water for 2 minutes, skimming away any foam, and drain well in a fine-mesh strainer.

Toss the nuts into the bowl with the spice mix. Stir to coat.

Spread the mixture evenly on the prepared tray, separating the nuts so they have room to dry and crisp. Bake for 20 to 25 minutes, using a spatula to mix the nuts every 5 minutes or so, until they give off a toasty smell.

Cool thoroughly before serving.

The mix can be stored in an airtight container at room temperature for up to 2 weeks.

Cocoa Nib and Nut Spice Mix

Makes 1 cup

ORIGINALLY EGYPTIAN, DUKKAH in Arabic means "to pound." Dukkah means different things to different people, but most mixes include cumin, coriander, salt, sesame, and a nut or grain. I've added cocoa nibs for an utterly original bittersweet flavor combo. Cocoa originated in Mexico and somehow skipped the Arab world along its trade route. The combination of our smoky flavors and the chocolate bean fragments is my own blend of these two flavor origins.

The textures and flavors in this mix go beautifully on fish, meat, or vegetables, folded into labneh, spread on bread in an olive oil paste, or sprinkled on soups and stews.

Technique is especially important here. Roasting each spice and nut individually allows you to smell for doneness. Grinding each ingredient individually ensures a uniform texture to the mix and prevents it from forming a paste. Remove the spices from the heat as soon as each becomes fragrant. Cool each ingredient completely before grinding to avoid trapping heat, which causes sogginess. Texture is a matter of taste. I like my textures finer, so the tastes blend together. Many prefer them coarser, with a crunchier texture.

½ cup whole almonds, with or without skins
1⅛ teaspoons coriander seeds
1⅛ teaspoons cumin seeds
½ teaspoon black peppercorns
2 tablespoons pumpkin seeds
2 tablespoons sesame seeds
3 tablespoons cocoa nibs or unsweetened Dutch-processed cocoa powder
1 teaspoon kosher salt

Preheat the oven to 300°F.

Place the almonds on a sheet tray. Roast for 10 to 12 minutes, until they smell toasty and have taken on a light golden-brown color.

While the almonds are roasting, heat a dry shallow pan on the stovetop over medium heat. Toast the coriander, cumin, and peppercorns, one at a time, for 2 to 3 minutes each or until they are fragrant and begin to make a crackling sound.

Set aside each spice to cool.

In the same pan, toast the pumpkin seeds and sesame seeds separately, until they begin to sound as though they are popping or crackling, 3 to 5 minutes. Set everything aside to cool completely before processing.

When completely cooled, pulse the coriander, cumin, and peppercorns to a fine powder in a food processor or blender. Empty into a small bowl.

Pulse the pumpkin seeds to a medium grind, the texture of coarsely ground pepper, and add to the bowl. Do the same with the cocoa nibs and almonds, being sure to do this in small batches. The high oil content of the ingredients requires small batches to prevent clumping.

Leave the toasted sesame seeds whole and stir into the mixture along with the salt.

The mix can be stored in an airtight container at room temperature for up to 2 months.

ADAAMEH · قضامة

Crunchy Chile-Roasted Chickpeas

Makes 1 cup

TEXTURALLY, THE CRUNCHY surface of roasted chickpeas yields a soft interior. They're a perfect vehicle to deliver the addictive taste trifecta of salt, sour, and heat. These treats used to come mixed into the nut and seed assortments my mother bought from the Arab markets, where we stocked up on staples. I'd sort through the packets, picking out every last chickpea. I could never get enough of them.

Once the chickpeas are boiled, this dish comes together with about 5 minutes of prep and 40 minutes of baking.

1 cup dried chickpeas or one 15-ounce can chickpeas, drained and rinsed
1 tablespoon extra-virgin olive oil
1 teaspoon lemon juice
1 teaspoon kosher salt
2 teaspoons Chile-Spice Mix (page 27) or Aleppo pepper

If using dried chickpeas, soak them overnight and boil until tender, 60 to 90 minutes. Drain thoroughly.

Preheat the oven to 400°F. Line a sheet tray with parchment paper.

Toss the chickpeas in the oil, lemon juice, salt, and spice mix until evenly coated. Spread on the prepared tray and bake until browned, 35 to 40 minutes, mixing every 10 minutes or so. Let cool completely.

The chickpeas can be stored in an airtight container at room temperature for up to 1 month. To re-crisp this snack, pop them into a 350°F oven for about 10 minutes and allow them to cool.

ZAYTOON · زيتون
Zingy Marinated Olives

Makes 2½ cups

WHILE BRINING FRESH olives is a rite of passage for Arabs, families in the diaspora often jazz up supermarket olives with spices to make them distinctly Arab and perfect for snacking or to serve alongside mezze. The trick is to find a variety of olive you love and then make it yours with your own blend of flavors. Olives cured in salt instead of vinegar brine need to be soaked overnight to reduce the salinity.

3 cups pitted or whole olives (green, black, or any mixture), drained

½ lemon, sliced ⅛ inch thick

1 dried arbol chile or ½ teaspoon Aleppo pepper or red chile flakes

4 garlic cloves, crushed but intact

2 or 3 sprigs of oregano or thyme

½ cup extra-virgin olive oil, plus more as needed to fill the jar

In a small bowl, mix the olives with the lemon slices, chile, garlic, and oregano.

Transfer to a 1-quart jar, immerse in olive oil, and seal with a tightly fitted lid. Marinate in the refrigerator for at least 3 days.

To serve, bring to room temperature or gently warm over low heat.

The olives can be stored in the jar in the refrigerator for up to 1 month.

Chapter Two

Base Sauces, Stocks, and Condiments

MAR'AT D'JAJ · مرقة دجاج
Arab-Style Chicken Stock

**Makes 8 cups of stock and
1 pound of shredded chicken**

IS THERE ANYTHING more comforting than
chicken stock, the soul-nourishing rich base for
soups and stews—and the secret weapon of moms?

My mother always kept some on hand to make us
chicken noodle soup, Arab-style. My recipe builds
on the warmth of seven-spice mix with the addition of sweet fennel, herby cardamom pods, and a
gentle peppercorn kick. I always make more than
I need and keep the remainder in the freezer; it
takes up less space when stored in a resealable
bag, laid flat.

**2 tablespoons neutral oil, such as
sunflower or canola**

**2½ pounds bone-in, skin-on
chicken thighs**

1 onion, quartered

4 garlic cloves

1 tablespoon kosher salt

1 tablespoon Seven-Spice Mix (page 26)

1 teaspoon fennel seeds

1 teaspoon black peppercorns

5 cardamom pods

2 bay leaves

Warm the oil in a stockpot over medium heat.

Working in batches, sear the thighs for 3 to
5 minutes on each side, until the skin crisps and
turns dark golden brown and the fat from the
chicken releases into the cooking oil.

When all the chicken is seared, wedge the onion
and garlic onto the bottom of the pan among the
chicken thighs. Sprinkle the salt, spice mix, fennel
seeds, peppercorns, cardamom, and bay leaves
over the chicken. Add enough water to cover the
chicken (about 8 cups). Stir to mix in the spices,
bring to a boil, and skim any foam from the surface.
Turn down the heat to a low simmer, cover, and
cook for 40 minutes. The chicken should be cooked
through but not falling apart. Remove the chicken
from the pot and set aside.

Strain the broth, reserving the stock and discarding the vegetable bits and any spice residue that's
collected in the bottom of the pot.

The chicken can be shredded and added back into
the stock along with some vegetables and noodles
to make a flavorful light soup or repurposed into
another meal such as the Shorbat Freekeh (page 168).
You can store it in the fridge for up to a week or in
the freezer for up to 3 months.

MAR'AT SAMAK · مرقة سمك
Classic Fish Stock

**Makes 12 cups (enough for all the recipes
in this book that call for fish stock)**

GROWING UP, WE rarely ate fish at home, except
when my mom fried frozen fillets to eat with rice.
Whenever my father got a craving for seafood,
he would pile us into the car for a visit to his favorite fish joint, the "No Name" restaurant on the
Boston Harbor. He loved fish and ordered it anytime we went out, which, on our spare budget, was
fairly infrequently.

Fish stocks are central to Arab cooking. You can ask
your local market to save you leftover fish bones
or reserve the bones and the head of fish you fillet
at home.

This stock adds special depth to seafood dishes,
including the stuffed squid Hibaar Mahshi
(page 191), the shrimp clay pot remix Zidbiyat
Gambari (page 193), and the rice and fish combo
Sayadiyah (page 195). If you are cooking halal,
you can skip the white wine.

Twenty minutes of simmering brings out the full
flavor and luscious gelatinous base. Less oily fish
such as halibut, snapper, and sole work best for
broth. If you're using an oilier fish such as salmon
or cod, reduce the simmer time to 10 minutes to
preserve the delicate flavor.

3 to 4 pounds fish bones and head
¼ cup neutral oil, such as sunflower
2 onions, cut into large chunks
**2 garlic heads, sliced midway root
to stem**
1 fennel bulb, coarsely chopped
2 large celery ribs, cut into large chunks
¾ cup white wine
12 cups water, plus more as needed
3 bay leaves

1 tablespoon black peppercorns
1 tablespoon coriander seeds
1 teaspoon kosher salt

If you are butchering your own fish and have bones,
it's a good idea to let them soak in cold water in
the fridge for 1 to 4 hours to remove any residual
blood. Drain and pat dry before using.

In a stockpot, heat the oil on medium-high heat.
Add the fish bones and head, rotating them to
get color. Once the fish has begun to brown,
about 10 minutes, remove the bones and head
and reserve.

Into the pot, add the onions, garlic, fennel, and
celery and sauté until softened, about 5 minutes.
Add the wine to deglaze the pot, scraping up any
browned bits stuck to the bottom of the pot. Allow
the wine to evaporate almost completely.

Return the bones and head to the pot and add
the water. Add additional water if needed to just
cover the fish. Bring to a boil, scooping away and
discarding any scum from the surface. Add the bay
leaves, peppercorns, coriander, and salt and lower
to a gentle simmer. Cover and cook for 20 minutes.

Strain the stock into a cooking pot if you're using
right away or into three 1-quart widemouthed jars
or deli containers to refrigerate or freeze for later
use. (If freezing, remember to cool in the fridge
first, leaving a couple inches of space in the jars
so that it doesn't crack the jars or containers once
frozen.) Discard the solids.

The stock can be stored in the refrigerator for up to
1 week or in the freezer for up to 3 months.

Spicy Red Pepper Paste

Makes 1½ cups

AT REEM'S, WE love making base condiments to incorporate into multiple dishes. This mildly spicy spread is delicious as a base for flatbreads and sandwiches and transforms into a great aioli when blended with egg yolk for fries (see page 157 for Batata Harra). Add a touch of honey or brown sugar, and you have a delicious barbecue sauce marinade.

Dibs Al Fleifleh is a milder version of harissa paste; bell peppers balance the chile with sweetness, and the lemon, in turn, dials down the sweetness with its acidity. The vegetables' liquids evaporate through slow cooking, intensifying the flavor.

This is a versatile condiment to have on hand. It can keep in an airtight container in the refrigerator for up to 3 weeks. If you will not be using it as frequently, you can freeze half and thaw when needed.

12 red Fresno chiles (about 12 ounces), stems, seeds, and veins removed

2 tablespoons kosher salt

4 or 5 large bell peppers (about 1½ pounds)

2 tablespoons extra-virgin olive oil, plus more to cover

1½ teaspoons ground cumin

1½ teaspoons ground coriander

1 teaspoon smoked paprika

2 tablespoons lemon juice

Preheat the oven to 400°F.

Finely chop the chiles and toss with the salt. Let sit for 30 minutes in a colander, until the chiles release their liquid.

While the chiles are draining, coat the peppers in 1 tablespoon of the oil and roast in the oven, until they are collapsed and blistered, 30 to 40 minutes. Remove the peppers from the oven, place in a bowl, and seal in plastic wrap and let steam. When the peppers are cool enough to touch, peel off the skins.

Turn down the oven temperature to 300°F.

Using a gloved hand or the weight of a mug, push down and drain as much of the salty liquid as you can from the chiles and discard the liquid. You should have about 1½ cups of chopped chiles.

Combine the chiles and peppers in a food processor or blender and add the cumin, coriander, paprika, and lemon juice. Blend on medium speed until smooth. Then gradually drizzle in the remaining tablespoon oil and blend until the sauce comes together.

Spread the sauce in a layer on a sheet tray and cook in the oven for 1 hour, stirring halfway through.

Once the cooked mixture resembles a thick paste, pour it into a sterilized 1-pint glass jar or deli container, pour additional oil over the surface to seal it, and cover.

The paste can be stored in the jar in the refrigerator for up to 2 weeks.

TARATOOR · طراطور
Lemon-Tahini Sauce

Makes 1 cup

THIS CREAMY, NUTTY, sour, salty, garlicky sauce is integral to everything. Okay, maybe not to *everything* but certainly to many wonders of Arab cuisine. It's easy to whip into a dipping sauce for falafel or thin with a bit of vinegar for salad dressing. Add some herbs, and it becomes a sauce for roasted fish. Mix with whole chickpeas, and you have a quick lunch to scoop up with vegetables. Its uses are endless. Enjoy this sauce with Falafel Mahshi (page 153) or as a condiment with Mashawi (page 182), slow-cooked lamb.

½ cup tahini

½ cup water

2 tablespoons lemon juice
(about 1 lemon)

2 garlic cloves, smashed and
finely chopped

1 heaping teaspoon kosher salt,
plus more as needed

In a small bowl, whisk together the tahini, water, and lemon juice until combined and smooth.

Add the garlic and salt to create a garlic paste. Whisk rapidly until the sauce is the consistency of crepe batter. Adjust the salt to taste.

The sauce can be stored in an airtight container in the refrigerator for up to 5 days.

TARATOOR'S NON-NEWTONIAN QUALITIES

Besides its versatility, the alchemy of taratoor is something of a miracle. When lemon's citric acid cuts through the oils protecting the tiny dry protein particles in tahini, they seize up and harden in much the same way cornstarch and water combine to create oobleck, a non-Newtonian substance, meaning neither liquid nor solid—except taratoor is delicious and packed with nutrients! Not unlike oobleck, if your taratoor hardens, you can loosen it back up with a splash of cold water.

TOUM · توم
Tangy Garlic Spread

Makes 2 cups

PERFECTED BY THE Lebanese, this tangy, fluffy spread is quintessential to Lebanese street food. Toum goes beautifully with grilled and roasted meats—shawarma, kabobs, roast chicken—and is equally delicious with fries. My favorite place for toum is Zankou Chicken, a Lebanese Armenian–owned chain of Los Angeles restaurants, famous for its spit-roasted chicken. During hot summer days with my grandparents, someone inevitably would decide we needed a break from the kitchen and plan an excursion to Zankou. No one bothered with the menu. We were there for the perfectly cooked rotisserie chicken, enrobed in bright lemony toum and served in cigar-shaped pita rolls with some extra toum added on the side.

Some people say it's the toum, not the meat, that makes the sandwich. Toum delivers the silkiness of aioli freed from the heaviness of egg yolk.

Just four ingredients and some ice water combine to make this magic. I perfected mine by searching out examples from Arab cooks and experimenting with technique. The secret, I found, is how you blend the ingredients in the emulsification process. Adding salt at the outset releases the garlic's water and helps it form a paste. Icy cold water preserves the freshness and brings down the heat from the motor of the blender; this allows the garlic, lemon, salt, and water to whip into creamy goodness without changing the chemistry. Start with a fresh head of garlic; pre-peeled garlic becomes too strong as it ages.

1 garlic head
¾ teaspoon kosher salt, plus more as needed
¼ cup ice water
2 tablespoons lemon juice (about 1 lemon)
½ teaspoon lemon zest
1½ cups neutral oil, such as sunflower

Separate the cloves from the garlic head and then peel. Halve the cloves and dig out the sprouts and germs from the centers to further mellow their pungency.

Combine the garlic and salt in a food processor and pulse, scraping down the sides until they form a paste. (If this amount is too small for your processor, you can mince the cloves on a cutting board, then sprinkle salt on top, and use the side of your knife to smash the garlic into a paste.)

Add the water, lemon juice, and zest to the food processor. Blend on medium speed until the mixture forms a white puree, about 3 minutes.

Gradually drizzle in the oil and continue mixing until the paste fluffs, 5 to 10 minutes.

Adjust the salt to taste.

The garlic spread can be stored in an airtight container in the refrigerator for up to 1 week.

TATBEELEH · تتبيله
Lemon-Garlic-Chile Relish

Makes about ¾ cup

TRADITIONALLY A LEMON-GARLIC vinai-grette, this condiment helps brighten dishes with an intense hit of citrus and flavors. I love it as a garnish on Hummus (page 138) or Ful Madammas (page 151), and I often splash it by the spoonful as a finisher on flatbreads, especially in the spring when I bake fresh tender veggies like asparagus and favas onto my Mana'eesh (page 77).

I've made this relish slightly less intense than the traditional version. When I can get it, I use green spring garlic for its milder, sweeter notes, and the rest of the year I blanch the cloves to tamp down the spice level. I also love to drizzle tatbeeleh over fresh herbs and fish like the Samaka Harra bil Tahini (page 197).

TIP • For all the crudo and fresh-seafood lovers, this makes an excellent topping for raw fish or oysters.

¼ cup finely chopped green garlic or 1½ tablespoons finely chopped blanched garlic (about 5 cloves)

1½ teaspoons finely chopped serrano or red Fresno chile (about 1 chile)

¼ cup white wine vinegar

¼ cup lemon juice (about 2 lemons)

¼ cup extra-virgin olive oil

1 teaspoon crushed coriander seeds

1 teaspoon Aleppo pepper or Chile-Spice Mix (page 27)

½ teaspoon kosher salt

If blanching garlic, place the peeled cloves in a small pot covered with cold water. Bring to a boil, then drain and shock in ice water. Once cool, drain, pat dry, and finely chop.

In a medium bowl, whisk all of the ingredients together.

The relish can be stored in an airtight container in the refrigerator for up to 3 weeks.

BASSAL · بصل
Onions Three Ways

MANY OF MY recipes require onions—lots and lots of onions. Not just as a base for stocks and sauces but as garnishes and pickles for various mezze dishes and meats. I also love to caramelize onions and fold them into dishes for extra sweetness. If you plan to tackle dishes such as Musakhan (page 173), Sayadiyah (page 195), or Mujaddarra (page 167), having ready-made caramelized onions comes in handy. My caramelized onion puree doubles as a sweet jam and can be used on charcuterie boards with cheese and bread or as a base condiment for a man'oushe (see page 77).

Caramelized Onions

Makes about 3½ cups

⅓ cup extra-virgin olive oil
3 yellow or white onions, thinly sliced into ¼-inch crescents (about 10 cups)
1½ teaspoons kosher salt

Heat a large pan (a 10-inch cast-iron pan works perfectly for this) over high heat. When hot, add the oil and warm until shimmering.

Add the onions and stir to coat with the oil. Cook on high heat for about 5 minutes, stirring every minute or so to make sure the onions get to a deep golden color but don't burn. Sprinkle in the salt and turn down the heat to medium. Spread the onions evenly over the pan and continue cooking, stirring occasionally.

Cook for 15 to 20 more minutes, stirring a few times in between. As the onion water evaporates, the onions should stick to the pan and start to brown. Allow the onions sufficient contact with the pan but stir before they burn. Continue stirring with increasing frequency as the onions soften and darken, until they turn a deep mahogany brown.

Store in an airtight container in the refrigerator for up to 1 week.

Caramelized Onion Puree

Makes about 2½ cups

1 recipe Caramelized Onions (previous)
2 tablespoons pomegranate molasses
½ teaspoon freshly ground black pepper
1 tablespoon kosher salt
6 tablespoons extra-virgin olive oil

In a blender, combine the onions, molasses, pepper, and salt and blend until it forms a smooth puree. Gradually drizzle in the oil, while mixing at high speed, until thick and emulsified.

Enjoy as a spread with bread and cheese or as a condiment in sandwiches or on flatbreads. The puree can be stored in an airtight container in the refrigerator for up to 1 week.

Quick-Pickled Red Onions

Makes 1½ pints

¾ cup apple cider vinegar
¾ cup water
¼ cup lemon juice (about 2 lemons)
2 tablespoons kosher salt
1 tablespoon sumac
1 large red onion, thinly sliced into ¼-inch crescents (about 1 cup)

In a medium bowl, combine the vinegar, water, and lemon juice. Add the salt and sumac and stir until dissolved.

Place the onion in a 1½-pint jar and pour the vinegar-lemon mixture over it. Store the jar in the refrigerator for up to 3 weeks.

Base Sauces, Stocks, and Condiments   43

Fermented Red Hot Sauce

Makes about 2 cups

LIKE VIETNAMESE GARLIC-CHILE sauce or Indonesian sambal, this go-to condiment holds a special place on the Arab chile lovers' table. Its secrets are time and good ingredients.

Shatta's traditional sun-dried fermentation creates an acidity that rounds out the taste. Fellow Palestinian chef Abeer Najjar figured out that dehydrating chiles in an oven replicates the intense flavor that results from the traditional sun-dried method.

Removing the moisture primes the chiles for safe fermentation and a longer-lasting shatta. I cheat a little by adding vinegar to speed up the fermentation at room temperature. To ferment, you will need a 16-ounce sterilized jar. To sterilize, submerge the jar for 10 minutes in boiling water. Remove the jar with tongs and dry completely on a rack before use.

You can adjust the spice level by removing half of of the chile seeds or all of the seeds for a mild and tasty hot sauce. Handle the chiles with gloves if you have them. Otherwise, make sure to wash your hands between steps to keep the heat out of your eyes and nose. Speaking from experience, it's not a mistake you're likely to make twice (or once, if you can help it).

Enjoy this with any mezze, main dish, or vegetable.

1 pound red Fresno chiles (or any available red chile), stems removed

2 tablespoons kosher salt, plus more as needed

2 tablespoons minced garlic (about 6 to 8 garlic cloves)

1 tablespoon apple cider vinegar

1 tablespoon Aleppo pepper or Chile-Spice Mix (page 27); optional

1 teaspoon sugar

Extra-virgin olive oil to cover

Preheat the oven to 300°F. Line a sheet tray with parchment paper.

In a food processor, pulse the chiles with the salt until you have a finely chopped, gritty paste. Spread the paste on the prepared tray and bake for 45 minutes, until most of the moisture has dried out.

In a small bowl, combine the paste, garlic, vinegar, Aleppo pepper, and sugar. Adjust the salt to taste.

Pour the mixture into the sterilized jar and pour in just enough oil to barely cover. Place cheesecloth or a coffee filter over the jar to cover. Allow to ferment in a draft-free spot away from direct sunlight. After at least 3 days, stir and taste with a clean spoon every day or two to check the flavor. I like to ferment mine for a week, but you can leave it to ferment for as long as you'd like, even for up to a year, under a thin layer of oil, in a sterilized jar.

Once fermented to your liking, shatta will keep in the refrigerator indefinitely, where fermentation will still continue, slowly intensifying the flavor.

SHATTA KHADRA · شطه خضرة
Tangy Green Hot Sauce

Makes 1 cup

PALESTINIAN COOKING BECOMES increasingly spicy the farther south you travel. Gaza, where my mother's family farmed citrus for generations, is where fresh chiles appear with most meals, often chopped into a salty lemon brine and speckled with herbs.

Cooks in my restaurant call it chimichurri. The two are similar, and many cultures have their own version of this herby spicy condiment. It's a sauce that goes well on just about everything, from hummus to nachos.

This easy recipe blends up beautifully in one simple step and takes just minutes from start to finish.

4 garlic cloves, crushed

2 serrano chiles, stems, seeds, and veins removed

2 teaspoons kosher salt

¼ cup lemon juice (about 2 lemons)

2 cups coarsely chopped parsley, stems included (about 1½ bunches)

1 cup coarsely chopped cilantro, stems included (about ½ bunch)

2 teaspoons ground cumin

3 tablespoons extra-virgin olive oil, plus more as needed

Combine all of the ingredients in a small blender or food processor on low to medium speed and puree until the mixture forms a thick pesto-like consistency flecked with herbs, about 30 seconds. If the mixture is too thick, add in more oil, a tablespoon at a time, until it's smooth. Adjust salt to taste. Scrape into a shallow bowl to serve.

The sauce can be stored in an airtight container in the refrigerator for up to 2 weeks.

KISHK · كشك

Fermented Yogurt and Bulgur

Makes 2 cups

THE SWISS ARMY knife of preserved Arab foods, kishk is served as a topping on flatbreads, crumbled over salads as a formidable challenger to blue cheese, or dried and rehydrated into a musky base as a thickener for comforting stews. Kishk is a funky fermented mix of cracked wheat in milk or yogurt that can be used right away, preserved in olive oil, or dried, powdered, and reconstituted when food is scarce. Our culinary traditions for preserving dairy are another ingenious way Arabs can make something out of nothing and save seasonal bounty for leaner times.

I grew up knowing kishk as a yogurt-based man'oushe spread with an extra kick, but it comes in all textures, from a wet spread to a dry crumble. It is used as a base in several recipes in this book, such as in Salatet Shamandar wa Kishk (page 212) and Mana'eesh Bil Kishk (page 80), so I encourage you to stock up.

For a milder version, this recipe can be made a few hours ahead and crumbled fresh over salads or kneaded daily for up to a week: the longer it's left to ferment, the headier the kishk.

⅔ cup bulgur #1 (fine size)
⅓ cup buttermilk
1 cup whole milk yogurt
½ teaspoon kosher salt

In a medium bowl, mix the bulgur with the buttermilk, yogurt, and salt until it's well-incorporated and looks like oatmeal. Seal with plastic wrap and set away from direct sunlight in a cool draft-free place for 24 hours.

The next day, hand-knead the mixture in the bowl. Replace the plastic wrap and leave to ferment for another 24 hours.

By the end of the third day, your "cheese" should develop a slightly fermented flavor and aroma. The kishk is ready once it's firm enough to crumble between your fingers. If the funkiness is to your liking, it can be broken into crumbles to use right away or stored in an airtight container in the refrigerator for up to 2 weeks. For a muskier spread, it can be left, covered, at room temperature and kneaded daily for up to a week.

If you want to keep it longer, spread your mixture on a sheet tray and bake on the oven's lowest setting for 4 to 5 hours, or until it's completely dried. Pulse the dried kishk in a food processor, until the shards reduce to a fine crumble.

The kishk can be stored in an airtight container in the refrigerator for up to 1 month or when dehydrated for up to 1 year. To rehydrate, add water, milk, or yogurt 1 tablespoon at a time until the consistency of the kishk is to your liking.

Part Two

THE ARAB
Street Corner Bakery

In the summer of 2010, my father, sister, and I arrived at Beirut–Rafik Hariri International Airport in Lebanon, to the kind of humidity that sends my curls fleeing in every direction. Before heading to my aunt's house, my cousins took us on a detour to Beirut's busy Hamra Street, packed with cafés and boutiques. We went there for one thing: hot out-of-the-oven mana'eesh.

The shops displayed fresh flatbreads, laid out in giant edible mosaics with every imaginable combination of toppings. We paused for a moment of awe, bellies rumbling at the smell of za'atar spice, melty and briny cheese, cured and spiced ground meats, fresh herbs, fragrant chopped tomatoes and cucumbers, olives, and spicy peppers. If you couldn't choose, the baker would gladly slather your man'oushe with two toppings, split right down the middle.

It seemed as if every block had at least one bakery, sometimes more. I remember scanning menu boards that filled entire walls of small shops, reading options in both Arabic and English, with ingenious combinations—everything from mortadella and cheese to chicken tandoori. The possibilities seemed endless.

I wish I could say we perused all the choices, carefully assessing our options, but since everything looked so good, we just grabbed the first man'oushe we found. There are no wrong choices on Hamra Street. With a warm bread in hand, folded in half and wrapped in paper, we strolled together, taking in the sights, sounds, and food smells of a bustling city. For the first time in a long time, I felt alive.

A few blocks over, Bliss Street ran past my mother's alma mater, the American University of Beirut (AUB), where students spilled out across the sidewalks, lining up for their favorite pick-me-ups from bakeries, eateries, and coffee shops. My sister, who had spent a semester at AUB, directed me to Snack Faysal, her favorite twenty-four-hour mana'eesh spot.

Munching on a man'oushe late one night, topped with Snack Faysal's special za'atar double-cheese "cocktail" combo, I could see how starkly misunderstood Lebanon—and the rest of the Arab world—was by the people I knew back home. Far from the tropes of a single-minded citizenry holding out against modernity, Beirut is the only place where a Virgin Megastore with a rooftop bar overlooks a bullet-ridden mosque. On one street you could find a woman celebrating the results of her plastic surgery beneath a revealing blouse crossing paths with a religiously covered woman, and neither would give the other a second glance. People of every generation and religious background fill Beirut's streets, all connecting through food,

suspending judgment, and enjoying life side by side, bite by bite.

By the time of this trip, following bouts of physical and mental illness in childhood and college, I had overcome despair. I'd remade myself as a devoted organizer, knocking on doors by day to recruit community leaders in the fight for justice and wielding a bullhorn by night, calling for a free Palestine and an end to the US War on Terror. The campaigns I championed resulted in living wages and better working conditions for Black and Brown hotel and airport service workers, affordable housing for residents fighting to stay in their neighborhoods, money for schools, and political power for community leaders who gained the skills and confidence to run for elected seats.

Black Lives Matter was on the ascent, and racial justice was gaining steam. Although I was living the life I'd imagined for myself, a nagging feeling kept re-emerging. Increasingly, I found myself at loose ends, a community organizer without my own community. The life of an organizer meant round-the-clock hours and little time to build a life outside of work. I often felt alone. After years of fighting on the front lines for others' voices to be heard, I had lost my own. I was burned out, and I desperately needed time to recharge. It was at this point my father asked me and my youngest sister, Manal, to take a trip with him to the homeland.

My father, Naim Assil, was born in Syria in 1946, the year that Syrians finally won independence from French colonial rule. That upheaval opened the way for revolutionary organizing. By high school, my dad's encounters with Palestinians taking refuge in Syria had a greater pull than the spot that awaited him on an elite club basketball team. (He always laments that he could have gone pro.)

In neighboring Egypt, Gamal Abdel Nasser was leading the overthrow of Egypt's dynastic monarchy and nationalizing the Suez Canal, a blow to British colonial forces who controlled the country's resources. Nasser's compelling vision called for a unified nation of Arabs, fighting for self-determination on their lands. A generation of young organizers, including my father, joined the call for Pan-Arabism, hoping to build a better future.

To avoid mandatory service in the Syrian army, my father moved to Egypt to study at Alexandria University, where he took to the streets between studies, knocking on doors, striking up conversations about the new future Nasser promised. As Pan-Arab unity grew, Europe and America strengthened the forces backing Nasser's opposition. The revolution collapsed, and thousands died fighting to preserve the housing, employment, health, education, and agricultural land they had gained through independence, gutting the dreams of my father and many in his generation. My father traded in his revolutionary fervor for an engineering career and turned to his faith, Islam, to guide his search for purpose.

By the time of this trip, nearly fifty years later, I was joining my father to visit the places that birthed his awakening. We were headed to Syria by way of Lebanon. I was there in search of my own purpose; he, to retrace the footsteps of his past and to show me where we'd come from.

My first days in Lebanon filled me with anxiety. I couldn't shake the sensation that I was an onlooker. Did my name, my looks, my food make me Arab, even if my thoughts carried me elsewhere? Would I feel the same sense of belonging my dad felt at the sight of the landmarks and people who had shaped him? I would soon find out.

The next leg of our journey took us from Lebanon across the eastern border into Syria. The crossing was a revelation. The guards, taken with my father's easy banter, waved us through, no passports needed. At home, no amount of documentation ever seemed sufficient to secure our place as Americans, and yet here, we were welcomed as kin, even before we had made it across the border. As we navigated toward the Assil family home in Damascus, the capital of Syria, I learned that at that point 180 people in the area called my father *khaloo*, meaning "uncle." Before each trip he took to Syria, my dad would map out his family tree—six sisters and two brothers, their children, and grandchildren—to plan the gifts he needed to bring and the stops he had to make. Sometimes it took some tape and extra paper to account for everyone, but still, to me, 180 felt like more Arabs than I'd ever met in my life.

Despite our lives apart, the family welcomed my sister and me, two "American" girls, as their own, which in the Syrian tradition meant feeding us endlessly. Their hospitality filled me with a joyful sense of belonging. In trying to find a word for the way in which Syrians care for others, it was described to me as *hanan*, a beautiful word meaning, in this context, "warmhearted kindness." What we lacked in language, with my choppy Arabic and their halting English, we made up for in humor and food. I wanted to freeze that sensation and take it home with me.

Each day centered on a big lunch, and we hopped from one home to the next to see family, feasting on treats like a side of Makdous (page 237), tiny baby eggplants, stuffed with a mix of sweet red peppers, walnuts, and garlic and then cured to tender perfection in olive oil. One weekend, we arrived at an aunt's mountain summer home to find her flanked by a team of at least ten women, circled around a heaping pile of dough for kibbeh (see page 162), meat-filled bulgur croquettes to be fried later in the evening.

The country was celebrating Ramadan, and an hour after sunset, once their fast was broken,

families spilled out of homes and mosques to enjoy the nightlife. On every street corner, bakeries whose facades opened onto the street pushed out stacks of Arab bread to lines of families waiting to buy bags for the morning suhoor, the pre-sunrise meal to sate fasters for the long day ahead.

Even families with little cash parked themselves on a patch of grass or dirt and brought out salty cheeses, breads, and cucumber spears accompanied by argeelah, a fruit-scented tobacco water pipe. They would strum ouds inlaid with mother-of-pearl to make beautiful lute-like melodies, while slapping out danceable rhythms on handheld tabla drums. Men walked the streets serving tea and street food like Ka'ak (page 85). The aroma of food filled every block. Shawarma and falafel shops anchored the street corners, and in between them, people sold fruits and nuts from the countryside.

Although the life I'd built was more than seven thousand miles away, it was here, sensing the ease among people, tasting fruits and vegetables from

nearby farms, and grabbing loaves warm from the oven, that I felt most at home.

Each night of our trip, when others had drifted off to sleep, my father and I would stay up to reflect on our days, something we hadn't done together in a long time. Leading up to the trip, we'd been nearly estranged. My path had veered far from his: I'd become an agnostic practicing Buddhism, an underpaid organizer, and an activist opposing the very government from whom he'd sought refuge. For years, he struggled to explain what I did for a living, but on this particular trip, Barack Obama's presidency provided him an easy answer. He proudly declared, "She's a community organizer, like Obama!" Faces would light up in recognition: "Ah! Like Obama!"

It was in those moments when I realized that my father's reluctance to accept my organizing career was not due to a lack of understanding of it but more so a fear that I might experience the same disappointment he did after a thwarted revolution.

My father, who had worked so hard to cocoon me in safety, had a hard time releasing me into a world he feared would be unwelcoming to a girl who took the path less traveled.

At the apex of our trip, we planned an escape from the city life of Damascus to the coast of northwest Syria on a guided tour to see sights my father had visited in his youth. At each of our stops, we arrived at a community that doubled as a place of refuge in the Syrian countryside for Armenians, Kurds, Turkmen, and Assyrians. In this part of Syria, we were the tourists, and they, Syrians, who alternated between their language of origin and Arabic. They welcomed us with a flourish of hospitality, serving up dishes from their own traditions.

We ate in Kasab, an ethnically Armenian mountain village, that was mostly Christian. Our meal featured fresh herbs, paper-thin breads, pickled vegetables, and meats enhanced with sour fruit like green plums—distinct from the Arab dishes my family prepared. The next day, we stopped for lunch along the Mediterranean coast in the Turkmen village of Umm al-Tuyour. A café owner hosted us with a selection of fresh fish grilled to perfection, served with sprigs of mint and parsley and wedges of lemon.

The Syria my father had left behind was now a place of refuge for people who had been dislocated from their homes by borders and conflicts. Was I any less Syrian than those families I'd encountered who had migrated into the countryside, carrying on their traditions even as they assimilated into Syrian life?

One day, our bus pulled over along the highway for a sightseeing stop. Across the way, a roadside vendor tended a wood fire beneath the steel dome of her griddle. I dashed over for a closer look. I stood, transfixed, as the rest of the group moved on. I studied her method, as she expertly

stretched even rounds of dough on a stiff pillow, its surface taut with thick canvas. She slammed stretched flatbreads onto the metal, which, I would later learn, is called a saj.

As soon as her dough hit the griddle, it began bubbling, and the steamy toasty smells made my mouth water. As she repeated the process, a thousand questions popped up inside me, but since I couldn't make out her heavy mountain Arabic dialect, I resolved to watch, as she patiently showed me with her hands and eyes. I observed her seamless movements, rearranging the flame and coals beneath the saj, flipping and adjusting the dough on different parts of the dome where the heat was higher or lower to ensure a perfectly baked flatbread.

On our return to Damascus, I wanted to see more bread making. It turned out that one of my uncles owned a bakery inside the walls of the legendary old-city market Souq al Hamidiyah, so we

went to see where the magic happened. Big mixers and tables for shaping dough gave me a sense of scale. Bags of Syria's special high-protein wheat flour lined the walls. We didn't know then that the Arab Spring was right around the corner. Neither did we know that the aftermath would produce a devastating war, resulting in wheat shortages that would force bakers to stretch their supplies with additions that would have been unthinkable then—cornmeal, barley, and even husks and bran. Bread is the lifeline of my people, so severing Arabs from their bread became a tactic of war on the Syrian people.

If bread is the lifeline of my people, then the bakery is king. Even when bakeries themselves became targets of military bombardment, people were willing to face rockets just to get their fix of daily bread. Each place where we stopped, even remote villages, had a bakery, whether run-down or well furnished. I loved overhearing bakers ask

about school, work, and health, as they baked families' homemade dough in the communal oven. The person who bakes the bread holds a special place as part of the extended family. I suddenly longed to be that baker. I longed for that kind of connection.

We made our way back to Beirut just days before our return to the United States, and I could already feel my loose ends coming back together through my discovery of bread, a vital implement for nearly every dish that Arabs eat. Bread is neither a rich nor poor food. It is the common denominator that connects us all.

I no longer remember all of the bakeries I saw in Lebanon and Syria. What I do remember is the feeling of life returning to my body after seeing mounds of savory and sweet breads. As far as the eye could see, there were stacks of Fatayer Jibneh (page 92), Fatayer Sabanikh (page 87), and Sfeeha Ba'albekiyyeh (page 90), dough wrapped in perfect geometric shapes around either cheese, spinach, or lamb filling, sitting next to mounds of sweets: nut-stuffed Ba'laawa bil Jowz (page 118), Ghraybe (page 263) shortbread cookies, and date-stuffed Ma'amoul Med (page 260). I remember the revelation that a bakery can spark life even in places where life has been most depleted. I knew then that my ancestors were trying to tell me something: my community back in California needed an Arab street corner bakery.

As my plane taxied onto the runway at San Francisco International Airport, I was already composing my resignation letter in my head. In just a few weeks, I would quit my organizing job and enroll myself in culinary school.

For the Love of Bread

THE BASICS OF BREAD MAKING

My earliest memory of bread was not the Arab bread of my mother and father's childhoods but rather of a yeasty sweetness wafting out of the smokestacks from the Wonder Bread factory we used to pass driving from our home in Sudbury, Massachusetts, to the Natick Mall. Even before I understood how to read street signs or recognize landmarks, I'd catch a whiff—something between malty caramel and toasty almonds—and my nose would tell me our location on the route. Although I now prefer the aromas and flavors of bread that hasn't been pumped with commercial yeast to speed up its fermentation, the smell of toasting Wonder Bread still fills me with indescribable joy.

When I teach Arab bread-baking workshops, I ask people what they love about bread, and nearly always, they say it's the smell and the memories that smell elicits; that smell connects them to their culture and warms them with nostalgia for their childhoods. As bread meets your senses—smell, touch, sight, and, of course, taste—it pushes everything else away, leaving no room for other problems.

When I entered culinary school and got serious about baking professionally, I was eager to learn the secrets to making great bread. I read every fermentation book I could get my hands on and enrolled in countless classes, but the language and approach felt intimidating and inaccessible.

I couldn't relate to the overwhelmingly white male voices and overuse of Eurocentric terminology coming through the pages of recipes and tutorials. I would often think to myself, "When should I use the word *levain*? Is it really any different from using the word *starter*? What is *biga*, then, and am I pronouncing that right?" It turns out they're all stages and procedures in the process of making sourdough starter.

Bread baking, it seemed, was the domain of white male bakers and chefs. I couldn't imagine myself thriving in this space or finding a mentor with whom I could feel excited, instead of feeling inadequate as I learned these concepts. That feeling of alienation was strong enough to keep me away from bread baking for years, focusing instead on sweet pastries.

But bread kept drawing me back. I was fascinated—and at times obsessed—with the alchemy of bread: just wheat, water, and salt, aided by hardworking yeast, that transform as if by magic into this life-sustaining food. Outside of the classroom, I studied the foundations of Arab baking by talking to elders, watching YouTube videos, and reading books in the library, discovering the sophisticated techniques and novel ingredients employed by Arabs over centuries.

Capturing "wild yeast" from the air to build sourdough bread starters was commonplace in villages spanning the Fertile Crescent, from Egypt to Lebanon. Each generation passed along its knowledge about the care and feeding of the living organisms fermenting their foods. Their wisdom was not confined to experts but was instead cultivated in homes from fathers to sons, mothers to daughters, and grandparents to grandchildren, since the act of baking bread was a family affair.

While I'm put off by the jargon of bread baking, it does bring out my inner nerd. I get as much joy from the science as from the connection to generations before me who used the same techniques I now use. Even today, after thousands of loaves, I get a little rush of excitement with each new batch of dough, watching, feeling, smelling its distinct features as it takes shape in my hands.

I've broken this section into savory and sweet breads and pastries. It is a mix of the best of both worlds: breads that inspired me during my visits to the Arab world, along with breads I've developed as a professional baker.

Khobz Arabi (page 71), or Arab bread, a 6- to 8-inch flatbread (depending on your desired thickness), is foundational to the cuisine of our region. This dough is used as a base for many recipes throughout the book, so I encourage you to learn and practice making it. There are two approaches to making it, and I offer both: a yeasted base dough as well as a sourdough base dough. You can use either. The sourdough entails more labor and commitment, such as building and maintaining your own starter, but it also leaves you with more flavor. Try both of them and see what works best for you. If you are strapped for time and still want to have a try at sourdough, many local bakeries freely offer their starters to give you a leg up.

Most of my bread recipes involve a stand mixer with a dough hook for ease and consistency, but if you are new to bread, I suggest starting by using your hands to get a feel for the construction of dough. You might even notice some buff contours in your forearms after a bit of practice! Ultimately, building gluten structure in naturally fermented sourdough requires heavy-duty mixing, so if you'd like a steady supply of fresh homemade bread, a KitchenAid mixer makes a good investment.

Below are a few key concepts in bread making that will help you understand the bread recipes in this book. If you have a question, chances are there are more details here that you can refer to for your bread-making process. Come back to this section as often as you would like or take a crash course now in order to approach the recipes in this section with more ease.

Measuring

I have included both weight and volume measurements in my baking recipes. While you may be more accustomed to using measuring cups and spoons, measuring weight on a scale will give you much greater accuracy, leading to more consistent results. Once you bake a perfect loaf, you'll be able to replicate your dough using weights, and it's easy to make tweaks by tracking small adjustments; that's hard to do with volume measures. In bread baking, even slight variations can cause slight changes in the product.

You can never scoop flour exactly the same way twice, so precision becomes important. Plus, weighing actually produces fewer dishes to wash later. Once your bowl is on the scale, you can pour each ingredient directly in and skip the measuring tools. For less than $20, you can pick up a small kitchen scale online or at most homeware stores. If measuring by volume is your only option, no matter; the smell of freshly baking bread will delight your senses every time. Just take care not to pack down the flour: scoop a heaping cup and scrape away the excess with your finger or a butter knife.

USING RATIOS

To scale the recipes up or down, I use ratios. This allows me to make ten pitas for a family breakfast or fifty for a special occasion, simply by recalculating the percentage. The formula for bread ratio pegs water, salt, and oil against the measurement of flour. The flour always represents 100 percent. If I am using 1 pound of flour, then a pound of flour is 100 percent. From there, 50 percent hydration means the recipe needs 8 ounces of water, 3 percent salt means 0.5 ounce of salt (0.03 multiplied by 16 ounces), and so on and so forth.

Kneading

Kneading the dough is the process by which you create the gluten structure that will tighten and eventually loosen enough to hold tiny pockets of gas; it's the inflation that differentiates puffy chewy bread from crunchy crumbly crackers. Kneading usually involves mixing wet and dry ingredients with a spoon or your hands until they merge into a shaggy goo and then turning the mass onto a lightly floured work surface. As you knead the dough, its texture begins to firm.

To knead by hand, grip the bottom edge of the dough farthest from you, curl it upward to the center of the dough mass, then push the dough away with your palm. Rotate the ball one-quarter turn and grab the bottom farthest away from you again, curl it up toward the center, and push it away with your palm. Continue the pattern: pull up, push away, rotate. For simplicity's sake, I refer to this as pull-push-turn. Keep some flour nearby, dusting the ball with small pinches to keep it from sticking to you or the board. You may be tempted to throw on lots of

extra flour if the dough is sticky. Don't. A slightly sticky dough grabs onto your work surface, and the resistance it creates actually functions as a second kneading tool. Allow the dough to stick to your hands for a bit. Eventually, you can rub them together with a sprinkle of flour and roll the bits back into your dough. With every turn, the dough becomes a bit smoother. This process takes about 5 minutes or up to 10 minutes for dough with more water content (wetter doughs take longer to stiffen up).

For some recipes, such as for my pita, you need to let the flour and water mixture sit for 15 to 20 minutes before kneading, a technique called autolyse. This allows the molecules to internally reconfigure to develop the dough structure themselves, giving you a head start on your kneading and making the process easier. My rule of thumb is: get the best structure you can while messing with the dough as little as possible. Dough that's overkneaded becomes tough and chewy, but this is more of a concern when you're using a stand mixer. It is nearly impossible to overknead dough by hand. You will tire out before that happens.

The First "Rise"

When bread dough rises, yeast is its main actor. Yeast is a living organism, technically a fungus, which needs food, warmth, and moisture to survive, much like us. There are two main types of yeast, and my breads use both: commercial and natural. I'll go into detail on natural yeast later (see page 63), but the most commonly used commercial yeast in home recipes—and the ones in this book—is active dry yeast. Most recipes require you to "bloom" the yeast with water and sugar, hydrating it back to life as it foams up.

ADJUSTING YEAST QUANTITIES

The recipes in this book call for active dry yeast. There's another kind of yeast called instant dry yeast, which is finer and dissolves more quickly, so you can add it directly to your dry ingredients without having to dissolve it first. If you only have instant yeast on hand, decrease the amount of yeast by about 20 percent. For example, 1 teaspoon of instant dry yeast is equivalent to 1¼ teaspoons of active dry yeast.

The rising caused by yeast is the process of fermentation. The yeast, once it comes into contact with flour and water, consumes starches within the flour, breaking them down into amino acids, natural sugars, and free fatty acids and producing alcohol and gases as by-products, which give yeasted bread its characteristic flavor and air pockets.

The longer the process, the more time for the molecules to build flavor and aroma. As time goes by, the dough gets more acidic because the alcohol turns to something like vinegar, just as it does for wine. The right balance of time and temperature in the rise creates just enough acidity to build flavor. Too little activity doesn't produce enough flavor, but too much activity overconsumes the sugars and breaks down the molecules of your new gluten structure, limiting the yeast's activity and collapsing the dough. To avoid this pitfall, many bakers ferment in the cold, where bacteria still thrive but yeast slows their activity; both can do their thing, nice and slow.

I'm a big fan of cold fermentation, or in baker's speak, "retarding" the dough in the refrigerator. It not only builds flavor but also creates stronger dough because the extended yeast activity allows more of the natural gluten formation. Every burst of gas sets protein molecules in motion, spawning more opportunities to link up and form new chains of gluten. A cold rise can be convenient, since it doesn't require a watchful two-hour wait for the dough to rise. You can make dough in the morning to bake in the evening or let the dough rise overnight to make fresh bread in the morning by refrigerating it during the rise. The natural process in my sourdough base recipe requires slow fermentation.

IS YOUR DOUGH READY?
A THREE-STEP TEST

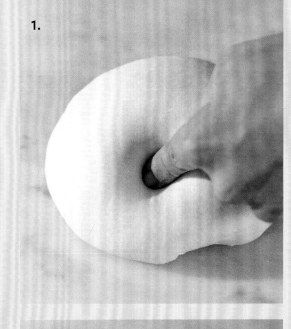

Groups of proteins bind and break to create bread's skeletal structure. Deriving from the Latin word for "to stick," gluten describes the proteins that form when flour meets water, generating an intricate web of protein chains that provide flexibility and structure to hold air pockets for leavened bread. The act of kneading binds the proteins into strong elastic chains, producing bread with a perfect crumb (a baking term meaning a well-distributed gluten network producing plenty of holes in the interior texture of the bread) and a flexible, satisfying tug between your teeth.

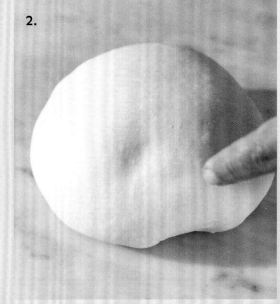

Each variety of wheat produces its own gluten structure; this means different flours yield different results. I use a combination of bread flour, which provides a stronger gluten structure to hold larger air pockets, and a little bit of all-purpose flour to counteract the strength of the bread flour and to create a more delicate chew. For my sourdough starters, I add rye flour for its super-ability to attract more wild yeasts than other flours do. The more yeasts, the more flavor.

There are three ways to tell when your dough's gluten structure is just where you want it and when to stop kneading: texture, elasticity, and strength.

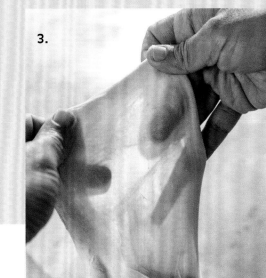

1. Texture: The dough appears smooth—like a baby's butt, we often say.

2. Elasticity: The dough springs back when you dimple it with your fingers.

3. Strength: A small piece of dough stretches thinly enough to see through, like a windowpane, without tearing.

Shaping, Rounding, and (Sometimes) Proofing

The bread recipes in this chapter involve shaping dough in different ways, most often into a ball. When your dough has risen, you want to turn it out of its bowl and cut it into the desired number of pieces while taking care to expel as little air as possible. Making rounds is like creating a dough balloon. You're pulling the dough's surface taut around the inner pockets of air. To do this, gently tug the dough from the top surface and tuck it beneath the ball to create a smooth top for your round. Tighten this shape by placing the round on an unfloured work surface, cupping your hands around the dough and shifting the ball in small circular motions, all while keeping it in contact with the work surface. The dough creates its own resistance, sticking to your work surface, helping to

tighten the molecules and forming a seam on the bottom. With practice, you may be able to roll two balls at a time by cupping a ball of dough beneath each hand and using your thumbs to pull and tuck the surface beneath your round.

Many of my recipes require only a short period of rest before rolling out and baking, but some, such as Ka'ak (page 85), call for shaping and then proofing your bread. Proofing means to let it rise again in its final intended shape. You want to bake your bread at the point it contains the maximum air and while the dough still has the strength to contain it. I give suggestions for proofing times in each recipe, but the best way to tell if your dough is fully proofed is by dimpling the surface with your finger. *Underproofed dough springs back; overproofed dough deflates. Just-right dough holds its dimple.* By this time, you will have noticed a considerable growth in the size of your dough.

Baking

Many of my bread recipes require intense high heat, which is not a simple feat in a home oven. The search for a scorching hearth is the very reason people carry their dough to the bakers who expertly tend communal ovens in the Arab world. Nevertheless, over time, I've discovered some tricks to re-create the experience of a bakery in your home kitchen. Breads in this book are baked in two ways: in the oven or over a high-heat griddle. The griddle mimics the convex griddle traditionally used to cook flatbreads, which go by the name of the surface on which they're cooked— saj breads. For oven breads, make sure to preheat well before baking. If you want to reproduce the effect of a clay oven, invest in a baking stone (see Pizza Tools, page 19) to warm on a low rack, for at least an hour, in advance. The initial boost of heat proofs the bread one final time in the oven,

maximizing the color and crust without drying it out.

One sign of good fermentation is the golden hue of a bread's crust. This is called the Maillard reaction, which is achieved by driving away moisture with heat, kicking off a chain of reactions that result in the caramelization of sugars on the bread's surface. Applying the right heat for the right time is critical for keeping the bread moist inside and beautifully crusted outside.

A few of my recipes, like Ka'ak (page 85), require a steam effect to develop a sweet crust on the outside and a fully baked moist bread on the inside, but most bake in high heat for a short time.

To Sourdough or Not to Sourdough?

One thing that makes the breads in my restaurant unique is they are made with "starter"—a fermented dough with natural yeast that allows for a slow rise. We spent three years building the starter, beginning with a small cup of starter brought over by a friend from Tartine Bakery. I debated whether to rely on natural fermentation to make thousands of rounds of dough a week. The wild yeasts can be tricky, and we struggled to scale up and manage inconsistencies in the beginning. But the wild yeast and bacteria create far more complex flavors than commercial yeast can do alone, so that is why I use both wild and commercial yeasts in my breads. At a certain point in 2019, we found our sweet—or shall I say sour—spot, creating a flatbread with delicious complexity that made it as interesting as the meats, cheeses, yogurts, and vegetables we serve on and with it.

I will never forget the day one of my regulars, a prominent Lebanese academic with strong opinions on Arab culture and politics, arrived for his dose of mana'eesh. He told me firsthand my bread was even better than the loaves made in Beirut. "It's like how it used to be made," he said emphatically. "Unfortunately, unless you go out to the villages, they don't make it like that anymore." I could think of no bigger compliment, and his praise solidified my commitment to learning about fermentation and continuing to perfect our bread at Reem's.

My obsession with natural fermentation is probably no coincidence; it's an ancient tradition dating back to the region of my ancestors, thousands of years before the invention of commercial yeast. In ancient Egypt, the creation of natural starter evolved from beer making. Breweries and bakeries often co-located and, not surprisingly, were run by women. Like many of the best inventions, the discovery was probably accidental. Most likely, the wild yeast spores spawned by beer brewing went to work on the flour and water which were mixed in the same clay pots for bread baking, and generated the same amino acids, alcohol, and gases that we now craft with great care to produce soft, chewy, heaven-scented bread. This discovery, several millennia later, connects me to bread as part of my own lifeline.

Way back before I started my bakery and before sourdough starter became popular for home bakers in the wake of the coronavirus pandemic, my only exposure to sourdough was at the iconic Boudin Bakery, located on Pier 39 in San Francisco. Though delicious as bread bowls with chowder, the loaves themselves didn't appeal to me at the time—I preferred the malty sweetness of quick-rise breads and disliked the sour element. When I joined the Arizmendi Bakery & Pizzeria, a sister to the famous Cheese Board Collective in Berkeley, California, in 2011, I knew I'd have my hands in lots of sourdough. Tending the live cultures and tasting the breads we produced, my taste shifted away from Wonder Bread and toward the nuanced world of sourdough and the endless range of flavors it introduces. My appreciation for fermentation took some time, not unlike the process itself.

Chapter Three

Khobz wa Mu'ajinaat · Savory Breads and Pastries

KHAMEERA · خميره

Basic Sourdough Starter

Makes about 1 cup

SOURDOUGH REQUIRES CARE, attention, and lots of loving.

When I started as a worker-owner at Arizmendi Bakery & Pizzeria, I stepped into well-established protocols for rotating and feeding the starter. We learned to take into account the weather, water temperature, flour-to-water ratio, and the frequency of feedings. Some days, our starter did not "look right," and we'd begin our detective work to find out why. How long had it been sitting? At what room temperature? Who fed it last? Did that person measure correctly? Once we'd tweaked the starter, we'd set it out to bask in the ambient room temperature to restore its gooey bubbly luster.

Building your own sour culture is simple and takes about 10 days. If fed correctly, it can last forever. Legend has it, some starters have been passed down as a nourishing heirloom over multiple generations. Reem's starter uses local rye flour, adding a touch of California love to our Arab breads. Rye hosts wild airborne yeasts and adds an element of whole grain complexity to the dough.

There's a life cycle for starters . . . they rise, crest, and then, left untended, they begin to decline (see the section on fermentation on page 60). When a starter has gone too long and descended into a bubbly soup, save ¼ cup, toss out the rest (don't think of it as waste but rather as energy expended), and begin feeding your starter again. In the bread world, that bit you save is called the mother, and I think of mine as a mother connecting me to my lineage.

1 cup/130g white rye flour
1½ cups/360ml lukewarm water
1½ cups/210g bread flour

DAY 1: In a medium bowl, stir the rye flour into ½ cup/120ml of the water, until the clumps dissolve. Cover the bowl with a dish towel and let it sit at room temperature for 48 hours.

DAY 3: Bubbles should begin to appear on the surface. Stir ¼ cup/35g of the bread flour into the mix until smooth. Put the mixture into a plastic container with high sides and cover it with a dish towel. Let it sit at room temperature for another 48 hours.

DAY 5: The starter should start to smell like sourdough bread and show large bubbles. Feed it another ¼ cup/35g of the bread flour and stir until fully incorporated and thick. The texture will be stiff and difficult to stir. Let it sit at room temperature for another 48 hours.

DAY 7: Remove ¼ cup of the starter into a new container with high sides and discard the rest. This becomes your "mother," the starter you'll use to jump-start your next batch of starter. Add another ½ cup/120ml of the water and another ½ cup/70g of the bread flour to your mother, scraping down the sides of the container and making sure everything is well incorporated. Let it sit at room temperature for another 48 hours.

DAY 9: Remove another ¼ cup of the starter and discard the rest. Add the remaining ½ cup/120ml water and the remaining ½ cup/70g bread flour to your mother and let it sit at room temperature for another day. By this time, your starter should be visibly expanding.

DAY 10: Your sourdough starter should reach its peak and be ready for the final feeding before use; see Basic Sourdough (page 68).

FEEDING YOUR SOURDOUGH STARTER

To maintain your starter, you should feed it on a regular basis. The following is my basic formula for maintaining a starter.

1 cup/140g bread flour
½ cup/65g white rye flour
½ cup/120ml water
1 tablespoon/15g Basic Sourdough Starter (opposite)

In a small bowl, combine all of the ingredients and mix with your hands. This will initially feel like a dry dough. (I like a less-hydrated starter, so I can detect more easily any rise or fall in its life cycle.) If the dough feels stiff, do not worry. It will come alive after 12 hours at room temperature, and your starter will then be ready to use.

STARTER CARE TIPS AND TRICKS

The following are helpful tips to maintain a healthy sourdough starter.

1. To maintain your starter for frequent use . . . If you're baking daily or even several times a week, keep your starter at room temperature and feed it daily, using the formula above to keep it bubbly.

2. To maintain your starter for infrequent use . . . If you're not baking weekly, keep your starter in the refrigerator. Once a week, pull it out of the refrigerator, feed it using the formula above, let it sit overnight at room temperature, and then return it to the refrigerator. It's helpful to designate a specific day of the week to feed it so you don't lose track.

3. To wake a sleeping starter for baking . . . Feed refrigerated starter about 12 hours before you plan to use it and then let it sit at room temperature. A starter that's fed the night before will be ready the next morning.

4. To grow your starter for bigger batches of dough . . . The Basic Sourdough recipe (page 68) will leave enough starter for future batches. If you're scaling up for a larger batch, double the portion you take from your mother and double the feeding formula for the starter.

THINGS TO LOOK OUT FOR

- If your starter is growing, is bubbly, and is sour smelling, it's in good shape.

- If your starter has been left for a long time in the refrigerator, it will separate into liquid on top and a darker mass below. Dump out the liquid and feed the base.

- If your starter is moldy, toss it out and begin anew.

- If you're feeding your starter weekly, 24 hours outside of the refrigerator without a feeding should be enough to get your starter going.

- If you're feeding your starter monthly, you'll need 48 hours outside of the refrigerator and two feedings.

'AJEENAH MUKHAMMARA · عجينة مخمره

Basic Sourdough

**Makes enough for 1 recipe of Arab Bread (page 71)
or Herby Za'atar Flatbreads (page 77).**

IF YOU HAVE successfully made your starter, congratulations. You are now ready to create Arab sourdough bread. Sourdough can be used for most of the bread recipes in this chapter. Refer to Using Ratios (see page 59) to scale up or down based on the percentages provided for each ingredient below.

Because this dough is made with sourdough starter and not commercial yeast, this recipe performs best when the dough is allowed to ferment in the refrigerator overnight. The slow fermentation allows the natural yeast to do its job, developing flavor and airiness in the dough. So, for best results, make this dough a full 24 hours before you plan to use it.

2 cups/480ml (57%) water

¼ cup/60g (7%) Basic Sourdough Starter (page 66)

6 cups/840g (100%) bread flour

2 tablespoons/18g (2%) kosher salt

3 tablespoons/45ml (5.6%) neutral oil, such as sunflower, plus more for greasing the bowl

To mix by hand: In a large bowl, combine the water, starter, and 3 cups/420g of the flour and use a sturdy wooden spoon to mix until everything comes together and forms a viscous, white gooey batter. Set aside, uncovered, at room temperature for 20 minutes. Add the remaining 3 cups/420g flour, salt, and oil and work together with your hands, squeezing the dough between your thumb and fingers in a lobster claw–type movement, until the mass forms a rough and shaggy ball. Turn out onto a lightly floured work surface and knead for about 10 minutes, or until the dough is smooth, springs back when dimpled, and stretches like a windowpane (see page 61).

To mix in a stand mixer: Combine the water, starter, and 3 cups/420g of the flour and, using the paddle attachment, mix until everything comes together and forms a viscous, white gooey batter. Set aside, uncovered, at room temperature for 20 minutes. Switch to the dough hook and add the remaining 3 cups/420g flour, salt, and oil. Mix at medium speed until the dough pulls away from the sides of the bowl, about 10 minutes.

Form the dough into a ball. Then coat a large bowl with oil and transfer the dough into the bowl. Cover the bowl with plastic wrap or a damp dish towel and let it sit for about 4 hours in a warm draft-free spot in your kitchen.

Proceed with your bread recipe or if you are not planning to use the dough right away, place the bowl in the refrigerator for up to 24 hours. When you are ready to use, remove the bowl from the refrigerator and set it out at room temperature 1 hour before baking.

'AJEENAH · عجينه
Basic Yeasted Dough

**Makes enough for 1 recipe of Arab Bread (page 71)
or Herby Za'atar Flatbreads (page 77)**

THIS DOUGH RECIPE forms a base for most of the breads in this chapter.

5½ cups/770g bread flour
2½ cups/590ml warm water (about 100°F)
1½ teaspoons/6g sugar
1 tablespoon/9g active dry yeast
1 cup/140g all-purpose flour
1 tablespoon/9g kosher salt
**¼ cup/60ml extra-virgin olive oil, plus
more for greasing the bowl**
Semolina flour for dusting

In the bowl of a stand mixer or in a large bowl, add the bread flour and then stir in 2¼ cups/530ml of the water. With the paddle attachment on low speed or using a sturdy spoon, mix until it resembles a thick batter. Set aside for 20 minutes.

While the flour and water mixture rests, stir together the remaining ¼ cup/60ml water, sugar, and yeast in a small bowl. Set aside until foamy, about 10 minutes. At this point, the yeast mix should give off a sweet fragrance and show a bubbly bloom.

To mix by hand: Use your hand to incorporate the yeast mixture, all-purpose flour, salt, and oil into the dough. Squeeze the dough between your thumb and fingers with one hand while holding the bowl with the other hand, until it forms a rough and shaggy ball. Turn out the dough onto a lightly floured work surface and knead until the dough is smooth, springs back when dimpled, and stretches like a windowpane (see page 61). This usually takes up to 10 minutes of kneading (see page 59).

To mix in a stand mixer: Add the yeast mixture, all-purpose flour, salt, and oil to the bowl and use the dough hook to mix the dough on low speed until everything comes together, scraping the bowl if needed. Turn up the speed to medium and mix until the dough pulls away from the sides of the bowl, 8 to 10 minutes, or until the dough is smooth, springs back when dimpled, and stretches like a windowpane (see page 61).

Form the dough into a ball. Then coat a large bowl with oil and transfer the dough into the bowl. Cover the bowl with plastic wrap or a damp dish towel and let it rise in a warm draft-free place for 1½ hours or until doubled in size. If you are not planning to use the dough right away, refrigerate for up to 12 hours until doubled in size.

KHOBZ ARABI · خبز عربي
Arab Bread

Makes ten 8-inch breads

IT'S AMAZING TO think that pita bread, or as we call it khobz arabi, became popular as an American food within my lifetime. While I was growing up, it was a rarity to find it unless we made our way to the Arab markets. My mom used to carve out some special room in the freezer to store the stacks we needed for our weekend breakfast mezze or for gatherings of guests. For those, she would flip the flat rounds back and forth over the open flame of our stove, filling the kitchen with the smell of fresh toasty bread.

Over time, I've tasted Arab breads in every imaginable size and thickness. This recipe makes ten 8-inch breads with just enough heft to give them a nice chew, although slightly thicker than the Lebanese pita we had growing up. If you like a "chubbier" pita, feel free to roll out to 6 inches instead. If you want a thinner pita, divide the dough into 12 pieces.

No matter how many times I make this recipe, I never tire of the sight of my bread rising into a beautiful bubble as it cooks. If the dough is strong and the heat is high, it will hold a lovely crust without deflating. To this day, I try to bake a symmetrical pocket evenly thick on both crusts. No matter the width, these beautiful breads go perfectly with just about any recipe in this book and form the base for an infinite combination of toppings.

This recipe is easy to make and freezes well if you have any leftovers—which would never happen in my household. My three-year-old son leaves no pita unconquered. Leftovers can also be repurposed for Fattet Lahme wa Hummus (page 159) or Salatet Fattoush (page 211).

**1 recipe Basic Yeasted Dough (page 69)
or Basic Sourdough (page 68)
All-purpose flour for dusting**

Divide the prepared risen dough into 10 pieces (about 137 grams each). Shape the pieces into rounds (see page 62), cover with a dry dish towel (or brush the dough with a bit of oil and cover gently with plastic wrap), and let rest for 20 minutes. If you are not baking right away, you can also shape and set aside in the refrigerator up to 24 hours until you are ready to bake.

When you are ready to bake, preheat the oven to 500°F. Arrange the oven racks on the upper and lower thirds of the oven; if you are using a baking stone, remove the lower rack from the oven, place the stone on the floor of the oven, and preheat the oven for at least 45 minutes.

Place the dough rounds on a lightly floured work surface, sprinkle them with flour, and pat each round into a 4-inch disk. Working your way around the rim of each disk, use your thumb and index finger to pinch the edges and stretch out the dough. (If the dough is resistant, allow the round to rest, covered with plastic wrap or a dish towel, for another 5 to 10 minutes.) Once you have pinched around the whole circle, sprinkle with a light dusting of flour. Continue the process for the remaining disks.

Using a rolling pin, roll out each round, up and then down once, shift a quarter turn and repeat the process, dusting with flour as needed, until you have an 8-inch disk. Continue the process for the remaining disks. Let the disks rest for another 5 minutes.

continued

If space is limited, stagger your disks on top of each other and dust with an ample amount of flour.

Sprinkle a thin layer of flour over two inverted sheet trays and place two or three disks on each one. To give the pita room to rise, remove the top rack of the oven. Place one of the sheet trays on the lower rack for 2 to 3 minutes or until the pita rise into a bubble and you see pleasing spots of brown.

Remove the sheet tray from the oven and transfer the pita in a single layer to a wire rack so they keep their shape. Place your next prepared sheet tray in the oven while your first sheet tray cools. Repeat the process, rotating between the two sheet trays, until all of your pita breads have been baked.

NOTE • If you're feeling brave and have a dough peel, you can also cook the khobz arabi directly on the baking stone for about 3 to 7 minutes or until the pita rises.

Cooled pita can be stored in a resealable bag at room temperature for 2 days or frozen for up to 6 months. To serve pita from frozen, throw them in the oven at 450°F for about 5 minutes. Enjoy this bread with all of your favorite mezze dishes.

KHOBZ OR PITA?

We call the flat round bread that is known as pita in the West, khobz arabi (Arab bread) or pita. It is unclear how the word *pita* caught on in the English language, but we know it is borrowed from the Greek word for bread. This word, *pisomi*, traces back to the ancient Greek word for "fermented pastry," which then made its way into Latin as *picta* (ever wonder why pizza sounds so similar?).

Bread itself has prehistoric roots in the Fertile Crescent, the boomerang-shaped region spanning from Syria to Iran that is known for its irrigation techniques and agriculture. Going all the way back to the Neolithic period, when people first learned to domesticate crops like wheat and barley, bread making marked our transition from hunter gatherers to makers and cultivators. The first known records for bread making originate in Mesopotamia (modern-day Iraq). Travelers and conquerors passing through the region brought the bread they had encountered and its methods back to their own cultures. That is the reason why Turkish, Greek, and Arab breads are so similar. Whether you call these breads khobz or pita, it's good to know the origin.

KHOBZ SAJ · خبز الصاج

Saj Bread

Makes six 12- to 14-inch flatbreads

SAJ BAKING REQUIRES the development of savvy culinary hands. I've been told that I'm not the only one who was hypnotized while watching women in Lebanese and Syrian villages spinning dough from one hand to the other, the disk thinning and expanding with each toss until becoming nearly translucent. The sheet of dough is then stretched on a stiff, round canvas-covered cushion and smacked onto a steel-carbon dome, kept hot by a massive burner emitting concentric flames, or wood fire if you're going old school, beneath it. Within seconds, the dough begins bubbling. It's then either topped with an herb mix like Za'atar (page 24) or flipped and cooked into a flatbread.

In my early quest to make bread to order for customers, I sent my uncle on a quest deep into the mountains of Lebanon to fabricate artisan griddles just for me. Eventually, two saj griddles arrived via Air France, and I got them released from the airport customs impound just in time for our debut at the San Francisco Ferry Building farmers' market, one of the most acclaimed markets in the country and the place that eventually built our fan base and helped land us our first brick-and-mortar location.

People gravitated to our stand like moths to a flame, mesmerized, just as I had been, watching the dough stretched and slapped on the hot saj with a resounding smack and then sprinkled with za'atar or cheese.

You can make this bread in your home by creating a makeshift saj from an inverted wok 10 to 16 inches in diameter.

The bread goes by many names, shrak for Palestinians, markook for Lebanese: whatever you call it, it's delicious. Eat saj bread dipped in mezze spreads or as a wrap for sandwiches as in Musakhan (page 173).

½ recipe Basic Yeasted Dough (page 69) or Basic Sourdough (page 68)
All-purpose flour for dusting

Divide the prepared risen dough into 6 pieces (about 114 grams each). Shape the pieces into rounds (see page 62) and cover with a dry dish towel (or brush lightly with oil and cover gently with plastic wrap) and let rest for 20 minutes. If you are not baking right away, you can also shape and set aside in the refrigerator for up to 8 hours until you are ready to cook.

When you are ready to cook, place the dough rounds on a lightly floured work surface, sprinkle them with flour, and pat each round into a 4- to 5-inch disk. Working your way around the rim of each disk, use your thumb and index finger to pinch the edges and stretch out the dough. (If the dough is resistant, allow the round to rest, covered with plastic wrap or a dish towel, for another 5 to 10 minutes.)

Once all of the 6 pieces are ready, invert a wok, bottom side up, over your largest stove burner and set the heat to medium.

Stretch the dough into a thin 12- to 14-inch disk, one piece at a time, using either the beginner, intermediate, or advanced method on page 74.

continued

Beginner Rolling Method

Intermediate Pizza Shop Method

Advanced Traditional Method

Beginner Rolling Method: Using a rolling pin, roll out each disk, up and then down once, shift a quarter turn, and repeat the process, dusting with flour as needed, until you have a 12- to 14-inch disk.

Intermediate Pizza Shop Method: Holding a disk aloft, continue to pinch and stretch the disk from its perimeter, allowing gravity to stretch the dough. When the disk is big enough to fit the knuckles of both hands beneath it, stretch gently in opposite directions, rotating 90 degrees between stretches. Continue the process, until you have a 12- to 14-inch disk. Gradually ease your knuckles out toward the edges to create an even round and to keep the center from thinning too much.

Advanced Traditional Method: Hold a disk palm up in one hand and rotate it, snapping your wrist to slap it with a spin into the opposite palm below. As the disk grows, let it drape across your palm and onto your forearm. Continue inverting the dough from palm to palm with quarter spins, making a motion that resembles an infinity loop, until it stretches to

12 to 14 inches. The more of your arm you use, the less likely the dough is to break.

Once the dough is ready, flip each disk onto your makeshift saj; it should bubble and brown in under a minute. The dough can be moved around if an undercooked area needs access to a hotter part of the saj's surface.

To make mana'eesh, spread or sprinkle on a topping (see page 78) as soon as the bread hits the surface of the saj; otherwise, flip the dough and brown both sides. Repeat the same process with each piece of dough. Stack the bread in a basket lined with a dish towel and serve warm.

Cooled bread can be folded and stored in a resealable bag at room temperature for 2 days or frozen for up to 6 months. To serve from frozen, thaw over a stove flame, in a toaster, or in the oven and serve warm.

MANA'EESH · مناقيش

Herby Za'atar Flatbreads

Makes eight 10-inch topped flatbreads

THE MAN'OUSHE (SINGULAR for mana'eesh) is the quintessential street food of the Levant. Wherever you go in the streets of Damascus, Beirut, or Jerusalem, you'll see professionals, students, families, and their children all enjoying piping hot flatbreads, usually slathered with herbaceous za'atar. They're eaten while walking down the street on the way to work or school, sitting in cafés, or around the breakfast table. Among my favorite memories in Syria and Lebanon is heading to one of the corner bakeries and ordering flatbreads by the dozen. Slid right out of the oven into pizza boxes, my cousins and I would rush back to an aunt or uncle's home and devour them without a single word exchanged.

In today's Arab world, bakeries offer book-length menus of every imaginable topping. But in the old days, according to my mother, every household would bring their own special toppings to the local baker, whether it was a family-secret za'atar formula or homemade cheese, to bake fresh in the inferno of an open oven.

I hope to one day bring back the tradition of the "communal oven." At the beginning of my bakery journey, I obsessed over Barbara Massoud's book *Man'oushé*. With its beautiful illustrations of flatbreads, it became my bible as I methodically worked, through trial and error, to perfect my dough. The more I read about mana'eesh, the greater my certainty that these flatbreads were the missing piece in Arab immigrants' US food experience.

1 recipe Basic Yeasted Dough (page 69) or Basic Sourdough (page 68)
All-purpose flour for dusting the dough
Semolina flour for dusting the pan

Za'atar-Oil Topping
¾ cup Za'atar (page 24)
¾ cup extra-virgin olive oil

Divide the prepared risen dough into 8 pieces (about 170 grams each). Shape the pieces into rounds (see page 62), cover with a dry dish towel (or brush the dough with a bit of oil and cover gently with plastic wrap), and let rest for another 30 minutes. If you are not baking right away, you can also shape and set aside in the refrigerator until you are ready to bake.

When you are ready to bake, preheat the oven to 500°F. Arrange the oven racks on the upper and lower thirds of the oven; if you are using a baking stone, remove the lower rack from the oven, place the pizza stone on the floor of the oven, and preheat the oven for at least 45 minutes.

Place the dough rounds on a lightly floured work surface, sprinkle them with flour, and pat each round into a 4-inch disk. Working your way around the rim of each disk, use your thumb and index finger to pinch the edges and stretch out the dough. (If the dough is resistant, allow the round to rest, covered with plastic wrap or a dish towel, for another 5 to 10 minutes.) Once you have pinched around the whole circle, sprinkle with a light dusting of flour. Continue the process for the remaining disks.

continued

Using a rolling pin, roll out each round, up and then down once, shift a quarter turn, and repeat the process, dusting with flour as needed, until you have a 10-inch disk. Continue the process for the remaining disks. If space is limited, stagger your disks on top of each other and dust with an ample amount of flour. Let the disks rest for another 5 minutes

To make the za'atar-oil mixture: In a small bowl, combine the za'atar and oil, gradually whisking or stirring until it is the texture of a viscous pesto.

Sprinkle a thin layer of semolina flour over an inverted sheet tray and place one disk on it. Spoon about 2 tablespoons (about 1 ounce) of the za'atar-oil topping onto the dough and use the back of the spoon to spread it nearly to the edges, leaving about a ⅛-inch rim.

Place the sheet tray on the upper rack and bake for 2 minutes, until bubbles start to form and the bread starts to develop a crust. Remove the sheet tray from the oven and, with tongs (or your hands if you dare!), transfer the par-baked flatbread directly onto the bottom rack or onto the stone and bake until the edges and the crust are brown about 3 minutes more. Repeat the process with the remaining rounds. Enjoy it sliced like a pizza or rolled up.

Variation: Za'atar and Cheese Topping "Cocktail" Style

This is a Lebanese favorite, for those who prefer two different toppings on the same flatbread. To make, spread 1 tablespoon of the za'atar-oil topping on one-half of the round and ¼ cup of grated melting cheese, such as mozzarella or Oaxaca, on the other half. Leave a ⅛-inch rim all around. Then bake according to the directions.

NOTE • If you're feeling brave and have a dough peel, you can also cook the flatbread directly on the baking stone for about 5 to 7 minutes or until the edges and bottom of the dough are spotted and golden.

ADD SOME LOVE TO YOUR MANA'EESH

I like to prepare various combinations of the following toppings for my mana'eesh before they go into the oven. These ingredients have a warming affect and make these flatbreads substantial meals. There is nothing like the taste of hot melted cheese and cured meats baked right onto my bread

Before the Oven

Charred or roasted seasonal vegetables

Sausage (I like sujuk, an Armenian spiced sausage, or merguez, a Moroccan spiced sausage)

Cured meat (I like basturma, sliced thin like prosciutto)

Feta or goat cheese

Aged cheese like Swiss or Gruyère

Garlic or tomato

Caramelized onions (see page 43)

Roast chicken or lamb

Tomato sauce

Spicy kishk (see page 80)

I finish off my mana'eesh with one or another of the following toppings to bring them to life with an element of healthy freshness. At Reem's, serving mana'eesh with a perfectly ripened avocado or fresh arugula is, indeed, adding some California love. These ingredients have a cooling effect and provide a perfect counterbalance to the heavier warming ingredients that go on before the oven.

After the Oven

Fresh vegetables, such as tomatoes, cucumbers, and arugula

Pickled vegetables

Avocado

Freshly chopped or whole herbs

Toasted nuts or seeds

Labneh or sour cream

Freshly squeezed lemon juice

Hot sauce

Man'oushe Is to Mana'eesh Like Goose Is to Geese

When I told my mother that I wanted to open a restaurant centered on man'oushe, her first reaction was, "You have to call it something else." After all, Arabic words were confusing enough for Arabic speakers—how would I help the American public know what to call it? I remember people asking me, "So, is it mana'eesh or man'oushe?" The easy answer, it's both!

Man'oushe is singular and mana'eesh is plural. Just as the English language has different ways to pluralize words, the Arabic language has innumerable ways as well. To educate our customers and have fun describing the food, we put up signs saying: "It's pronounced *Man-ooo-Shay*! It's okay. We'll still love you and feed you—even if you can't pronounce it." Or "It's kinda like an Arab pizza. But not really. . . ." We used illustrations describing many ways to eat a man'oushe. In no time, we had customers with no prior connection to Arab culture walking up and pronouncing the man'oushe of their choice perfectly and without hesitation because it had become part of their daily routine.

When Reem's started as a market stand in San Francisco's Mission District, I would glimpse people walking by with a warm man'oushe in one hand and in the other, a bag of fresh produce. It was so magical that I might very well have been walking in the streets of Beirut.

Every time I hear this, I smile from ear to ear, knowing that an organic culture shift is underway. And I remember the response I gave to my mom: "Man'oushe will be in the English language of our future. It's that good."

MANA'EESH BIL KISHK · مناقيش بالكشك
Funky Red Pepper and Cheese Flatbreads

Makes four 10-inch flatbreads

I STOPPED COUNTING the number of times my Lebanese customers prodded me for their beloved spicy, funky kishk man'oushe. Confusingly, they would just call it by its topping, kishk, which in essence is a tomato and onion sauce, thickened with fermented yogurt and bulgur. The mixture takes a few days to ripen and develops a creamy texture, and the fermentation produces a funky version of a pimento cheese spread.

1½ cups Fermented Yogurt and Bulgur (page 47)

⅓ cup Spicy Red Pepper Paste (page 38) or store-bought harissa paste

¾ teaspoon Aleppo pepper (optional)

½ teaspoon ground cumin

¼ cup extra-virgin olive oil

¾ teaspoon kosher salt

1 cup finely diced yellow onions or shallots

1 cup finely diced Roma tomatoes (about 4 tomatoes)

½ recipe Basic Yeasted Dough (page 69) or Basic Sourdough (page 68)

All-purpose flour for dusting the dough

Semolina flour for dusting the pan

1 cup grated mozzarella, Oaxaca, Jack, or other melting cheese for topping

Fresh arugula, tomatoes, or other vegetables for serving

In a medium bowl, combine the fermented yogurt and bulgur, red pepper paste, Aleppo pepper, cumin, oil, and salt and mix. Fold in the onions and tomatoes until the mixture forms a spreadable paste. Set aside.

Preheat the oven to 500°F. Arrange the oven racks on the upper and lower thirds of the oven; if you are using a baking stone, place it on the floor of the oven and preheat for at least 1 hour.

Place the dough rounds on a lightly floured work surface, sprinkle them with flour, and pat each round into a 4-inch disk. Working your way around the rim of each disk, use your thumb and index finger to pinch the edges and stretch out the dough. Once you have pinched around the whole circle, sprinkle with a light dusting of flour. Continue the process for the remaining disks.

Using a rolling pin, roll each round up and down, shift a quarter turn, and repeat the process, dusting with flour as needed, until you have a 10-inch disk. Continue the process for the remaining disks. Let the disks rest for another 5 minutes.

Sprinkle a thin layer of semolina flour over an inverted sheet tray and place a disk on the tray.

Spoon about ⅓ cup of the yogurt-red pepper topping onto each of the rounds and use the back of the spoon to spread it nearly to the edges, leaving about a ¼-inch rim. Then sprinkle ¼ cup cheese on top of each round.

Place the sheet tray on the upper rack and bake for 3 minutes, until bubbles start to form and the bread starts to develop a crust. Remove the tray from the oven and transfer the par-baked flatbread directly onto the bottom rack or onto the stone and bake until the edges are brown about 3 minutes more. Repeat the process with the remaining rounds.

NOTE · If you're feeling brave and have a dough peel, you can also cook the flatbread directly on the baking stone for about 5 to 7 minutes or until the edges and bottom of the dough are spotted and golden.

Crispy, Spiced-Meat Flatbreads

Makes five 10-inch flatbreads

THIS DISH IS ubiquitous in the Arab Levant, served as breakfast, lunch, dinner, snacks, and party food. The name translates simply to "meat in dough," and the magic comes in the preparation of wafer-thin bread, topped with the finest possible layer of delicately spiced vegetable-flecked meat to create a bite that's simultaneously crispy and succulent.

Growing up right outside of Watertown, Massachusetts, a town known for its Armenian community, my mom would take us to her favorite source for lahm bi ajeen, Sevan, which was owned by a Lebanese Armenian family. We would drive home with bags full of flatbreads, stacked and layered with parchment paper, filling the car with the smell of spiced meat and fresh bread that made my mouth water.

I love a bright confetti of finely diced vegetables, so I sweeten my spread with Dibs Al Fleifleh (page 38), onions, tomatoes, and a green serrano chile. To make all of the flavors come to life, as the breads come out of the oven, I top them with a squeeze of lemon and a dollop of yogurt. I've seen people eat this iconic street food open-faced or folded. There is no wrong way to eat lahm bi ajeen.

½ recipe Basic Yeasted Dough (page 69) or Basic Sourdough (page 68)

1 yellow onion, finely chopped or grated (about 1 cup)

1 cup finely diced tomatoes (about 1 tomato)

2 tablespoons minced garlic (about 6 cloves)

1 small serrano chile, stems, seeds, and veins removed, finely diced (about 1 teaspoon)

1 tablespoon kosher salt, plus more as needed

⅓ cup Spicy Red Pepper Paste (page 38) or store-bought harissa paste, plus more as needed

½ teaspoon ground allspice, plus more as needed

1 teaspoon ground cumin, plus more as needed

1 teaspoon ground coriander, plus more as needed

½ pound ground lamb or beef

2 tablespoons extra-virgin olive oil

All-purpose flour for dusting the dough

Semolina flour for dusting the pan

Garnish
Leaves from 6 sprigs of parsley
1 lemon, sliced into 4 wedges
½ cup whole milk yogurt

continued

Divide the prepared risen dough into 5 pieces (about 137 grams each). Shape the pieces into rounds (see page 62), cover with a dry dish towel (or brush the dough with a bit of oil and cover gently with plastic wrap), and let rest for 30 minutes. If you are not baking right away, you can also shape and set aside in the refrigerator until you are ready to bake.

When you are ready to bake, preheat the oven to 500°F. Arrange the oven racks on the upper and lower thirds of the oven; if you are using a baking stone, remove the lower rack from the oven and place the pizza stone on the floor of the oven and preheat the oven for at least 45 minutes.

In a medium bowl, combine the onion, tomatoes, garlic, chile, and salt and toss together. Using a fine-mesh sieve, drain the mixture for about 20 minutes, pressing gently until it's mostly free from any excess water (about ½ to 1 cup of liquid should release).

In another medium bowl, combine the red pepper paste, allspice, cumin, coriander, ground meat, and olive oil. Add the drained onion-tomato mixture and work together with your hands, until the mixture has a pasty consistency.

Using a rolling pin, roll out each round, up and then down once, shift a quarter turn, and repeat the process, dusting with ample amounts of flour, until you have a 10-inch disk. Continue the process for the remaining disks. Let the disks rest for another 5 minutes.

Sprinkle a thin layer of semolina flour over an inverted sheet tray and lay a disk onto the tray. Scoop about ½ cup of the meat mixture onto the dough and, using your fingers and palm, spread the mixture into a thin even layer onto each of the bread rounds, until it spreads nearly to the edges, leaving about a ⅛-inch rim.

The Armenian Influence on Lahm bi Ajeen

Baalbek-style, Aleppo-style, Armenian-style—many have adapted this bread. Some like it a little sweeter, with pomegranate molasses. Some a little spicier. As with many foods that travel, lahm bi ajeen is known by several names, including lahmajun, most notably in Turkey. Though the origins of the dish come from the Arabic name (which literally translates to "meat in dough"), it was Armenians, working in Ottoman kitchens, who introduced and then propagated the dish. Treated as second-class citizens after their conquest by the Ottomans, Armenians suffered a wrenching genocide, still unrecognized by Turkey, in World War I. For Armenians, as for Palestinians, the preservation of their food became key to resisting their erasure.

In every community where they found refuge, Armenians have excelled culinarily, particularly in the bakeries. In Bourj Hammoud, Beirut's Armenian neighborhood, Armenian bakers pump out thousands of lahm bi ajeen every day in bakeries that stud the one-mile stretch of little Armenia. I sometimes joke that if the Arabs and Turks are fighting over their claim to something, chances are, it's Armenian. Such is the case with lahm bi ajeen.

Place the sheet tray on the upper rack and bake for 3 minutes, until bubbles start to form and the bread starts to develop a crust. Remove the tray from the oven and, with tongs (or your hands if you dare!), transfer the par-baked flatbread directly onto the bottom rack or stone and bake until the edges are brown and a bottom crust forms, about 3 minutes more. Repeat the process with the remaining disks.

Garnish with the parsley, lemon wedges, and a dollop of yogurt.

NOTE • If you're feeling brave and have a dough peel, you can also cook the flatbread directly on the baking stone for 5 to 7 minutes or until the edges and bottom of the dough are spotted and golden.

KA'AK · كعك
Sesame-Crusted Bread Pouches

Makes 8 bread pouches

THIS IS ONE of my all-time favorite breads in the Arab world. I have vivid childhood memories of old men on horse-drawn carts slinging toasty-brown loop-shaped loaves to passersby. There's something irresistible and tantalizing about bread stacked on a tall stick or hanging fresh from wire hoops, in much the same way as it's hard to pass up funnel cakes flying fresh out of the booth at a state fair.

Many vendors keep bowls of Khalta Harra (page 27), a chile-spice mix; Za'atar (page 24); or sumac on hand and split the puffy pouch of the bread to stuff with these spices and occasionally with Picon cheese, an iconic French brand of semi-soft spreadable cheese, introduced to Lebanon in the 1960s during my mother's childhood. She enjoyed these school-morning snacks, grabbed straight from the carts, some of which were even equipped with little toasters to serve them piping hot.

You can also use these pouches as buns for sandwiches such as the Kafta (page 179) or Falafel Mahshi (page 153).

1 recipe Basic Yeasted Dough (page 69) or Basic Sourdough (page 68)

All-purpose flour for dusting the work surface

Neutral oil, such as sunflower, for greasing the pan

½ cup sesame seeds

Semolina flour for dusting the pan

1 cup cold water or ice cubes

Follow the instructions for making the dough through its first rise and until it has doubled in size. Gently ease the dough from the bowl, cradling it with both hands to minimize deflation.

Divide the dough into 8 pieces (about 170 grams each). Tuck the edges under, as if you are starting the process of making rounds (see page 62). Let rest for 5 minutes.

Place a round, smooth side down, on a lightly floured work surface. Gently tug the sides and then fold the left and right ends to meet in the center. Pinch the ends to form a 4-inch seam in length, resulting in an elongated round. Flip and rotate the round 90 degrees, so the wide side now faces you. To seal the seam, flip the round, seam side down, and cradle it between your index fingers and thumbs, rocking the dough back and forth a few times against the friction of the table, until the dough has tightened. Your dough should start to look like a football. Repeat with the remaining pieces and place them on a lightly oiled sheet tray.

Leave the pieces of dough, covered with plastic wrap or a dish towel, to proof in a draft-free place for 2 hours, until they are puffed and doubled in size.

Remove the dough from the baking tray and shape each piece into a "purse," a rounded pouch, topped with thinner handles. Gently tug the pointy ends of each inflated football and roll them out under your palms, until the dough resembles a 10- to 12-inch-long baguette with a fat belly and skinny tapered ends. Repeat the process for the remaining pieces.

continued

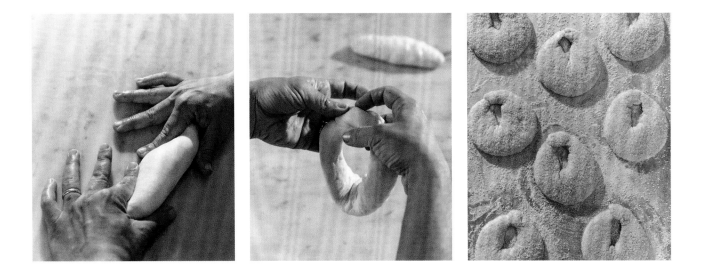

Return to the first piece, wrap one end over the other, tuck the tail beneath, and gently press to seal, forming a lopsided circle. Gently press the pouch of the purse—the loop's fatter center—to flatten it. As you do so, the size of the hole will shrink to about an inch. Repeat the process for the remaining pieces.

Place the sesame seeds in a shallow tray. Using a spray bottle or pastry brush, lightly coat the top of each purse with water. Dunk the wet side into the sesame seeds.

Sprinkle a thin layer of semolina flour over a sheet tray. Flip each purse, sesame side up, onto the prepared sheet tray. Let the dough rest, covered with plastic wrap or a dish towel, for another 45 minutes to an hour at room temperature. They are ready when an indentation remains after you've pressed your finger into the dough.

While the dough is resting, preheat the oven to 500°F. Place the water in a shallow nonglass pan at the bottom of the oven to create a steam effect; this will help the loaves expand properly and develop a nice crust.

Bake for 6 minutes and then rotate and bake for another 6 minutes, or until the crust and seeds take on a deep golden-brown color.

Ka'ak are delicious eaten warm, or they will last a few days stored in a paper bag at room temperature and used for sandwiches or toast.

NOTE • One way to create a proofer to aid the yeast in its important work and cut your time in half is to place the dough, uncovered, on the middle rack of a closed, turned-off oven above a pan filled with 2 to 3 cups of boiling water on the bottom rack. Let the dough sit for 45 minutes to 1 hour.

Spinach and Onion Turnovers

Makes 24 turnovers

EQUALLY AT HOME on the plates of vegans and meat lovers alike, spiced spinach and onion flavors burst from these pyramid-shaped, crispy-seamed turnovers. The trick to a perfect seal is to squeeze out as much moisture as possible from the spinach mixture before placing it on the dough, so that when the spinach cooks, it won't steam and pop the pie open, exposing its innards for all to see. If your pie opens, don't be hard on yourself. My mom never cared. The turnovers are still equally as delicious!

I always thought of fatayer as a baking affair prepared by women to be enjoyed at a big azoumeh, which in Arabic translates to "house party." So, I was shocked the first time I saw burly men making them en masse in bakeries in Lebanon, where men hold more of the large-scale production-type jobs.

Fatayer makes a great seasonal dish as well. It can be stuffed with chard, purslane, lamb's-quarters, or a host of greens that are often used in Lebanon. Starting with triple-washed baby spinach that is widely available and reasonably priced saves the extra step of rinsing and drying and will give you a head start on producing spinach with a minimum of water content.

This same dough is used in other turnover recipes: Fatayer Jibneh (page 92) and Sfeeha Ba'albekiyyeh (page 90).

Fatayer Dough
¾ cup/180ml warm water (about 100°F)
1½ teaspoons/4g active dry yeast
1 teaspoon/4g sugar
2¾ cups plus 1 tablespoon/385g all-purpose flour, plus more for dusting

1½ teaspoons/5g kosher salt
⅓ cup/80ml extra-virgin olive oil, plus more for greasing the bowl

Filling
12 cups/32g spinach leaves, cleaned and coarsely chopped
1½ teaspoons/5g kosher salt
2 cups/280g red onion, finely diced (about 1 small red onion)
⅓ cup/80ml extra-virgin olive oil
1 tablespoon/15ml lemon juice (about ½ lemon)
½ teaspoon/2g lemon zest
3 tablespoon/18g sumac
¼ teaspoon/1g freshly ground black pepper
¼ teaspoon/0.5g ground allspice
½ cup/60g toasted pine nuts or coarsely chopped toasted walnuts (optional)

Olive oil for brushing the tops

To make the dough: In a small bowl, combine ¼ cup/60ml of the water with the yeast and sugar and set aside in a draft-free space for 10 minutes or until foamy.

In the bowl of a stand mixer or in a large bowl, combine the flour and salt.

To mix by hand: Using your hands, slowly drizzle in the oil until the flour forms a fine crumble. Form a well inside the crumble, add the yeast mixture and the remaining ½ cup/120ml water, and use your hands to pull the flour mixture into the wet mix a little at a time. Continue working with your hands, until you get shaggy pieces of dough. Turn

continued

out onto a flat work surface and knead until the dough is smooth, dimples, and stretches like a windowpane (see page 61). This usually takes up to 10 minutes of kneading (see page 59).

To mix in a stand mixer: Using the paddle attachment on low speed, slowly drizzle in the oil, until the flour forms a fine crumble. Switch to the dough hook and add the yeast mixture and the remaining ½ cup/120ml water and mix on medium speed until the dough pulls away from the sides of the bowl, 8 to 10 minutes. You should hear the dough slap the sides of the bowl.

Form the dough into a ball. Then coat a large bowl with oil and transfer the dough into the bowl. Cover the bowl with plastic wrap or a damp dish towel and let the dough rise in a warm draft-free place for 1½ hours or until doubled in size. If you are not planning to use the dough right away, refrigerate for up to 12 hours, until doubled in size.

To make the filling: In your largest bowl, sprinkle the spinach with the salt. Rub the salt into the leaves, using your hands, and let it sit for 5 to 10 minutes.

Meanwhile, in a separate medium bowl, combine the onion with the oil, lemon juice and zest, sumac, pepper, allspice, and pine nuts.

Once the spinach has softened, scoop as much as you can hold in one hand, cup it with your other hand, and squeeze it over a sink to draw out excess water. Continue removing as much moisture as possible from the remaining spinach and then add it to the onion-spice mix until it has all been incorporated. Set aside.

To make the turnovers: When the dough has doubled in size, punch it down and, using a bench scraper or knife, divide the dough into quarters. Cut each of the quarters into 6 pieces for a total of 24 pieces (about 25 grams each). Shape each piece into a smooth round (see page 62) and place on a sheet tray. Cover with plastic wrap or a damp dish towel and let the rounds rest for another 5 minutes.

Working with about six rounds at a time, roll out or hand-press each round on a lightly floured work surface with a floured rolling pin or floured fingers, flipping the dough and dusting beneath with flour, until the dough is ⅛ inch thick and each round is about 4 inches in diameter. Cover the remaining rounds with plastic wrap or a damp dish towel to prevent them from drying.

Preheat the oven to 400°F. Line an 8 by 13-inch sheet tray with parchment paper.

Mound 2 packed tablespoons of the filling in the center of each disk. Lift three edges of the circle with one hand, holding the point where they meet at the center and, with the other hand, pinch the seams together from top to bottom to form pronounced ridges (about ⅛ inch) along the seams (see page 93). Make sure to pinch the seams together well to prevent the spinach from bursting out of the dough while the disks cook. If your seams are not closing, it may mean your dough has dried. Dip your finger in a bowl of water and trace the edges of the disks to hydrate. Repeat this process four more times, until all of the turnovers have been shaped.

Place the turnovers on the prepared sheet tray ¼ inch apart, brush the ridges with oil to accentuate the crunch, and bake for 10 to 12 minutes or until the sides turn golden and the ridges darken to a caramel color. Serve warm or at room temperature.

Once cooled, the turnovers can be stored in an airtight container in the freezer for 3 months and can be reheated, directly from the freezer, in the oven.

SFEEHA BA'ALBEKIYYEH · صفيحة بعلبكية
Baalbek-Style Meat Turnovers

Makes 24 turnovers

JUICY ON THE inside and crisp along the corner seams, these small savory squares of dough that encase exquisitely spiced meat are emblematic of Baalbek, a city at the center of the Beqaa Valley, known as the Fertile Crescent in the north of Lebanon and the "Napa" of Lebanon. I've always been drawn to Baalbek, which traces its history back thousands of years, including conquests by the Phoenicians, Romans, and the Ottoman Empire. Right along with the Roman temples, sfeeha are among the region's top tourist attractions.

On the outskirts of Baalbek, the road to the Syrian border is studded with bakeries and butcheries, where you can pick up a favorite meat mix at one spot and ferry it down the street to a bakery to spread on a flatbread or tuck into a pastry. On road trips from Lebanon to Syria, my family loved stopping at these spots for lunch to watch bakers produce these turnovers at lightning speed, pinching precise balls off the big mound of dough with machinelike precision to fill with raw meat and then bake in a high-heat hearth.

These turnovers work equally well on a mezze spread, as party appetizers, or as take-and-bake protein snacks. Proceed with caution, though: after one, it's near-impossible to stop eating them.

1 recipe Fatayer Dough (page 87)

½ cup pine nuts

1 red onion, finely diced (about 2 cups)

¼ cup whole-milk regular or Greek yogurt

2 tablespoons tahini

2 tablespoons pomegranate molasses

1 tablespoon kosher salt

2 teaspoons ground cinnamon

2 teaspoons ground allspice

1 teaspoon freshly ground black pepper

1 teaspoon Aleppo pepper (optional)

12 ounces ground lamb or beef

2 tomatoes, finely diced and strained of excess liquid (about 1½ cups)

All-purpose flour for dusting

2 tablespoons pomegranate seeds (optional)

Olive oil for brushing the crusts

Follow the instructions for making fatayer dough (see page 87) through to the point where it is portioned into 24 pieces.

Preheat the oven to 300°F.

Spread out the pine nuts on a sheet tray, toast for 8 minutes. Set aside. Turn the oven up to 400°F.

To make the filling: In a large bowl, combine the onion, yogurt, tahini, molasses, salt, cinnamon, allspice, black pepper, and Aleppo pepper. Add the meat and knead the mixture with your hands until just incorporated. Do not overknead! Gently fold in the tomatoes and ¼ cup of the pine nuts.

Line an 8 by 13-inch sheet tray with parchment paper.

Working with about six rounds at a time, roll out or hand-press each round on a lightly floured work surface with a floured rolling pin or floured fingers, flipping the dough and dusting beneath with flour, until the dough is ⅛ inch thick and each round is about 4 inches in diameter. Cover the remaining rounds with plastic wrap or a damp dish towel to prevent them from drying.

Mound 2 tablespoons of the filling in the center of each disk. Top with a pinch of the remaining ¼ cup pine nuts and a pinch of the pomegranate seeds. Form the dough into a traditional square shape around the filling by pinching the edges together in four corners, leaving a small ½-inch open square in the center (see page 93). If your seams are not closing, it may mean your dough has dried. Dip your finger in a bowl of water and trace the edges of the disks to hydrate. Repeat this process until all of the turnovers have been shaped.

Place the turnovers on the prepared sheet tray ¼ inch apart, brush the tops with oil, and bake for 10 to 12 minutes or until the sides turn golden and the ridges darken to a caramel color. Serve warm or at room temperature.

Once cooled, the turnovers can be stored in an airtight container in the freezer for 3 months and can be reheated, directly from the freezer, in the oven.

FATAYER JIBNEH · فطاير جبنة

Cheese and Nigella Seed Turnovers

Makes 24 turnovers

THIS IS A great treat to impress your friends: boat-shaped turnovers with golden seams and a burst of flavor from the Akkawi cheese and nigella seeds inside. Bread-based dishes like this one, and the small dishes like olives and pickles that accompany them, can be served at any time of the day, from breakfast, to picnics, and right through to dinner.

This recipe calls for Akkawi cheese and nigella seeds; both are commonly found in Arab markets. If you want to make this with ingredients on hand, you can substitute any crumbly melting cheese like mozzarella or Oaxaca and black sesame seeds.

1 recipe Fatayer Dough (page 87)
1½ cups melting cheese, such as Akkawi, mozzarella, or Oaxaca cheese
All-purpose flour for dusting
1½ tablespoons nigella seeds
Olive oil for brushing the tops

Follow the instructions for making the dough through to the point where it is portioned into 24 pieces.

In a food processor, pulse the cheese until you get a fine crumbled cheese. If you are using a drier cheese such as Akkawi, add a couple tablespoons of water to form a paste so that the cheese doesn't fly around while you form the turnovers.

Working with about six rounds at a time, roll out or hand-press each round on a lightly floured work surface with a floured rolling pin or floured fingers, flipping the dough and dusting beneath with flour, until the dough is ⅛ inch thick and each round is about 4 inches in diameter. Cover the remaining rounds with plastic wrap or a damp dish towel to prevent them from drying.

Preheat the oven to 400°F. Line an 8 by 13-inch sheet tray with parchment paper.

Mound 2 tablespoons of the cheese in the center of each disk and sprinkle with a pinch of nigella seeds. Form the dough into a canoe shape around the filling by pinching opposing sides of the circle and pulling them gently in opposite directions (see page 93). If your seams are not closing, it may mean your dough has dried. Dip your finger in a bowl of water and trace the edges of the disks to hydrate. Repeat this process until all of the turnovers have been shaped.

Place the turnovers on the prepared sheet tray ¼ inch apart, brush the tops with oil, and bake for 10 to 12 minutes or until the sides turn golden and the ridges darken to a caramel color. Serve warm or at room temperature.

Once cooled, the turnovers can be stored in an air-tight container in the freezer for 3 months and can be reheated, directly from the freezer, in the oven.

Spinach and Onion Turnovers

Baalbek-Style Meat Turnovers

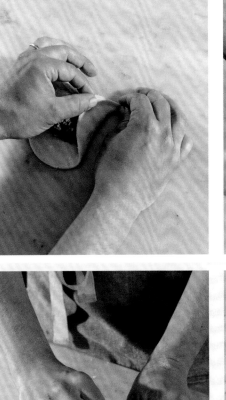 

Cheese and Nigella Seed Turnovers

Chapter Four

Halaweyat Bil Furn · Bakery Sweets

SAMNEH · سمنة
Clarified Butter

Makes 1½ cups

CLARIFIED BUTTER IS a key ingredient in Arab pastries. Clarifying is the process of removing the water and milk-fat solids from the butter, yielding a richer, slightly nuttier taste.

Clarified butter provides not only deep flavor but also health and technical cooking benefits. Once the sugar, protein, and moisture are boiled and skimmed away, the butter can withstand higher cooking temperatures and longer cook times, allowing pastries like Ba'laawa bil Jowz (page 118) sufficient time to turn golden and bake through every layer without burning the top.

The process produces more of butter's healthy fatty acids and removes the lactose, making it safer for most people with lactose intolerance. With its moisture removed, clarified butter lasts longer, adding it to the list of Arab food-preservation techniques. Also known as ghee in South Asian cooking, the butter takes easily to infusions of whole spices and dried herbs during the boiling process, enriching its flavor and adding further health benefits.

I love keeping the milk solids, browning them, and spreading them on toast for a special treat.

1 pound unsalted butter

In a small pot, melt the butter, barely bubbling, over medium-low heat, until foamy, about 20 minutes. Be careful not to let the butter boil or bubble aggressively because the milk solids could emulsify or start to brown. Using a fine-mesh skimmer or a wide flat spoon, periodically scoop the milk solids from the surface.

Cover the mouth of a quart jar with a strainer and a layer of cheesecloth to catch any remaining milk solids and slowly pour the butterfat into the jar. Be careful to leave behind any extra water in the bottom of the pot; this looks like a milky white liquid. Set aside to cool.

The milk solids can be recouped from the strainer and brushed on breads or vegetables as a delicate, sweet finisher.

The butter can be stored in an airtight container at room temperature for up to 6 months or, refrigerated, for up to 1 year.

ATTAR · قطر

Blossom Syrup

Makes 2 cups

ATTAR IS THE signature ingredient that sweetens most Arab desserts and pastries. Orange blossoms and rose petals mingle to infuse this all-purpose syrup with the scent of springtime. In addition to the added flavor, lemon juice keeps the syrup from crystallizing.

In lieu of baking with sugar directly, Arabs often opt to control sweetness by drizzling and, in some cases, drenching pastries in this rich syrup. Pastries hot out of the oven are often met right away with syrup. My general rule of thumb on syrup: room-temperature syrup on hot pastry or hot syrup on cooled-down pastries but never cold on cold, since it will not absorb as well, and never hot on hot, since it may become mush.

Keep this syrup on hand for both the recipes in this chapter and for the recipes in the special occasion desserts chapter. It also mixes well as a simple syrup in cocktails, tea, and coffee.

2 cups sugar
1 cup water
1 tablespoon lemon juice
1 tablespoon orange blossom water
1 tablespoon rose water

Combine the sugar, water, and lemon juice in a medium pot and bring to a boil, stirring until the sugar has dissolved. Decrease the heat and simmer, uncovered, until the syrup thickens enough to coat the back of a spoon, about 7 minutes. Add the orange blossom and rose waters and cook for 3 minutes more. Set aside to cool.

The syrup can be stored in an airtight container in the refrigerator for up to 3 months.

SFOOF · سفوف

Orange-Turmeric Cake

Makes twelve 2-inch squares

THE LICORICE SCENT of anise and the citrusy orange play beautifully off the earthy spice notes of turmeric in this vibrant, sun-colored cake. Serving this family favorite reminds me of the ways my grandmother used to befriend neighbors and make community wherever she went. This Lebanese village cake spoke to her country roots, as she adapted to city life in Beirut.

The key to this cake's delicate crumble is mixing just enough. Cutting the butter into the flour saturates the grain without activating the gluten: too much mixing, and the cake will become gummy. Greasing the pan with tahini instead of butter provides a nutty finish and a subtle heft to the bottom crust. If you don't have tahini, butter works fine. The heartiness of the buttermilk makes this a good breakfast pastry, mid-afternoon snack, or a treat for guests.

Tahini or melted unsalted butter for greasing the pan

1 orange, sliced into ⅛-inch-thick rounds for garnish

1½ cups/300g sugar

1 cup/240ml buttermilk

½ cup plus 2 tablespoons/150ml orange juice (about 4 small oranges)

2 tablespoons/30ml orange blossom water

1½ cups/250g fine semolina flour

2 cups/300g plus 2 tablespoons/18g all-purpose flour

1½ teaspoons/6g baking powder

1½ teaspoons/4g ground turmeric

1 teaspoon/3g anise seeds

¾ teaspoon/2g kosher salt

¾ cup/158g melted Clarified Butter (page 96), ghee, or vegetable oil

Preheat the oven to 350°F. Grease a 9 by 13-inch straight-sided baking pan with the tahini.

Halve the orange rounds until you have 12 nice pieces. Set aside.

In a medium bowl, combine the sugar, buttermilk, orange juice, and orange blossom water and mix until the sugar has dissolved.

In the bowl of a stand mixer or in a large bowl, combine the semolina flour, all-purpose flour, baking powder, turmeric, anise seeds, and salt.

To mix by hand: Slowly drizzle in the clarified butter. Use a fork or your hands to rub the butter into the flour mixture until the flour is fully saturated and forms fine crumbles. Make a well in the center of the flour mixture and, with a mixing spoon or spatula, pour in the wet ingredients and mix until almost no lumps remain. (The batter will resemble cornbread.)

To mix in a stand mixer: Using the paddle attachment on low speed, slowly drizzle in the clarified butter, until the flour mixture is fully saturated and forms fine crumbles. Pour in the wet ingredients and mix until almost no lumps remain. (The batter will resemble cornbread.)

Pour the batter into the prepared pan and spread evenly. Lay down three even vertical rows of four orange slices.

Bake for 30 to 35 minutes or until a toothpick inserted into the center comes out clean. Serve warm or at room temperature.

The cake can be stored in an airtight container in the refrigerator for up to 1 week.

NAMOURA · نمورة
Tangy Coconut-Semolina Cake

Makes twenty 3-inch squares

CRUSTY ON TOP, delicate and crumbly in the center, this blossom-infused Arab favorite is as easy to make as it is gratifying to eat and serve. No wonder my grandma always had a stash on hand as an after-breakfast treat or post-swim pick-me-up.

During my pastry training, I churned out volumes of cakes, but what I quickly realized was these formal methods were not new, at least not to me. I remembered my grandmother's cakes and in particular this namoura, something deeply traditional but also entirely expressive of my own tastes. I already knew how to make great pastry—my grandmother and our people had been doing it all along—and this settled in me a lingering uncertainty about where I belonged.

The namoura served in commercial bakeries is denser and sweeter than I prefer. My namoura draws on the flavors I love but also marries them with my pastry training: flour and eggs fluff up the center, while semolina flour forms a deeply satisfying crust, helping to soak up the blossom syrup. I added lemon zest to emphasize the subtle tang of the yogurt and reduced the sugar to heighten the coconut's nutty profile.

This cake holds up well and can be made a day or two in advance and stored, covered, in the refrigerator. Bring to room temperature before serving.

Tahini or melted unsalted butter for greasing the pan

4 eggs

¾ cup/145g sugar

1½ cups/335g labneh or whole milk Greek yogurt

1 cup/240g neutral oil, such as canola or sunflower

1 cup/75g unsweetened shredded coconut

2 tablespoons/30ml orange blossom water

Zest of 1 lemon

1⅓ cups/180g all-purpose flour

1⅛ cups/180g semolina flour

1½ teaspoons/7g baking soda

1½ teaspoons/5g kosher salt

¼ cup/32g whole almonds, with skins

1 cup/240ml cold Blossom Syrup (page 97)

Preheat the oven to 350°F. Grease a 9 by 13-inch straight-sided baking pan with the tahini.

In the bowl of a stand mixer or in a large bowl, combine the eggs and sugar.

To mix by hand: Whisk the eggs and sugar vigorously until the mixture becomes pale and fluffy, about 5 minutes. Using a spatula, fold in the labneh, oil, coconut, orange blossom water, and lemon zest.

In a separate medium bowl, combine the flours, baking soda, and salt. Sift the dry ingredients into the wet ingredients one-third at a time and fold in with the spatula until fully incorporated and no pockets of flour remain.

To mix in a stand mixer: Using the whisk attachment, beat the eggs and sugar on high speed until the mixture has tripled in size and is pale yellow, 2 to 3 minutes. Decrease the speed to low and add the labneh, oil, coconut, orange blossom water, and lemon zest. Mix for 1 minute more until fully incorporated and no pockets of flour remain.

In a separate medium bowl, combine the flours, baking soda, and salt. Add the dry ingredients to the wet ingredients one-third at a time and mix on low speed until fully incorporated and no pockets of flour remain.

Using a rubber spatula, scrape the batter into the prepared pan and spread evenly.

Bake for about 40 minutes or until a toothpick inserted into the center comes out clean. The top should be crusty and a deep golden brown.

While the cake is baking, fill a kettle with water and place over high heat until boiling. Place the almonds in a heatproof bowl and pour the water over the almonds, leaving them to soak until cool. Once the almonds are cool enough to touch, drain the water and squeeze each nut between your fingers to pop them out of their skins.

When the cake has finished cooking, let it rest for about 10 minutes on a wire rack. While it's still hot, cut it into diamond-shaped pieces, four rows horizontally and five rows diagonally to make 20 pieces. (You will have some scrap pieces that make a good snack.) Press a skinless, hydrated whole almond or almond sliver in the center of each piece and seal them in by pouring the cold syrup over the hot cake, allowing the syrup to soak into the crevices and edges.

NOTE • My general rule of thumb on syrup: cold on hot or hot on cold but never cold on cold, since it will not absorb as well, and never hot on hot, since it may become mush.

MA'AROUK · معروك
Aleppan Braided Brioche

Makes 1 loaf

THE ALEPPANS DESERVE a place in the heart of all bread lovers for their delicately spiced and syrup-glazed take on the soft, puffy bread we know here as challah. This braided brioche is a treat served mainly during Ramadan.

Bread bakers over the ages have created fancier versions with dates and other fillings, but I opted for its simplest form because making it takes me back to my challah-braiding days at the worker-owned Arizmendi Bakery & Pizzeria. Every Friday, we would produce challah for the Sabbath. I became a pro at braiding dough—an afternoon weaving the long, soft ropes, alive with molecular activity, was therapy. When I discovered this Aleppan specialty, I was immediately hooked, not just for its proximity to challah (which I love), but for the way it incorporates two beautifully Arab ingredients—anise and sesame seeds—imparting a faint sweetness.

The secret ingredient that lends a nutty floral flavor to this bread is mahlab, adding a level of complex flavor to many breads in the region. Mahlab is the pulverized pit of a St. George cherry. It can be found in Arab grocery stores and is well worth having in your pantry if you want to bake the sweet breads and pastries in this book.

Dough
1 tablespoon/11g active dry yeast
2½ teaspoons/10g sugar
¾ cup/180ml whole milk, warmed to skin temperature (about 100°F)
2¾ cups/385g all-purpose flour, plus more for dusting
1 teaspoon/3g kosher salt
1 teaspoon/2g ground mahlab (optional)
¾ teaspoon/2g ground anise
2 tablespoons/50g whole milk yogurt
2 tablespoons/50g melted unsalted butter
1 egg
Neutral oil, such as canola or sunflower, for greasing the bowl

Egg Wash
1 egg yolk
1 tablespoon/15ml heavy cream

3 tablespoons/30g sesame seeds
(I like a mix of black and white)

Syrup
4 or 5 cardamom pods
1 cup/200g sugar
½ cup/120ml water
1 teaspoon/5ml lemon juice

To make the dough: In a small bowl, dissolve the yeast and sugar in the milk. Mix until well incorporated and set aside in a draft-free place for 10 minutes or until foamy.

In a separate small bowl, combine the flour, salt, mahlab, and anise.

To mix by hand: Add the dry ingredients to a large bowl. Make a well in the center and pour the yeast mixture into the middle. Add the yogurt, butter, and egg in the well and mix the wet ingredients together until well incorporated. Slowly bring the flour into the middle and mix with your hands. You should have a shaggy, sticky dough. Using a bowl scraper or spatula, gently flip the loose, sticky dough onto a lightly floured work surface and

continued

knead for about 10 minutes or until the dough is smooth, springs back when dimpled, and stretches like a windowpane (see page 61).

To mix in a stand mixer: Combine the yeast mixture, yogurt, butter, and egg in the bowl and, using the paddle attachment, mix on medium speed until well incorporated. Switch to the dough hook, decrease the speed to low, and slowly pour in the dry ingredients. Increase the speed to medium and mix for 5 to 8 minutes, until the dough is shiny and elastic.

Place the dough in an oiled bowl and cover with plastic wrap. Let it rest in a warm draft-free place for 1 to 2 hours or until the dough has doubled in size.

Once the dough has risen, cut it into 3 pieces (about 252 grams each) and roll each piece into lengths about 16 inches long. Pinch the three ropes together at the top and braid the three strands. Pinch them together again at the other end.

Line a sheet tray with parchment paper.

Cradle the braided dough with your hands on both sides and transfer it to the prepared sheet tray. Gently brush the braid with the oil. Gently cover the braid with plastic wrap and allow it to proof for about 25 minutes or until the braid has doubled in size and the dough bounces back about halfway when indented with a finger poke.

Preheat the oven to 400°F.

To make the egg wash: Beat the egg yolk and cream together and brush it onto the dough.

Sprinkle the seeds over the dough.

Bake for 15 to 18 minutes until golden brown.

While the bread is baking, make the syrup: Crack the cardamom pods, pressing them on a hard surface with the flat side of a knife. In a small pot, combine the sugar and water and bring to a boil. Add the lemon juice and cracked cardamom pods and simmer until thickened, 5 to 7 minutes. Remove from the heat and set aside. Make sure the syrup cools before you brush it over the bread.

As soon as the bread comes out of the oven, place it on a wire rack and brush it with the syrup. Let cool and serve.

The bread can be stored in an airtight container at room temperature for up to 3 days; thereafter, it makes lovely French toast.

NOTE • My general rule of thumb on syrup: cold on hot or hot on cold but never cold on cold, since it will not absorb as well, and never hot on hot, since it may become mush.

To Aleppo, With Love

On my trip up the Syrian coast back in 2010, my father and I never made it to Aleppo. In Arabic, we call Aleppo "Halab." Halab was the promised land for food lovers from the West and from the Arab world alike. One of the oldest cities in the world, Aleppo reigned as the heart of culture and food, packed with outdoor markets and produce and fed by surrounding acres of citrus groves and orchards. But more importantly, Aleppo's rich gastronomic display was a result of the role it had played for generations as a refuge for the diverse range of Arabs, Kurds, Armenians, and Circassians who contributed their food traditions to this magical place.

I speak of Aleppo in the past tense with tenderness because it no longer exists as it once did. The devastation of war has brought this magnificent city to its knees. I carry the stories from my father and our friends of the region's specialty spots known only to locals— from sweet shops to expertly carved kebob spindles. The city was a gourmet destination indeed.

LAFAA'IF SAFARJAL · لفائف سفرجل
Quince and Cheese Pastry Rolls

Makes 8 rolls

SAVORING MY FIRST mouthful of pastry amid a burst of buttery flakes at the famous Panadería Rosetta in Mexico City, I knew instantly I had to make my own Arab version of this fruit and cheese confection. Like a croissant or kouign-amann, this crunchy, caramelized wonder is accomplished by repeatedly rolling and folding yeasted dough around the best butter you can find, until the gluten proteins dance their intricate dance with the sugars, salts, and fats to produce a delicately layered pastry whose complex molecular structure would make even a physicist proud. The name for this method is lamination, a process of alternating layers of dough and butter to create flakes of soft, delicate dough. I build an extra layer of depth into the flavor of this dough by creating a pre-ferment base called a poolish.

Anything wrapped in dough reminds me of the yeasted pastries we love in the Arab world; adding fruit and cheese to the mix kicks it over the top. We love cheese in our sweets! The Mexican guava paste I tasted in Mexico City reminded me of the perfumed jams we make from quince during the brief window when they reach their peak ripeness (see page 245). You can also buy these preserves in any Arab grocery store. If quince is unavailable, this recipe works equally well with any of your favorite fruit preserves, including kumquat, apricot, plum, cherry, and rose.

Luis, the head baker at Reem's, descends from three generations of bakers from the Yucatan and rolls beautifully laminated dough that I could swear was baklava in its original form. I hope this pastry honors both his heritage and mine.

This recipe takes patience and time (about 5 hours of inactive time); it's great to make on a Sunday or spread over the course of a couple of days. If you decide to freeze your laminated dough between folds to make the rolls over more than one day, remember to leave ample time for the block of dough to thaw before it can be rolled again.

Poolish
¼ cup plus 3 tablespoons/105ml water
¾ cup plus 2 tablespoons/100g bread flour
1 teaspoon/4g active dry yeast

Dough
1 cup/240ml whole milk, at room temperature
2 teaspoons/8g active dry yeast or 1 tablespoon/15g Basic Sourdough Starter (page 66)
3¼ cups/455g bread flour, plus more for dusting
¼ cup/50g sugar
1 tablespoon plus 2 teaspoons/15g kosher salt
Neutral oil, such as sunflower, for greasing the bowl

Butter Block
2 sticks/227g cold unsalted butter, cut into 1-inch-thick slices

Egg Wash
1 egg
2 tablespoons/30ml heavy cream

1 cup/256g ricotta cheese
1 cup/320g quince (see page 245) or other fruit preserves

continued

To make the poolish: In a small bowl, combine the water, flour, and yeast and mix with your hands or a spoon until it forms a batter. Let it sit, covered with plastic wrap, in a warm place for 2 to 3 hours or in the refrigerator overnight. (If refrigerated, allow a half hour for the poolish to come to room temperature before you're ready to make the dough.)

To make the dough: Add the milk and yeast to the poolish, using a spoon to break it up, and then stir.

In a separate medium bowl, combine the flour, sugar, and salt and mix with a whisk or with your hands.

To mix by hand: Make a well in the center of your bowl of dry ingredients and pour in the milk-poolish mixture. Using cupped fingers, pull the flour bit by bit from the sides. Squeeze handfuls and use the edge of your palm to squeegee the last bits, until the flour is fully incorporated. The dough should be wet and gooey. If it's firm, add warm water, 1 tablespoon at a time (up to ¼ cup), until it loosens up. Let the dough sit, uncovered, for 15 minutes to relax. Using a bowl scraper or spatula, gently flip the loose, sticky dough onto a lightly floured work surface, knead for 5 to 10 minutes or until the dough is smooth, springs back when dimpled, and stretches like a windowpane (see page 61).

To mix in a stand mixer: In the bowl of the stand mixer with the dough hook attached, add the milk, yeast, and poolish and mix at low speed, slowly incorporating the dry ingredients into the wet. The dough should be gooey but firm. If it is too firm, add warm water, 1 tablespoon at a time (up to ¼ cup), until it loosens up. When everything is incorporated, let the dough sit, uncovered, for 15 minutes to relax. Increase the speed to medium and mix until the dough pulls

away from the sides of the bowl, about 5 minutes, or until the dough is smooth, springs back when dimpled, and stretches like a windowpane (see page 61).

Form the dough into a ball. Then coat a large bowl with the oil and transfer the dough into the bowl. Cover the bowl with plastic wrap or a damp dish towel and let it rise in a warm draft-free place for 1½ hours or until doubled in size.

To make the butter block: While the dough is rising, place the butter pieces edge to edge between two pieces of parchment paper, forming a square, and pound it lightly with a rolling pin, until it softens and the pieces merge. Once the butter is malleable, roll it into an 8 by 10-inch block. Straighten up the sides with the edge of your palms. Using a small knife, cut and move any uneven edges to square-up any rounded corners. Keep the butter covered between two pieces of parchment and chill in the refrigerator.

Once the dough has risen, transfer it to a sheet tray and push with your hands or with a lightly floured rolling pin into a rectangular shape about 12 by 16 inches. Cover with plastic wrap and chill in the freezer for 25 to 30 minutes.

Take the butter block out of the refrigerator 10 to 15 minutes before using, so it is malleable and does not break into pieces when you roll it.

Remove the dough from the freezer and position the widest side near you on a lightly floured surface. Remove the butter block from its parchment paper mold, and place it in the middle of the rectangle with the long side perpendicular to you, leaving 1 inch of dough above and below it.

continued

Fold over both sides toward the center so they cover the butter completely and then press the edges together to create a seam down the middle. Position the block with the narrow side facing you so you can roll in the direction of the open sides. Starting from the center each time, use a rolling pin to roll the dough up to the top edge and then down to the bottom, until it forms a long narrow rectangle nearly two-and-a-half times its original length, about 30 inches.

Rotate it 90 degrees and fold the dough, bringing the right side over the center and then the left side over it to the edge to create a trifold that is 8 by 10 inches.

Return the dough to the freezer for 20 minutes to relax the gluten molecules.

Remove the dough from the freezer and transfer it to your floured work surface. Repeat the rolling and folding process. Position the block so you can roll it toward its open sides. Roll it back out to nearly two-and-a-half times its size, rotate 90 degrees, fold it into thirds, cover in plastic wrap, and return it to the freezer to relax for 20 minutes.

Remove the dough from the freezer and repeat the rolling and folding a final time, then cover with plastic wrap and return the dough to the freezer to relax for another 20 minutes for one last time.

To make the egg wash: In a small bowl, beat the egg and cream together with a whisk or a fork. Set aside.

Remove the dough from the freezer and transfer to a floured work surface. Continue to add more flour to prevent sticking as you roll out the chilled dough to a 12 by 16-inch rectangle that is about ¼ inch thick. Cut away all four edges to reveal the lamination.

Line a 13 by 18-inch sheet tray with parchment paper.

To form your rolls, use a knife or bench scraper to divide the dough into eight equal strips. Tug gently at the ends to taper them. Wrap each strip around your fingers like a spiral phone cord, tucking in the ends to meet at the center and forming a ringed wall around a thin floor.

Place the rolls bottom side down, spaced at least 2 inches apart, on the prepared sheet tray.

Brush the rolls with the egg wash and loosely cover with plastic wrap. Let sit in a warm draft-free spot such as in a turned-off oven or on top of the refrigerator until at least doubled in size, 1½ to 2 hours.

Preheat the oven to 400°F.

Once the dough has doubled in size, press a spoon into the center of each roll to form a depression, then fill each roll with 2 tablespoons of the cheese, topped with 2 tablespoons of the preserve.

Bake for 20 to 25 minutes, rotating halfway in between, until the rolls are dark golden brown. Serve warm out of the oven.

These pastries are most delicious freshly baked on the day of but can be stored in an airtight container in the refrigerator for up to 2 days and revived in an oven or toaster.

KHALIAT NAHAL · خلية نحل
Yemeni Honeycomb Bread

Makes two 9-inch cakes or one 16-inch cake

KHALIAT NAHAL IN Arabic translates to "bee-hive." Baked closely together in a round pan, pollinated in the center with a dollop of creamy cheese, and sticky with honeyed syrup, these Yemeni buns bake into a honeycomb pattern. I stumbled on this delectable treat in Dearborn, Michigan, the promised land for Arab American foodies. I was on tour promoting *We Are La Cocina*, a collection of stories and recipes with my sister entrepreneurs from La Cocina's kitchen incubator program.

Our crew made our way to Qahwah House, a café that brewed every imaginable roast of Yemeni coffee, served in both modern pots and traditional rakwahs, tiny long-handled copper vessels, kept warm over a low candle. *Qahwah* is the Arabic word for "coffee," which originated in Yemen in the fourteenth century. A wall of photos showed the cultivation of coffee beans on the café owner's family farm in Yemen. There was something familiar about walking into Qahwah House. As soon as I caught the fragrant scent of Arabic coffee, it transported me straight to my grandmother's back patio. But what felt novel to me were the Yemeni pastries, which lined the front counter, fragrant with honey, another of Yemen's celebrated ingredients. Every time I discover a new sweet from the Arab world, it makes me smile—how much I have yet to learn about the wondrous expansiveness of the region's culinary arts.

Dough
1½ teaspoons/6g active dry yeast

¼ cup/50g sugar

¾ cup/184ml warm whole milk (about 100°F)

3 cups/420g bread flour, plus more for dusting

1 teaspoon/3g kosher salt

2 tablespoons/50g plain full-fat yogurt or labneh

1 egg

6 tablespoons/83g unsalted butter, softened

Neutral oil, such as sunflower, for greasing the bowl and pans

Filling
8 ounces/227g mascarpone or cream cheese

Syrup
⅓ cup/80ml honey or Blossom Syrup (page 97)

⅓ cup/80ml water

½ teaspoon/3ml orange blossom water

½ teaspoon/3ml rose water

1 teaspoon/5ml lemon juice

Topping
¼ cup/60ml milk

3 tablespoons/30g sesame seeds

To make the dough: In a small bowl, dissolve the yeast and a pinch of the sugar in ¼ cup of the milk. Mix until well incorporated and set aside in a draft-free place for 10 minutes or until foamy.

continued

To mix by hand: In a large bowl, combine the flour, the remaining sugar, and salt and mix until well incorporated.

In a separate medium bowl, combine the remaining ½ cup milk, yogurt, and egg with the yeast mixture and whisk in the butter.

Make a well in the center of the flour mixture and pour the milk-yeast mixture into the middle. Use a mixing spoon to slowly incorporate the dry into the wet and mix until it forms a shaggy, sticky mass. Using a bowl scraper or spatula, gently flip the loose, sticky dough onto a lightly floured work surface and knead for about 10 minutes or until the dough is smooth, springs back when dimpled, and stretches like a windowpane (see page 61).

To use a stand mixer: Pour the yeast mixture into the bowl with the remaining ½ cup milk, yogurt, and egg. Using the paddle attachment, mix until fully incorporated. Switch to the dough hook and on low speed, add the flour, the remaining sugar, and salt and mix. When the dough starts to look shaggy and comes together, add the butter. Increase the speed to medium and continue to mix for another 5 minutes, until the dough clings to the paddle and slaps the sides of the bowl. It should feel smooth and elastic.

Place the dough in a lightly oiled bowl and cover with plastic wrap. Let it rest in a warm draft-free place for about an hour. When the dough completes its first rise, gently lift it out of the bowl and divide it into 6 pieces, then cut those 6 pieces into 6 pieces to create a total of 36 pieces (about 21 grams each).

Line two 9-inch pans or one 16-inch round pan with parchment paper and rub thoroughly with oil.

Shape each dough piece into rounds (see page 62), then let the dough relax for 10 minutes. Use your fingers to flatten each round into a 2-inch-diameter disk. Place 1 teaspoon of mascarpone cheese at the center of each round. After all the rounds are topped, go back to the first round. Bunch the edges to envelop the cheese and pinch together to seal. Place edge side down in the center of the pans. Repeat the process, spacing the dough balls ½ inch apart, creating concentric circles. Stagger the balls to make a honeycomb-shaped formation.

Once all the dough balls are filled and formed, cover with plastic wrap or a dish towel and let rest for another 1 to 1½ hours. The dough balls should grow and just touch each other.

While the dough is resting, make the syrup: In a small pot, combine the honey and water and heat until the honey is dissolved. Add the orange blossom and rose waters and lemon juice. Set aside to cool completely before using.

Preheat the oven to 375°F. Brush the dough with the milk and sprinkle with the sesame seeds.

Bake for 20 to 25 minutes until golden brown. As soon as the cakes come out of the oven, drizzle with the cooled honey syrup.

Allow the bread to cool slightly before serving. Slice into wedges and enjoy with your favorite tea or coffee.

The cake can be stored in an airtight container in the refrigerator for up to 3 days.

NOTE • My general rule of thumb for syrup is cold on hot or hot on cold but never cold on cold, since it will not absorb as well, and never hot on hot, since it may become mush.

Coffee Culture and Resistance

Coffee and its rituals are a cornerstone of Arab hospitality. The first source for roasting the magical bean into a beverage dates back to Sufi monasteries in the south of Yemen five hundred years ago—two hundred years before beans from anywhere else made it onto the market. My first experience of this community was in Oakland's Yemeni cafés, where coffee, bubbled to perfection in small copper pots, took center stage.

I got to know more about the hardships Yemenis face through my work at the Arab Resource and Organizing Center. Working-class Yemenis make up a large part of the Arab community in Oakland and San Francisco. As Islamophobia climbed in the early years of the Trump administration and a new spate of racist violence targeted Arabs and Muslims, war deepened the world's worst humanitarian crisis unfolding in Yemen.

The Yemenis I've met bear scars both emotional and physical. Despite the involvement of the US government, the war receives little coverage here. Perhaps that's part of the reason federal policies restricting Yemenis from sending remittances back home to family members receive almost no notice, even as famine and starvation spread rapidly. When the Muslim Ban prohibited travel, Yemenis were among the hardest hit; many US families were separated, and some were detained and deported by Immigration and Customs Enforcement. They took up the slogan "Banned and Bombed" to express the Yemeni experience in the United States.

Local officials and civil rights groups denounced the policies, but the Yemeni community knew that to reverse the harm, they would also have to mobilize, organize, and build political power.

I am inspired by the transformation I've seen in this community as a result of organizing, but I'm equally inspired by the way we can use ancient traditions of hospitality to create a sense of home away from home, here, even today. While we work to overturn harmful policies and provide support for a community suffering a humanitarian crisis, we can lift our spirits and remind ourselves of our innate power and the legacies that bind us.

LAFAA'IF FOUSTIK · لفائف فستق
Pistachio-Cardamom Sticky Buns

Makes 18 buns

GOOEY CARAMEL ROLLS laced with cardamom
and pistachios make for a heavenly Arab twist on
a fan-favorite breakfast pastry, sticky pecan rolls.
I learned to make these at Arizmendi Bakery &
Pizzeria, a worker-owned bakery, where I landed
my first professional baking position.

I took the morning shift, starting work hours before
the sun rose to prepare hot sweet breads for early
risers. I gradually pushed through my grogginess
to develop speed and efficiency. I remember the
early days, working alone in the morning silence,
rolling out brioche to fill a whole butcher-block
table and slathering it with melted butter, sugar,
spices, and pecans. The sun would make its way
to the window, lighting up the sugary mix with a
golden glimmer.

My body found a rhythm to move with grace through
rolling, cutting, weighing, and nesting swirls of
dough one against the next. Those were healing
days for me. The work took me out of my head and
into my body. It was meditative. Being a baker
not only fulfilled my yearning for connection to
community, but it also guided me on a necessary
path to rediscover myself and to deal with the
trauma I had experienced in my body as an Arab in
the diaspora.

TIP • The caramel filling comes out bubbling hot and
tempting, so be sure to let it cool just a bit, until the
filling firms up enough not to drip or burn. At Arizmendi,
we called it goo and saved it to fold into our granola
recipe—nothing went to waste.

It's helpful to pull out the butter a half hour ahead of time
so it will already be at room temperature when you start.

Dough
½ cup/120ml heavy cream
½ cup/120ml buttermilk
2 teaspoons/8g active dry yeast
2½ cups/350g all-purpose flour,
plus more for dusting
¼ cup/50g sugar
1½ teaspoons/5g kosher salt
⅓ cup/75g softened unsalted butter
1 egg
Neutral oil, such as sunflower,
for greasing the bowl and pan

Filling
⅔ cup/150g unsalted butter
1 cup/200g packed light brown sugar
1 tablespoon/15ml rose water (optional)
¾ teaspoon/1.5g ground cardamom
⅛ teaspoon/0.5g kosher salt
1¼ cups/150g coarsely chopped
pistachios

To make the dough: In a small saucepan over low
heat, combine the cream and buttermilk and warm
just until the mixture feels warmer than your
skin (about 100°F). Then whisk in the yeast until
dissolved and set aside in a draft-free place for
10 minutes or until foamy.

To mix by hand: In a large bowl, combine the flour,
sugar, and salt. Using a spoon or your hands, mix
in the butter until the mixture forms a crumble.
Make a well in the center of the crumble mixture,
pour in the yeast mixture, and add the egg. Stir
the wet mixture in the middle with a large mixing
spoon or spatula and slowly bring in the flour
mixture from the sides, until it forms a shaggy,
sticky dough.

Using a bowl scraper or your hands, turn out the dough onto a lightly floured work surface and knead for about 10 minutes or until the dough is smooth, bounces back when dimpled, and stretches like a windowpane (see page 61).

To mix in a stand mixer: Add the egg to the bowl and, using the whisk attachment, beat until smooth. Pour the yeast mixture into the bowl. Add the flour, sugar, salt, and butter. Switch to the paddle attachment and mix on medium speed until well combined and a loose ball forms around the paddle, 1 to 2 minutes. Switch to the dough hook and knead for 7 to 10 minutes or until the dough is smooth, springs back when dimpled, and stretches like a windowpane (see page 61).

Shape the dough into a ball. Then coat a large bowl with oil and transfer the dough into the bowl. Cover the bowl with plastic wrap or a damp dish towel and let it rise in a warm draft-free place for 1 to 1½ hours or in the refrigerator overnight for a slow rise. The dough should at least double in size.

To make the filling: In a medium saucepan, melt the butter over low heat. Add the brown sugar and rose water and whisk until bubbles form to make a thick, viscous syrup. Whisk in the cardamom and salt. Lightly grease a 9 by 13-inch baking pan with oil. Spread ¼ cup of the filling into the prepared dish and set the remainder aside.

When the dough is ready, transfer the ball to a lightly floured work surface and use a floured rolling pin to roll out to an 8 by 20-inch rectangle. Position the wide side nearest you. Spread the remaining "goo" over the dough, leaving a ½-inch border, then sprinkle on the pistachios. Roll the dough away from you into a long cylinder.

Using a sharp knife, cut the roll into eighteen 1-inch slices (about 60 grams each) and place each bun, cut side up, nested against each other, in the gooey baking dish. Let rest in a warm place for about 20 minutes to proof the dough before baking.

Preheat the oven to 350°F.

Place the baking dish on the middle rack in the oven and bake for 30 to 35 minutes or until the buns are brown and bubbly. Use a spatula to flip the hot buns, gooey side up, onto a serving plate. Let cool before eating.

The buns can be stored in an airtight container at room temperature for up to 3 days.

عجينة فيلو
Hand-Rolled Phyllo Dough

Makes twenty 12 by 17-inch sheets

THE FIRST TIME I saw bakers making phyllo dough, it was life changing. I'd returned from a trip to the Arab world with my dad, where I had obsessively tracked down every bakery I could find. One fall, while visiting my father outside of Boston, he and I went to Watertown, or as we called it—little Armenia—where countless Lebanese Armenian bakeries had set up shop. We stumbled upon a small bakery in a shopping plaza with a big sign that read: Voted Best Baklava in Boston!

On the day we wandered in, a young woman about my age and a man who looked to be her father stood on opposite sides of an enormous six-foot butcher block, engrossed in the task at hand: stretching a sheet of spectacularly thin dough. Watching the process fascinated me, but it was the product itself that rocked my world. Theirs was an ultra-delicate, soft, delicious dough, layered around nuts and sweet fillings. How was it, I wondered, they could create a dough this soft and yet so strong that it never ripped when stretched thin?

The difference between this house-made dough and the shipped-in-boxes of stuff I'd had before was like night and day. I silently vowed that one day I would feature this homemade dough in my own bakery. It turns out that it's harder to make than it looks, and it's taken generations, descending from the Ottoman Empire, to perfect the skill of making this dough.

If you feel inclined, give making it a try! You might discover a natural-born skill. And if you do, it will set your baklava apart a million times over.

6 cups/840g all-purpose flour, plus more for dusting

3 teaspoons/9g kosher salt

2 cups/480ml warm water (about 100°F)

½ cup/120ml neutral oil, such as sunflower or canola oil, plus more for greasing the bowl

2 tablespoons/30ml apple cider vinegar

Cornstarch for rolling and dusting

To mix by hand: In a medium bowl, combine the flour and salt. Make a well in the center and then pour the water, oil, and vinegar into the middle. Slowly bring the flour into the middle and mix with your hands. You should have a shaggy dough that comes together. Using a bowl scraper or spatula, gently flip the loose dough onto a lightly floured work surface and knead until the dough is smooth and elastic, 5 to 10 minutes. Your dough should be strong and stretch like a windowpane without ripping.

To mix in a stand mixer: Combine the flour, salt, water, oil, and vinegar in the bowl. Using the dough hook, mix on low speed for 2 to 3 minutes, until it comes together. Increase the speed to medium and mix for another 5 minutes, until you hear the dough slap the sides of the bowl.

Place the dough in a lightly oiled bowl, cover with plastic wrap or a dish towel, and let rest in the refrigerator for at least 2 hours. This will allow the dough to become elastic and make it easier to work with during the next steps.

Place the cornstarch in a wide bowl. Set aside.

To roll out the dough: When the dough is well rested, divide it into 20 pieces (about 70 grams each). Roll the pieces into small balls and cover them with plastic wrap or a damp dish towel to prevent drying.

Work with only 5 pieces at a time and place the rest of the dough in the refrigerator. Dip the first piece of dough in the cornstarch. On a floured work surface, roll out the dough to a 5-inch disk about ⅛ inch thick, rotating 45 degrees with each turn, then set aside. Repeat the same process with the remaining 4 pieces.

Using a fine-mesh sieve, lightly dust the five disks with a teaspoon of cornstarch each. Stack the disks and, with a flat (not tapered) rolling pin, very gently and slowly roll out the sheets, rotating them 90 degrees every so often, until the sheets are about 12 inches wide by 17 inches long. If the layers begin to stick together, take a moment to dust with more cornstarch between them. Transfer and restack the five sheets of phyllo onto parchment paper, re-dusting each layer with cornstarch, and cover with another piece of parchment paper to prevent drying. Place them in the freezer and repeat this process four more times, until you've rolled out all 20 pieces of dough.

To store: Stack all four batches in their parchment dividers, loosely roll (don't press tightly) the entire stack, and slip the whole thing into a resealable bag or wrap thoroughly in plastic wrap. Freeze for up to 3 months. When ready to use, thaw in the refrigerator overnight or at room temperature for a few hours.

Finding the Best Phyllo

Not all phyllo is created equally. The key to a good phyllo is sufficient oil content to keep it soft but sufficient strength to prevent breakage with handling. The ratio of flour-to-fat content also affects the browning. I like a dough that holds its shape and doesn't break apart when it flakes and yet remains delicate to the bite. A great dough browns evenly but doesn't get so crispy that it shatters with handling or, more importantly, when it's being eaten. You can find phyllo in the frozen section of most grocery stores. My favorite brand is Kronos because of its delicate texture; it has served us well at Reem's.

BA'LAAWA BIL JOWZ · بقلاوة بال جوز
Spiced Walnut Baklava

Makes 24 pieces

WHEN I FIRST opened Reem's, I wanted to be an exclusively savory bread bakery. But then I started getting the million-dollar question: "What about baklava?" The Greek version is well-loved and assimilated in the American palate; its square shape, with cinnamon-spiced walnuts, is the relatable guy next door.

I knew I wanted to make baklava to rival the best I'd ever tasted. With its delicate pastry-like flakes, crisped in clarified butter, its layers held to one another with blossom-scented syrup and sandwiching a spiced-nut crumble, baklava had served as a cultural emissary of my childhood. Sharing it made me feel accepted.

Ba'laawa, the Arabic word for baklava, can be stuffed with a range of fillings, and I offer some of my favorites here and in the next few recipes. Making ba'laawa is straightforward, and, once you find your groove, painting each sheet in broad strokes with melted butter can be meditative, even therapeutic.

Two things are essential for the success of this dish: clarified butter to allow the sheets of dough to crisp and reach a golden brown without burning and cooled syrup poured onto hot-from-the-oven pastry. Cooled syrup preserves the flaky texture, averting the sogginess in some commercially produced ba'laawa.

I sometimes joke that ba'laawa embodies my spirit: it's delicately layered, nutty, and sweet—and it can easily be buttered up.

Filling

2 cups walnuts

¼ cup sugar

½ teaspoon cinnamon

1 teaspoon orange blossom water

1 teaspoon rose water

1 recipe Hand-Rolled Phyllo Dough (page 116) or 1 package store-bought phyllo dough, defrosted and at room temperature

1 cup melted Clarified Butter (page 96) or ghee, plus more for greasing the pan

1 cup Blossom Syrup (page 97)

Preheat the oven to 350°F. Line a 9 by 13-inch sheet tray with parchment paper. Using a pastry brush, coat the parchment and sides of pan with melted clarified butter.

To make the filling: In a food processor, combine the walnuts, sugar, and cinnamon and pulse to a fine crumble. Drizzle in the orange blossom and rose waters and pulse a few more times, until the mixture dampens. Do not overblend or the crumble will form a paste. Set aside.

To prepare the dough: Unroll the phyllo dough on a cutting board or work surface. Using a sharp butcher knife, cut the dough in half, splitting the long side down the middle to make forty 8½ by 12-inch sheets. Stack one on top of the other and cover with plastic wrap or a damp dish towel to prevent drying.

To assemble the baklava: Start with one stack and form the base of the pastry by layering the dough, one sheet at a time, onto the prepared sheet tray and brush each sheet from edge to edge with the melted butter. (Note: If using hand-rolled phyllo, you may need to gently brush away any excess cornstarch/flour mixture from the dough.) The first few layers may tear when brushing, so drizzle rather than brush on about a tablespoon of melted butter instead. When you have layered twenty sheets, sprinkle the nut filling evenly across it and lightly pat the filling down. Layer and brush the second stack of twenty dough sheets to form the top crust of the pastry. Place the tray in the refrigerator to chill the dough for about 20 minutes to help everything set before cutting.

Remove the tray from the refrigerator and, using a sharp knife, cut the dough (still in the pan) as follows: make two vertical and three horizontal cuts to divide the pastry into twelve evenly-sized squares. Next, make diagonal corner-to-corner cuts, dividing the squares into twenty-four triangles; take care to cut all the way through. Spoon the remaining melted butter over the pastry and into the crevices.

Bake for 50 to 60 minutes or until golden brown.

While the baklava is baking, prepare the syrup and set aside to cool.

Remove the baklava from the oven and pour the syrup evenly over the top. Let the baklava cool and serve at room temperature.

The baklava can be stored in an airtight container, layered between wax or parchment paper, in the refrigerator for up to 1 week. Enjoy cold or at room temperature.

ESH EL BOL BOL · عش البلبل

Pistachio Birds' Nests

Makes 40 small nests

IS IT POSSIBLE to love a recipe simply for its name? These delicacies are as cute as the creation they imitate. They're formed by wrapping coiled phyllo dough around bright green candied pistachios (in this case, in the form of a paste). My fondest memories of these sweets come from Shatila Bakery in Dearborn, Michigan, the promised land for Arabs in America. Every year we were sent one of their iconic red boxes of baklava sweets, and sure enough, I would find these little birds' nests waiting for me.

I use a pistachio paste to make up the center, but these can be filled with virtually any sweet treat, including pastry cream, chocolate, or other candied nuts.

TIP • To form and scrunch the rolls, you will need a ¼-inch wooden dowel. When I don't have a dowel on hand, I tape two chopsticks together to extend past the widest part of the phyllo dough.

1 cup melted Clarified Butter (page 96) or ghee, plus more for greasing the pan

1 recipe Hand-Rolled Phyllo Dough (page 116) or 1 package store-bought phyllo dough, defrosted and at room temperature

Paste
½ cup pistachios
¼ cup confectioners' sugar
1 teaspoon orange blossom water
1 tablespoon Blossom Syrup (page 97), plus more as needed

Preheat the oven to 350°F. Line a 9 by 13-inch sheet tray with parchment paper. Using a pastry brush, coat the parchment with melted butter.

To prepare the dough: Unroll the phyllo dough on a cutting board or work surface with the short side facing you. With a sharp knife, score the dough down the middle to make 40 long pieces. Stack one on top of each other and cover with plastic wrap or a damp dish towel to prevent drying.

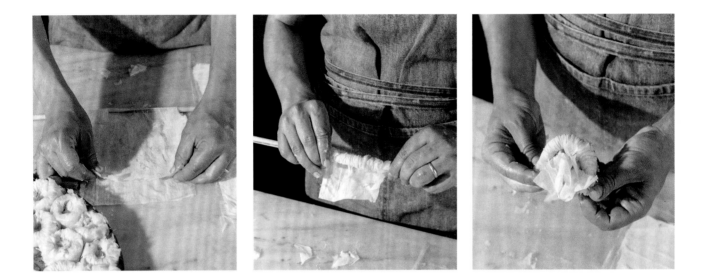

To assemble the nests: Place one sheet of phyllo on a clean work surface with the shorter side facing you. Lightly brush the butter across the top, center, and bottom of the phyllo sheet.

Fold the edge of the phyllo closest to you up to 1 inch below the top edge. Place the dowel on the bottom folded edge, align the end of the dowel to the left edge of the phyllo, and begin to loosely roll the phyllo around the dowel, stopping at the inch of extra dough. Lift the dowel and gently scrunch the phyllo, accordion-style, to the left end. Slide it off the dowel and gently shape it into a circle, with the reserved inch of phyllo forming the center of the nest. Your nest should resemble a scrunchie. Place the nest on the sheet tray. Repeat with the remaining sheets of phyllo, placing them close together but not touching. Bake until lightly golden, about 15 minutes.

To make the paste: While the nests are baking, combine the pistachios, sugar, orange blossom water, and syrup in a food processor and blend until it forms a nice smooth paste; add more syrup if it seems too dry.

After the nests come out of the oven, place a teaspoon of paste in each center and drench with the remaining syrup. Let the nests cool and serve at room temperature.

The nests can be stored in an airtight container, layered between wax or parchment paper, in the refrigerator for up to 1 week. Enjoy cold or at room temperature.

Hazelnut-Praline Baklava Rolls

Makes 40 rolls

BAKLAVA, HAPPILY, CAN take many shapes. The name for one of the most popular, asaabe', translates to "fingers" in Arabic. These rolls are scrunched to create fine ridges for a maximum wow effect, lined up side by side in a tray, baked, and then bathed in a milky syrup.

This dessert is loosely based on a baklava called sütlü nuriye that I once saw in a Turkish bakery. It's a version of baklava made lighter by thinning the sugar syrup with milk. I loved the milky texture with the hazelnut. In this recipe, I added praline to the hazelnut mixture and swapped honey for sugar in the syrup to add depth.

In one version of the dessert's history, a price ceiling on baklava, imposed in the aftermath of a Turkish military coup in the 1980s, raised the cost of producing traditional pistachio-filled baklava, forcing the closure of many baklava shops in Istanbul. But one shopkeeper was determined not to close down because of that; instead, he created a new type of baklava and substituted hazelnuts for the pistachios to make a cheaper but equally delicious alternative. His invention caught on, and it remained in the baklava arsenal when shops reopened and the regulations were lifted. Stories like this remind me of the resilience people in this region have and the creative deliciousness they can produce, even in the face of adversity.

TIP • To form and scrunch the rolls, you will need a ¼-inch dowel. When I don't have a dowel on hand, I tape two chopsticks together to extend past the widest part of the phyllo dough.

1 cup hazelnuts

½ cup sugar

2 tablespoons water

1 cup melted Clarified Butter (page 96) or ghee, plus more for greasing the pan

1 recipe Hand-Rolled Phyllo Dough (page 116) or 1 package store-bought phyllo dough, defrosted and at room temperature

Syrup

1½ cups whole milk

½ cup honey

2 tablespoons orange blossom water

Preheat the oven to 350°F.

Spread the hazelnuts evenly on a sheet tray and toast for 10 minutes or until golden. Remove the sheet tray from the oven and rub the nuts in a dish towel to remove their skins. Skip this step if the hazelnuts are pre-blanched. Remove any remnants of skins from the tray and return the nuts to the tray.

In a medium saucepan, combine the sugar with the water. Cook over medium-high heat until the sugar has melted and turns a deep amber color. Pour the caramel mixture over the nuts on the sheet tray and let them cool completely to harden, about 10 minutes.

Break the nut brittle into the bowl of a food processor and pulse to a fine crumble. Take care not to overblend or the crumble will form a paste. Reserve ¼ cup for garnish.

continued

Line a 9 by 13-inch sheet tray with parchment paper. Using a pastry brush, coat the parchment with melted butter.

To prepare the dough: Unroll the phyllo dough on a cutting board or clean work surface. Using a sharp butcher knife, cut the dough in half lengthwise to make two equal stacks. Cover the stacks with plastic wrap or a damp dish towel to prevent drying.

To assemble the baklava: Position one sheet with the widest side (about 17 inches) facing you and brush with the melted butter. Place a second sheet on top and, again, brush with butter. Sprinkle with 2 tablespoons of the hazelnut brittle.

Place the dowel at the end facing you (widest) and roll the layered phyllo gently all the way up. Place a hand on each end of the rolled phyllo and gently push both ends toward the center to scrunch like an accordion. Slide the scrunched roll off the dowel and place on the narrow end of the prepared sheet tray. Repeat this process until all of the dough has been scrunched into lines of rolls. Chill the dough in the refrigerator for about 20 minutes to help everything set before cutting.

Remove the tray from the refrigerator and, using a sharp knife, cut the shaggy ends to create clean edges. Then cut the rows into fourths. Line up the pieces: you should have four columns of ten rows each for a total of 40 pieces. The rows may be touching, and that's okay. Pour the remaining butter over the crevices.

Bake for 25 to 30 minutes or until the rolls are crisp and deep golden brown. Let the rolls cool to room temperature.

While the rolls are cooling, prepare the milk syrup: In a small saucepan, combine the milk and honey and bring to a boil, stirring until the honey dissolves. Once bubbles form, turn the heat to low and simmer for 10 minutes. Add the orange blossom water and remove from the heat.

Pour the hot milk syrup over the pan of rolls and allow them to soak up the syrup for at least 30 minutes, then sprinkle with the reserved hazelnut brittle and serve.

The rolls can be stored in an airtight container, layered between wax or parchment paper, in the refrigerator for up to 1 week. Enjoy cold or at room temperature.

بسكويت الشوكولاتة والطحينة

Chocolate Chip–Tahini Cookies

Makes 24 cookies

THIS IS AN Arab take on the classic chocolate chip cookie, but with a twist. Ultra-chewy in the center, crispy on the edges, and topped with toasted sesame seeds, flecks of halawa candy, and salt flakes, these cookies will seem original and, at the same time, deeply familiar. If you're looking for a way to impress a vegan friend, the search is over.

Halawa is the Arabic name for the tahini-based candy known in the United States as halvah. It's a crumbly melt-in-your-mouth sesame fudge, dating back thousands of years all the way to the Byzantine period, originating in present-day Istanbul. A thirteenth-century book on Arab cookery, *Kitab al-Tabikh*, documents seven different variations of this beloved treat. You can have fun with halawa, swirling in nuts, chocolate, or dried fruit.

TIP • To make a good halawa, you need to make correct candy syrup. If you don't have a candy thermometer, place a bowl of iced water next to your syrup. After a few minutes of boiling, test the syrup by placing a spoonful in your water. It is at the right stage when it forms a firm ball that can be rolled between your fingers and is slightly malleable when you squeeze it.

Crumble

1 cup/258g tahini
¾ teaspoon/2g kosher salt
¾ cup/150g sugar
3 tablespoons/44ml water

¼ cup/40g sesame seeds

Dough

2¾ cups plus 2 tablespoons/400g all-purpose flour
2½ teaspoons/9g baking powder
1½ teaspoons/6g baking soda
2 teaspoons/6g kosher salt
2 cups/340g packed light brown sugar
⅔ cup/144g coconut oil at room temperature (melt if mixing by hand)
½ cup/120ml oat milk
2 teaspoons/10ml vanilla extract
1 cup/160g 70% dark chocolate, coarsely chopped
1 teaspoon/3g Maldon salt (optional)

To make the crumble: Stir the tahini well and then combine with the kosher salt in a heatproof bowl. (Wrap a damp dish towel into a little nest and place beneath the bowl on a countertop to make stirring easier.)

In a small pot, combine the sugar and water over medium heat and stir continuously. Using a candy thermometer, take the temperature of the mixture. When it reaches 250°F, carefully drizzle the syrup into the tahini, while stirring the mixture constantly using a wooden spoon. Continue stirring until the tahini begins to look grainy and becomes

continued

difficult to stir, then on a tray spread in a ¼-inch layer, and allow to cool to room temperature. The mixture should look crackly on top and become dry to the touch, almost like fudge. Cool to harden slightly and then break it with your hands into small crumbles (around the size of chocolate chip morsels). You should have about 3 cups of the crumble. Reserve 1 cup for the topping.

Preheat the oven to 300°F.

On a small sheet tray, toast the sesame seeds for about 12 minutes or until light golden brown. Set aside.

Increase the oven temperature to 350°F.

To make the dough: In a medium bowl, combine the flour, baking powder, baking soda, and kosher salt. Set aside.

In a stand mixer fitted with the paddle attachment or in a large bowl, combine the brown sugar and coconut oil and, with the mixer on medium speed or with a mixing spoon, cream until homogenous, about 5 minutes. Add the milk and vanilla and mix until thoroughly combined. Gradually add the flour mixture to avoid spatter and mix until well incorporated. Fold in the crumble and the chocolate.

Line a cookie sheet with parchment paper or a Silpat.

To form the cookies: Using a 2-ounce scoop, portion the dough (each should be about the size of a golf ball), and set 3 inches apart on the prepared cookie sheet. Refrigerate for 10 minutes to chill to help the cookies keep their shape when they bake.

After the dough has chilled, coat the top of each cookie with a sprinkling of the reserved crumble, ½ teaspoon of the sesame seeds, and a pinch of Maldon salt.

Bake for 14 to 16 minutes, rotating the pan after 7 minutes, until the cookies are crisp on the edges and soft but not raw in the center. Let cool completely.

The cookies can be stored in an airtight container in the refrigerator for up to 3 days. These cookies can be frozen and thawed when ready to enjoy.

AWAMEH · عوامة
Glazed and Spice-Sprinkled Donut Holes

Makes 36 donut holes

I KNOW I am not alone in my obsession with donuts. My favorites are the little donut holes; in just a bite or two, the only evidence remaining is a trace of glaze or sprinkles on my fingers.

While growing up, I never missed the chance to indulge in the cider donuts from nearby farms during apple-picking season or the donut holes saved for me by the cashier at the Dunkin' Donuts near my college campus. I'd buy up bags of Munchkins and freeze them for late-night snacks.

When I travel, I love tasting different renditions of fried dough. Inspired by the beignets at New Orleans' famous Café Du Monde, I set about making a donut hole I would love. After much experimenting, I got a dough with a texture that falls somewhere between pancake batter and a brioche dough.

Scoop these into donut holes with whatever spoon you have on hand or shape them with an ice cream scoop. The donut holes will double in size. I would encourage you to use the weight measurements, since the final product will then be closer to the intended result than if you use the volume measurements. If you don't have a scale, that's okay. Just pay attention to the textural clues in the recipe.

TIP • This recipe accounts for glazed and sprinkled donuts. If you want only one topping, double either topping.

Dough
1 cup/240ml warm milk (about 100°F)
1½ teaspoons/6g active dry yeast
2¼ cups/315g all-purpose flour
2 tablespoons/25g granulated sugar
¾ teaspoon/2g kosher salt
2 eggs
½ cup/110g unsalted butter, melted

Glaze
2 cups/200g confectioners' sugar
¼ cup/60ml water
2 teaspoons/10ml lemon juice
½ teaspoon/2ml orange blossom water

Sprinkles
⅓ cup/61g granulated sugar
1 teaspoon/2g ground cinnamon
½ teaspoon/1g ground cardamom
½ teaspoon/1g ground anise
¼ teaspoon/0.5g ground nutmeg
⅛ teaspoon ground cloves

Neutral oil, such as sunflower, for frying and coating the scoop

Line a 13 by 18-inch sheet tray with paper towels. Set a wire rack over a second sheet tray.

To make the dough: In a small bowl, combine the milk with the yeast and set aside in a draft-free space for 10 minutes or until foamy.

To mix by hand: In a large bowl, combine the flour, granulated sugar, and salt. Make a well in the center and pour the yeast mixture into the middle. Add the eggs and butter. With your hand, slowly work the flour into the wet mixture to create a thick batter. Embrace the gooey strands sticking to your fingers as you activate the gluten. Use the outer edge of your hand or a bowl scraper to scrape and fold the batter in on itself for about 5 minutes, turning the bowl a quarter rotation with each fold.

To mix in a stand mixer: Combine the yeast mixture with the flour, granulated sugar, salt, eggs, and butter in the bowl. Using the paddle attachment, mix on medium-low speed, scraping down the sides of the bowl if needed. Mix until ribbons or strands form a batter-like dough and begin to pull away from the sides of the bowl, 3 to 5 minutes.

Cover the bowl with plastic wrap and leave it at room temperature for 1½ hours in a warm draft-free place or refrigerate overnight. It will bubble up, creating a wet dough that makes long strands if you lift a finger full of it from the bowl.

To make the glaze: Combine the confectioners' sugar, water, lemon juice, and orange blossom water in a shallow bowl. Set aside.

To make the sprinkles: Combine the granulated sugar, cinnamon, cardamom, anise, nutmeg, and cloves in a shallow bowl. Set aside.

To fry the donut holes: Fill a medium pot with about 4 inches of oil or enough to immerse the donut holes. Heat the oil over medium-high heat (350°F) until hot but not smoking. A droplet of batter should sizzle instantly when it hits the oil.

Fill a small bowl with enough oil to coat an ice cream scoop between uses.

Scoop balls of dough, about an inch in diameter, into the hot oil. Leave some space for the donut holes to bounce around and fry in batches one layer at a time. After about a minute, flip with a slotted spoon or tongs and cook for another minute. When they're done, the donut holes will be evenly brown and feel much lighter than they look. A toothpick pierced through the center should come out clean.

Using a slotted spoon or tongs, lift the donut holes from the fryer and place on the prepared baking sheet. Scoop the next batch into the oil. While the next batch is frying, use tongs to twirl and flip each donut in the bowls of glaze and sprinkles and then transfer to the wire rack. Serve warm or at room temperature. Donuts can be stored in an airtight container at room temp for up to 2 days.

Part Three

THE
Arab Table

By the time I reached my teens, a typical weeknight meal featured a hodgepodge of dishes passed back and forth across our table: spiced rice and vermicelli with stewed green bean loubieh leftovers, perhaps supplemented by last-minute vegetable chow mein Chinese takeout (halal to please my father) and General Tso's chicken in sweet spicy sauce (to please us kids).

My mother, a grad student, would rush in from a forty-five-minute commute and then whip together dinner to head off the pending state-of-hangry threatening her home. The nightly news, turned up a little too loud, would sedate my dad in the next room, where he dozed after work. I would be pacing my room, guessing at my physics assignments to avert my father's offers of help (he always took too long). And my sister Dalyah would hang out with her best friend, Elissa, the unofficial fourth Assil sister. My baby sister, Manal, would cling to our mother's side, still acclimating to after-school care. It took a small miracle to get us all to the table.

The Arab table, for me, begins with my mother, Iman Kishawi. Today, she is a scientist with a PhD and a twenty-year career working on the human genome project, proving it's never too late to return to your passion.

But it wasn't always that way. After a brief courtship, my parents married and made a hurried exit from Beirut, where civil war raged on the streets outside, and came to America, where my father landed his first engineering job. My mother jokes that if someone had arrived at her doorstep offering to move her to the North Pole, she would have gone immediately.

Instead, she landed in Lancaster, Pennsylvania, where she discovered the ultimate American delicacy, peanut butter and jelly, to the detriment of her waistline. She consumed these confections along with her first introduction to American culture: the daytime soap opera *General Hospital* and its incredulous adventures of Luke and Laura, who died and came back to life, reuniting in their love for one another several times. In place of bombs, F-16 fighter jets, and the hum of urban life, horse-drawn buggies pulled Amish families from farm to town. To say she felt shell-shocked would be too ironic.

Where my grandmother was extravagant, sliding plates over one another until the table overflowed with vegetables, preserves, pickles, cheeses, and spreads, my mother was ultra-practical, packing vegetables, grains, and meat into masterful one-pot meals.

Nutrition and flavor ruled my mother's kitchen; impressing guests was lower on her list. She knew how to layer spices and aromatics into stews like Shorbat Freekeh (page 168), a rich smoky concoction of cracked green wheat, that even to this day, tastes like home each time I take my first bite.

When we moved to Sudbury, a small suburb of Boston, our table expanded to feed more than just my mother and father. The Arab table became a calling for her to nourish those she loved. If we came home asking why we weren't doing taco Tuesday like the rest of the kids, my mother would sauté some ground meat in tomato sauce, spiked with Arab seven-spice mix, spoon it into tortillas, and voilà, it became Arab taco night. She kept her pantry stocked to feed family members who were passing through, whether on their way to begin university studies or nursing heartbreak.

After playing this role for half a decade, my mother decided she had been at home long enough. She overcame my father's reluctance, convincing him that our family needed two incomes. She wanted to be a scientist and set about resuming her studies at the University of Massachusetts Lowell. As part of her PhD program, my mother took a research job at the laboratories of Massachusetts General Hospital in Boston. Every day, no matter what else might have been happening, she would dash out the door to feed her lab cells. We joked that she cared more about her cells than her kids.

With my mother's daily departure, we became latchkey kids, raised on afternoon TV, including *Saved by the Bell* and *The Fresh Prince of Bel-Air*. The cupboards soon filled with instant ramen, mac and cheese, and giant square pizzas from Sam's Club. Dinner became a grab-and-go affair, and we rarely ate at the same time. For us, the comforts and tradition of the Arab table were overcome by the demands of working parenthood in America.

I missed the years when our home was a bed and breakfast for uncles and cousins who filled our table with Arabic and laughter. I began to long for the times when our aunts lavished us with family meals on our trips to Lebanon, Syria, and Palestine. There, no matter the hardships, the family gathered each day: men returned from work, food flooded the table, and everyone sat together at mealtime.

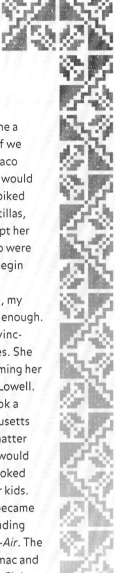

Despite the economic and political instability all around them, there was a sense of connectedness at those tables that I loved.

In America, we had stability but no table. The Arabic phrase we use to call family to the table for the first meal of the day, *khalleena nitrawwa'*, means "let's relax." Here, we'd shake cereal from a box and dash out the door to school. There was no tirwaa'a (in other words, no leisurely breakfast), no fetching fresh falafel from the street corner to add to the mosaic of small plates, stacked with fruits and vegetables and spread with olive oil–coated labneh and cheeses.

My mother, too, struggled with these contradictions. She had arrived in this country with a master's degree in microbiology, only to take up a post in the kitchen, when, in fact, she did not even know how to cook. She deferred her professional ambitions for eight years to fulfill family and social expectations as a wife and mother. It was nearly impossible to do everything well all the time, and yet our freezer full of fatayer proved her determination to try.

While she had less time for meals, she still remained vigilant against blows that scraped away at our identities. Protecting us from the hardships of being Arab in America sometimes meant taking matters into her own hands. In middle school, two older boys often waited at the end of the block, ready to pepper me with insults and threats on my daily walk to school. I'd bow my head and pick up my pace, until I felt safe enough to catch my breath. One day, one of the boys taunted me, "Go back to Arabic." I answered in the same nonsense way, "Go back to Italian." That day, I had come home crying one time too many, and my mother marched down the street to confront one of the boys. With a few choice words, issued at very close range, and a handful of his shirt in her grip, the bullying stopped. No one ever braved a second encounter with my mother.

One day, I returned home from school in tears. Our social studies unit on cultures of the world had screened a film from the 1970s about Arabs that depicted an Arab family around the dinner table. In place of the invocation *yislamu idayk*—"God bless your hands"—murmured almost reflexively by everyone I knew to celebrate the cook, the film's dramatic climax hinged on Arabs burping to show appreciation. As my classmates laughed, I felt shame and embarrassment.

The next day, my mother stormed the school and demanded that they establish an alternate lesson plan; however, there wasn't an existing one that depicted Arabs as we really are. So, she made one herself and volunteered to teach it. At the end of the month of Ramadan, our month of fasting, she came to the school as a guest speaker and shared ma'amoul, our special nut- or date-stuffed cookies with a delicate melt-in-your-mouth semolina crust pressed into decorative molds. Every year thereafter, she found a way to arrive at school with sweets and teach a lesson about Arab culture.

Her ferocity wasn't reserved just for our battles. She fought to be recognized even in everyday transactions. I cannot count the number of times she confronted store clerks who heard her accent and made the mistake of underestimating her. "Do you think I'm clueless just because I have an accent?" she would say, while disputing even small matters at the register. We'd try to play it down, embarrassed by her escalations. But in hindsight, I realize she was demonstrating what it means to stand up for yourself.

I get my courage from my mother. She's not a diplomat; she's an advocate. She wanted to protect us from forces that would cause us to question our worth. Education was our ticket to financial independence, and she made sure we had the best. Throughout my life, I have witnessed my mother stand by the side of women dealing with abusive husbands, fighting unsuccessful battles against cancer, and standing up to unfair conditions in their workplaces. But she struggled in her own household to get support from all of us to keep our house in order.

She wasn't as religious as my father, but she felt constant pressure to enforce his strict rules, telling us we couldn't go places or do things that she might have thought were okay. She had little time to herself, and when tensions erupted, she'd dash out of the house and escape alone to a theater to watch whatever happened to be on screen.

In my search for purpose, I have returned again and again to the Arab table as a place that shapes my identity.

The Arab table, for me, is a place of contradiction. The table I create in my adulthood resists patriarchy and concedes to a nurturing maternal impulse. It can feel good, generous, even spiritual to cook for others. And it can feel oppressive when it's expected of me.

Ironically, when I finally found my way to the kitchen, I confronted an industry dominated by white men. Like my mother, I made it my mission to set my own terms. But it hasn't been easy.

Still, I'm excited to raise a feminist child and to demonstrate that family, to me, is larger than just my household: it's my co-workers, community, friends, and comrades, struggling just like me. I've stationed my Arab table at the crossroads of my many communities.

Chapter Five

Mezze · Small Plates

HUMMUS · حمص
Chickpea-Tahini Spread

Makes about 1½ cups

LEARNING TO MAKE great hummus requires tasting along the way and trusting what you taste. My grandmother knew just what she was looking for when she made hummus, but she still called me over to ask my opinion, feeding me the answers she wanted: "Do you think it needs a little more lemon?" We'd squeeze another half of a lemon into the mix. "Do you think it has enough salt?" She'd pour a half-teaspoon into my palm to tip into the food processor . . . and we'd taste it again. Round and round we'd go, adding and tasting, thinning it with broth from the beans as needed, until everyone agreed it was perfect.

For my grandmother, recipe portions were a starting point, but her real secret to perfect hummus came from pouring in dabs of lemon and tahini. She'd adjust the amounts, depending on how flavorful and ripe her lemons were. And she never skimped on the tahini.

In my grandmother's time, to get the smoothest-textured hummus, cooks used to rub the boiled beans together to remove the skins. Today, with powerful food processors, few people take this step. In my restaurant, I boil the beans, rub them together with my hands, and pour off the skins that float to the top several times. This process, for me, is meditative and produces a creamier result.

My grandmother's method, layering in the ingredients, is the one I still use. The hummus continues to form its taste and texture long after it's left the blender. The lemon's acid binds with the tahini to thicken the spread, and any hummus that goes into the fridge emerges thicker and filled with a garlic-infused bloom. If you need to, thin it with ice water and restore the texture to your liking with a whisk or a spoon.

This hummus recipe can be used as the base for Hummus bil Awarma (page 141); as a nice vegan platform for Tatbeeleh (page 42), a lemon-chile relish; or for the classic dish Qudsiyah by spooning Ful Madammas (page 151), stewed fava beans, on top.

This recipe is perfect for a two-person household but easily doubles or triples for a family or a party.

¾ cup dried chickpeas, or one 15-ounce can chickpeas, drained and rinsed
¼ teaspoon baking soda (for dried chickpeas only)
2 garlic cloves
5 tablespoons lemon juice (about 2 lemons), plus more as needed
1½ teaspoons kosher salt, plus more as needed
¼ cup ice water, plus more as needed
½ cup tahini
2 tablespoons extra-virgin olive oil, plus more as needed
1 teaspoon sumac for garnish
1 teaspoon Aleppo pepper or Chile-Spice Mix (page 27) for garnish

If using dried chickpeas, soak the chickpeas overnight or for at least 12 hours.

Drain the chickpeas, place them in a small pot with the baking soda, and cover the beans with about 6 inches of clean water. Bring to a boil, skim, discard the residue from the water's surface, and decrease the heat to a simmer over medium heat. Cook, uncovered, until the beans soften, about 30 minutes. Test for doneness by squeezing a bean between your thumb and forefinger. A perfect bean crushes easily but does not turn to mush. Drain in a colander when done cooking.

Immerse the beans in a bowl of cold water and rub between your palms, pouring off any skins that float to the surface. Drain and repeat two or three times. If using canned chickpeas, repeat the same step, rubbing off as many skins as you can. Reserve 2 tablespoons for garnish.

Combine the remaining chickpeas, garlic, lemon juice, and salt in a food processor and pulse. Add the ice water. Blend at high speed for 5 minutes, until no lumps remain. (Yes, that's right, for 5 minutes. Set a timer and walk away.) At the 5-minute mark, slowly drizzle the tahini into the mixture on medium speed. The mix should be airy and form stiff peaks. If it's the texture of ice cream, it's too thick, so add additional ice water, as needed. Adjust the lemon juice and salt to taste.

When ready to serve, scoop the hummus onto a plate or into a shallow bowl. Use the back of a spoon to form a moat between the outer edge and the center. Drizzle your canvas copiously with olive oil and garnish decoratively with the reserved whole chickpeas, sumac, and Aleppo pepper. Hummus can be stored, ungarnished, in an airtight container in the refrigerator for up to 3 days.

Loaded Hummus (and I Don't Just Mean the Awarma on It)

I'm going to fill you in on a little secret: if it don't got chickpeas, it ain't hummus. The word *hummus* means "chickpea" in Arabic—not "dip." Calling it black bean hummus is like calling a hamburger ham. You can understand how someone might make that mistake, but you know the instant you hear it that it's wrong. If you want to have fun with flavors, you can add tahini and lemon to just about any vegetable and call it mutabal (see pages 146–150); just don't call it hummus.

Maybe the sensitivity I and many Arabs feel about hummus has to do with the way we've been cut out of a food story so integral to our culture. Hummus has become synonymous with Israeli food in America (the Israeli company Sabra has more than 60 percent of the market share for hummus in the United States), even though the origins of hummus likely stretch back to Egypt.

The real test for me comes in a too-familiar discomfort that starts deep in my belly when a customer praises my hummus, saying it reminds them of Israel. I'm expected to affirm their experience and create a connection between us, but that affirmation makes me feel invisible. In that story, Palestinians are cast in a supporting role, affirming an Israeli story, and requiring me to shrink and disappear.

There is also the harmful idea of "hummus kumbaya," a phrase my friend, Palestinian cookbook author Leila Haddad, uses to describe the idea that eating hummus somehow diminishes our differences. Israelis may make and eat hummus the same way we do, but it doesn't make us the same if Palestinians are denied basic rights like land-ownership, freedom, and basic human dignity that Israelis afford themselves.

Yes, we all eat hummus, but that doesn't negate occupation and apartheid. Enjoying our foods while rejecting our right to exist is why Palestinians have fought for ownership of our foods in the face of Israel's infusion of millions of "gastrodiplomacy dollars" to make the appropriation of Palestinian foods seem normal and commonplace. Our food is an assertion of our existence and our connection to the land.

Hummus with Spiced Lamb

Makes 4 to 6 servings

IT'S HARD TO keep from snacking on the choicest shreds of this gorgeous confit of crispy lamb breast. That cut is the fattiest part of the lamb, and slow-roasting it allows it to cook in its own fat and become moist and tender. Harvest the spice-steeped lamb fat into a glass jar to use later for spectacular home fries or roasted vegetables.

Lamb breast is a specialty cut of meat, but it's well worth it. The most flavorful parts of the lamb lie between the tissue of the breast. You will most likely have to special order it from the butcher. If you have a hard time sourcing breast, lamb shoulder chops make a great substitute, either bone-in or deboned. You may need to extend the cooking time if the shoulder is cut more than 1 inch thick.

1½ teaspoons kosher salt

2 tablespoons Chile-Spice Mix (page 27), plus more for garnish

2 tablespoons extra-virgin olive oil, plus more for garnish

1½ pounds lamb breast or shoulder, cut into 1-inch-thick slices

2 tablespoons neutral oil, such as sunflower

1 recipe Chickpea-Tahini Spread (page 138)

In a small bowl, whisk together the salt, spice mix, and oil to make a viscous paste. On a small sheet tray, rub the lamb with the rub and let it sit, covered, at room temperature for 2 hours or marinate in the refrigerator overnight.

If the lamb has been marinated overnight, remove it from the refrigerator 1 hour before cooking to bring it to room temperature.

Preheat the oven to 350°F.

Pour the oil into a cast-iron skillet or heavy pan and warm over medium-high heat. When the oil is hot, sear the lamb, browning each side for about 3 minutes or until a deep golden char is achieved. Cover the pan with aluminum foil and bake for 1 to 1½ hours or until the meat softens and easily pulls away from the bone.

Once cool enough to touch, pull the meat from the bone, coarsely chop it into bite-size pieces, and shred the pieces into strands. Reincorporate the juices and rendered fat into the pulled chopped meat.

Just before serving, reheat the cast-iron skillet and crisp the lamb, pressing the strands with a spatula, browning the bottoms and then flipping the meat to do the same on the other side. You should have a varied texture with a mix of crispy and soft pieces.

When ready to serve, scoop the hummus onto a plate or into a shallow bowl. Use the back of a spoon to form a moat between the outer edge and the center. Spoon the hot crispy lamb, along with its juices, into the well and garnish with a bit more oil and spice mix.

The lamb can be stored in an airtight container in the refrigerator for up to 3 days.

BABA GHANOUJ · بابا غنوج
Charred Eggplant Salad

Makes 4 to 6 servings

THIS IS A bright, creamy, pomegranate-eggplant salad, but hold the tahini, please. It's a mystery why baba ghanouj, one of our most widely known dishes, is so different in the United States from that in the Arab world. When we talk about baba ghanouj in the Levant, we are referring to a tart salad of creamy roasted eggplant, brightened with pomegranate molasses and flecked with tomatoes—which is what this is!

If you're looking for an eggplant spread made with garlic and tahini, you'll find recipes under mutabal (see pages 146–150). Eat this baba ghanouj with bread, or it's also delicious as a side salad.

2 large globe eggplants (about 2 pounds)
Olive oil, for rubbing eggplants,
plus more for drizzling
2 garlic cloves, minced
¼ cup lemon juice (about 2 lemons)
Zest of 2 lemons
½ teaspoon ground cumin
1 teaspoon kosher salt, plus more
as needed
⅛ teaspoon freshly ground black pepper
1 small Roma tomato, finely diced
½ red bell pepper, finely diced
½ red onion, finely diced
1 tablespoon coarsely chopped parsley
1 teaspoon pomegranate molasses

Cook the eggplants directly on the burner of a gas stove or in the oven. On a gas stove, sear the eggplants directly over a medium-high flame. Rotate every 5 minutes until the globes are completely blackened, about 15 minutes total. Alternately, preheat the oven to 450°F. Place the eggplants on a sheet tray, poke them all over with the tines of a fork, rub them with the oil, and place the tray in the oven and cook for 25 to 30 minutes, until the eggplants collapse in on themselves, and the skins are blackened.

Place the cooked eggplants in a bowl and seal the bowl with plastic wrap to let the eggplants steam in their own juices.

In a medium bowl, combine the garlic, lemon juice and zest, cumin, salt, and black pepper.

When the eggplants have cooled enough to touch, split them lengthwise. Using a spoon, scrape out the pulp, discarding the skins and stems. For a milder flavor, scrape the seeds off the strands of pulp.

Use a fork to mash the pulp into the lemon-garlic mix. Fold in the tomato, bell pepper, and onion. Adjust the salt to taste.

When ready to serve, scoop the eggplant mixture onto a serving plate, drizzle it with the olive oil, and garnish it with the parsley and molasses. Baba ghanouj can be stored, ungarnished, in an airtight container in the refrigerator for up to 5 days.

MUHAMMARA · محمرة
Roasted Red Pepper–Walnut Spread

Makes scant 3 cups

I REMEMBER THE first time I served this spread at an event. Several people reacted the same way: "It's like an Arab romesco sauce!" I wonder if the Catalonians intersected with Arabs during the time when they conquered Spain to inspire this tomato, almond, and pepper sauce, but in the end, it doesn't matter. All great things travel, and muhammara is a great thing.

The Arabic word *muhammara* translates literally to "something that is red," so the trick to this dish is to choose peppers with the deepest ripe-red hue possible to create the perfect sweet pepper spread. The secret ingredient is a backdrop of sweet and tart pomegranate molasses to brighten all the other flavors. Snack on this with fresh flatbread or toss it into your pasta. There is no wrong way to eat muhammara.

4 large red bell peppers (about 1½ pounds) or one 15-ounce can roasted red peppers, drained and rinsed

1⅓ cups walnuts, plus 2 tablespoons, chopped for garnish

½ cup panko bread crumbs

2 garlic cloves

1 tablespoon pomegranate molasses

2 tablespoons lemon juice (about 1 lemon)

1½ teaspoons Aleppo pepper or Chile-Spice Mix (page 27)

¾ teaspoon kosher salt, plus more as needed

½ teaspoon ground cumin

¼ cup extra-virgin olive oil, plus more for drizzling

2 tablespoons pomegranate seeds (optional) for garnish

2 tablespoons chopped parsley (optional) for garnish

Preheat the oven to 400°F. Line a sheet tray with parchment paper.

If you are using fresh bell peppers, place them on the prepared tray. Roast the peppers until the skins are charred, about 30 minutes, turning them over once or twice. Transfer to a resealable bag or a bowl covered with plastic wrap and set aside. Once cool, tear the peppers open and remove the stems, seeds, and skins.

Combine the walnuts and bread crumbs in a food processor and process to a cornmeal-like texture. Add the roasted peppers, garlic, molasses, lemon juice, Aleppo pepper, salt, and cumin. Pulse until smooth, scraping down the sides of the bowl as needed.

With the processor running, slowly add the oil and blend until the oil is completely incorporated. Adjust the salt to taste.

When ready to serve, scoop the pepper mixture, chilled or at room temperature, onto a serving plate. With the back of a spoon, create little divots for the oil to fall into. Drizzle with the oil and garnish with the chopped walnuts, pomegranate seeds, and parsley.

The spread can be stored, ungarnished, in an airtight container in the refrigerator for up to 1 week.

MUTABAL · متبل
Eggplant-Tahini Spread

Makes 2 cups

THE TAHINI-LACED EGGPLANT version of this dish is ubiquitous in Arab restaurants and homes across the United States. Growing up, we called it baba ghanouj, but I later learned that in the Arab world, baba ghanouj means a more citrusy eggplant salad. There, this dish of mashed vegetables with creamy tahini is more commonly called mutabal, which means a dish that's made tastier or more flavorful with spices. When people refer to mutabal, the default vegetable is eggplant, but it actually can be made with just about any vegetable, as I share in the following two recipes.

With each variation, the preparation of the vegetable distinguishes the dish. In the case of eggplant, roasting makes it tastier, and I char mine for a smoky flavor. Most versions I taste today are too watered down and too garlicky—the smokiness of the cumin and charred eggplant in this version achieves the complexity I prefer.

2 large globe eggplants (about 2 pounds)
Olive oil, for rubbing eggplants,
plus more for drizzling
¼ cup tahini
¼ cup lemon juice (about 2 lemons)
1 teaspoon lemon zest
2 garlic cloves, minced
½ teaspoon ground cumin
1 teaspoon kosher salt, plus more to taste
Pinch of freshly ground black pepper

Garnish
1 teaspoon pomegranate molasses
(optional)
2 tablespoons pomegranate seeds
1 tablespoon coarsely chopped parsley

Cook the eggplants directly on the burner of a gas stove or in the oven. On a gas stove, sear the eggplants directly over a medium-high flame. Rotate every 5 minutes, until the globes are completely blackened, about 15 minutes total. Alternately, preheat the oven to 450°F. Place the eggplants on a sheet tray, poke them all over with the tines of a fork, rub them with the oil, and place the tray in the oven and cook for 25 to 30 minutes, until the eggplants collapse in on themselves and the skins are blackened.

Place the cooked eggplants in a bowl and seal the bowl with plastic wrap to let the eggplants steam in their own juices.

In a medium bowl, combine the tahini, lemon juice and zest, garlic, cumin, salt, and pepper.

When the eggplants have cooled enough to touch, split them lengthwise. Using a spoon, scrape out the pulp, discarding the skins and stems. For a milder flavor, scrape the seeds off the strands of pulp.

Use a fork to mash the pulp into the tahini-garlic mix, creating a chunky dip. Adjust the salt to taste.

When ready to serve, scoop the eggplant mixture onto a serving plate. Use a spoon to create a well in the center and drizzle in the oil, then garnish with the molasses, pomegranate seeds, and parsley.

Mutabal can be stored, ungarnished, in an airtight container in the refrigerator for up to 3 days.

Beet-Tahini Spread

Makes 3 cups

THE NATURAL SWEETNESS and electric magenta of this dish contrast beautifully with any of the spreads in this book. When the season is right, I love to make a trio of mutabal dips, including the Mutabal Arra' (page 149) and the Mutabal Silik (page 150), lined up like a carnival flag.

This spread starts off sweet, then gets a little spicy, and ends with an earthy, savory flavor that will make you want to go back for more. Like most of the spreads in this chapter, it tastes even better when made a day ahead, giving all of the flavors a chance to meld. This makes a lovely dip for bread, carrots, radishes, and cucumbers.

4 red beets (about 2 pounds)

2 teaspoons extra-virgin olive oil, plus more for drizzling

3 teaspoons kosher salt, plus more as needed

2 garlic cloves, minced

1 serrano chile, stems, seeds, and veins removed, halved lengthwise

¼ cup lemon juice (from about 2 lemons), plus more as needed

½ teaspoon cumin seeds, toasted, or ¼ teaspoon ground cumin

½ cup tahini, plus more as needed

1 tablespoon coarsely chopped herbs, such as cilantro, dill, or fennel fronds for garnish

Preheat the oven to 400°F.

In a medium bowl, coat the beets in the oil and 1 teaspoon of the salt. Tear four lengths of aluminum foil and tightly wrap each beet individually in the foil. Roast the beets in the oven for about 1 hour, until caramelized and tender (a knife or cake tester should go through them with little or no resistance). Remove the beets from the oven and cool in the foil.

For this next step, I save old towels I don't mind staining. When cool enough to handle, remove the beets from the foil, wrap each beet in a towel, and rub the peels away.

Coarsely chop the beets and place them in a food processor or blender. Add the garlic, chile, lemon juice, cumin, and the remaining 2 teaspoons salt and blend for about 5 minutes, until creamy and smooth. Slowly drizzle in the tahini and continue blending until the tahini is fully incorporated. Scrape down the sides of the bowl as needed. Adjust the salt and lemon juice to taste. If you want a thicker spread, blend in more tahini, 1 tablespoon at a time.

When ready to serve, scoop the mixture onto a serving plate, drizzle it with the oil, and garnish it with the herbs.

This spread can be made ahead of time and stored, ungarnished, in an airtight container in the refrigerator for up to 1 week.

Butternut Squash–Tahini Spread

Makes 3 cups

I LOVE WHEN fall rolls around and beautifully shaped winter squash fill the farm stands; ridged and smooth, green and orange, I feel an urge to cook them all. This spread of sweet pomegranate-roasted butternut squash balances with the acidity of fresh lemon and a little bite from the garlic and pepper and works equally well with acorn, pumpkin, and other winter squash. It's beautiful served on its own, scooped with Khobz Arabi (page 71), or used as a complement to the other mutabal spreads in this chapter. The squash can be roasted ahead for quick assembly; once roasted, the dish comes together in fewer than 5 minutes.

1 butternut squash, halved lengthwise and seeds removed (about 2½ pounds)

1 tablespoon extra-virgin olive oil, plus more for drizzling

1 tablespoon pomegranate molasses

1 teaspoon kosher salt

2 tablespoons lemon juice (about 1 lemon)

Zest of 1 lemon

¼ cup tahini

2 garlic cloves, minced

1 serrano chile, stems, seeds, and veins removed

2 tablespoons coarsely chopped parsley for garnish

1 tablespoon pomegranate seeds (optional) for garnish

Preheat the oven to 350°F.

In a 9 by 13-inch glass baking dish, rub the squash with the oil, molasses, and salt. Roast cut side up for 1½ hours, until the edges caramelize and the flesh is soft when pierced with a fork.

Remove the dish from the oven to cool.

While the squash is cooling, combine the lemon juice and zest, tahini, garlic, and chile in a medium bowl.

Scoop the squash pulp out of the skin and add to the lemon-tahini mixture. Use a spoon to thoroughly incorporate the mixture into a thick, chunky spread.

When ready to serve, scoop the squash mixture onto a serving plate, drizzle with the oil, and garnish it with the parsley and pomegranate seeds.

This dip can be made ahead of time and stored, ungarnished, in an airtight container in the refrigerator for up to 1 week.

MUTABAL SILIK · متبل سلق
Chard-Tahini Spread

Makes 2 cups

CREAMY, NUTTY TAHINI plays beautifully off of Swiss chard's deeply vegetal minerality, mixed with a one-two punch of garlic and lemon for a spread that's as tasty as it is nutritious. This is the kind of dish I've seen in Lebanon, where seasonal produce gets integrated into menus, but never in the United States.

To showcase the seasonality in Arab cuisine, I first introduced this dish at the Culinary Institute of America during their Worlds of Flavors event as part of a rainbow trio with red beet and golden butternut squash mutabal. I spent anxiety-filled hours convincing myself my dishes were more than "just dips." But tasting each one side by side, I realized that I was providing a dish that was not only visually stunning but also one with the perfect balance of earthy, sweet, and acidic flavor. This recipe is an exceptionally flavorful play on this hearty green. And, really, who couldn't use an excuse for a few more greens in their diet?

2 bunches green Swiss chard

4 garlic cloves

¼ cup lemon juice (about 2 lemons), plus more as needed

1 teaspoon lemon zest

2 teaspoons kosher salt, plus more as needed

¼ cup olive oil, plus more for drizzling

½ cup tahini

1 tablespoon sumac (optional) for garnish

1 teaspoon Aleppo pepper (optional) for garnish

Bring a large pot of water to a boil. Remove the tough ends of the chard stalks and reserve for another use. (It's okay for some stems to remain.) Rinse the chard and blanch it in boiling water for about 2 minutes or until tender. The leaves should pluck easily from the stalks but still hold together. Drain and run under cold water to stop the cooking process. Squeeze well with your hands to remove excess water.

Chop the chard and add it to a food processor along with the garlic, lemon juice and zest, salt, and oil to make a smooth paste. Blend at medium speed until the leaves form small pesto-like flecks. Drizzle in the tahini and pulse until it's a uniform pale green color. Scrape down the sides of the bowl as needed. Adjust the salt and lemon juice to taste.

When ready to serve, scoop the chard mixture onto a serving plate, drizzle it with the oil, and garnish with the sumac and Aleppo pepper.

This dip can be made ahead of time and stored in the refrigerator in an airtight container for up to 2 days before it loses its vibrant color.

FUL MADAMMAS · فول مدمس
Fava Mash with Roasted Garlic

Makes 6 to 8 servings

FUL MADAMMAS WAS my mother's go-to weekend breakfast. A creamy, mild fava stew, cooked low and slow, this stew reduces to a simple and hearty canvas for an infinite array of fresh toppings. Dried unpeeled or canned favas work equally well. Arab grocers stock many varieties of favas, and, using canned, which my mother opted for, will get you from the stove to the table in a matter of minutes if your garlic is roasted ahead.

Favas are among the oldest-known cultivated plants, so it's no wonder that ful is a staple across the Arab world and likely traces its roots to ancient Egypt. Recipes vary from house to house and region to region. I've lightened the fava beans with a mix of chickpeas, the way most Palestinians do, and given it heady notes of caramelized onion and roasted garlic.

For an extra kick, top it with Tatbeeleh (page 42), a lemon-chile relish, and a mix of any fresh herbs you have on hand; to add a Gazan flair, sprinkle on some freshly chopped chiles and dill at the end. If you want to route toward Jerusalem, turn it into the classic dish Qudsiyah by spooning ful on top of a fresh plate of Hummus (page 138). It's eaten, of course, with warm Khobz Arabi (page 71).

This dish makes a perfect centerpiece in a breakfast mezze, spread with crudités, sliced cheeses, boiled eggs, and olives.

1½ cups small dried fava beans or one 28-ounce can fava beans with its liquid

⅛ teaspoon baking soda (for dried fava beans only)

2 heads garlic

3 tablespoons extra-virgin olive oil, plus more for roasting the garlic and for garnish

¼ teaspoon kosher salt, plus more for roasting the garlic and as needed

1 small yellow onion, finely diced

2 garlic cloves, finely chopped

½ teaspoon ground cumin, plus more as needed

One 15-ounce can chickpeas, drained

1 tablespoon lemon juice (about ½ lemon)

½ pint cherry tomatoes, halved

4 sprigs of parsley, stems removed and coarsely chopped

½ bunch scallions, ends trimmed and finely chopped

If you are using dried beans, immerse them in hot water and the baking soda and soak them overnight at room temperature. Drain thoroughly and then rinse the beans.

Place the favas in a small pot and add water until waterline is 2 inches above the beans. Simmer until soft, about 45 minutes. Reserve 1½ cups of the cooking liquid. If you are using canned beans, skip this step.

Preheat your toaster oven or home oven to 400°F to roast your garlic.

continued

Slice the stem ends of the garlic heads about a ¼ inch down, revealing the tops of the cloves. Set the heads on a piece of aluminum foil large enough to fully enclose them. Drizzle the heads with about a tablespoon of olive oil, sprinkle with a pinch of salt, and tightly close the foil.

Roast for about 1½ hours or until the heads smell fragrant and toasty and the insides are golden brown and tender. When the garlic is cool enough to handle, unwrap and simply squeeze the heads from the bottom to release the roasted cloves. Discard the heads and set the roasted cloves aside for garnish.

In a medium saucepan, warm 3 tablespoons oil and sauté the onion over medium heat, until lightly caramelized. Add the chopped garlic cloves, ¼ teaspoon salt, and cumin and sauté until they smell aromatic, 2 to 3 minutes. Add the fava beans with their reserved liquid (just enough to cover the beans), then simmer, stirring occasionally, until the beans are tender and smashable, about 30 minutes.

Turn off the heat and, with a potato masher or the back of a spoon, smash the beans until only half or less of the whole beans remain. If the stew dries out, add some water until you get the texture you want. I like a cross between mashed and whole beans. Turn the heat to medium-low, add the chickpeas, and simmer until warmed. Adjust the salt and cumin to taste.

Remove the pot from the heat. Stir in the lemon juice and roasted garlic. To serve, spread in a serving bowl, drizzle with the oil, and top with the tomatoes, parsley, and scallions.

This dish can be enjoyed warm or at room temperature or made ahead and stored, ungarnished, in an airtight container in the refrigerator for up to 3 days.

FALAFEL MAHSHI · فلافل محشي
Chile-Onion–Stuffed Falafel

Makes 14 stuffed falafel balls

WHEN I SET out to create my restaurants, I swore I'd never serve falafel. I even included that pledge in an early version of my tagline: "Beyond the falafel and shawarma." I wanted to prove Arab cuisine's rich complexity and bust out of the confines to which we'd been reduced. But people asked for falafel so often that we could no longer ignore the demand. I gave in, and Reem's began to serve what would become one of our best sellers.

I came across this chile and onion stuffing, a Jerusalem specialty, while researching my perfect falafel. Arabs like to stuff just about everything, even falafel. These crispy balls deliver a silky caramelized onion surprise and a burst of spice with every crunch. Do not use canned beans, since they are already cooked; the crunch that makes falafel irresistible comes from frying rehydrated uncooked beans.

Falafel are best eaten fresh from the fryer. They're delicious dipped into Taratoor (page 39), a lemon-tahini sauce, rolled into a delicious round of Khobz Saj (page 73), a griddle-cooked flatbread, and served with any of the pickles in this book.

Feel free to get creative with the filling. At Reem's we sometimes fill ours with a soft-boiled egg and call it a fleg.

TIP · This falafel is easily scaled up so that you can make enough to cover your falafel needs for multiple meals. Pack any extra mix in gallon-size resealable bags and press to flatten; keep frozen until ready to use. To use, thaw the bag at room temperature or submerge in warm water, then proceed with stuffing and frying.

1¼ cups dried chickpeas

2½ cups coarsely chopped yellow onions (about 1 onion)

1½ tablespoons coarsely chopped garlic (about 3 cloves)

1 serrano chile, stems, seeds, and veins removed

1 cup chopped parsley, with stems

1 cup chopped cilantro, with stems

2 teaspoons kosher salt

1½ teaspoons ground coriander

1 teaspoon ground cumin

½ teaspoon ground ginger

¼ teaspoon ground cardamom

¼ teaspoon baking powder

Filling

2 cups finely diced red onions (about 1 large onion)

2 tablespoons extra-virgin olive oil

1 tablespoon sumac, plus more as needed

1 tablespoon Tangy Green Hot Sauce (page 45), sambal, or your favorite hot sauce, plus more as needed and for serving

½ teaspoon kosher salt, plus more as needed

Neutral oil, such as sunflower or canola, for frying

⅓ cup sesame seeds for coating

1 recipe Saj Bread (page 73) for serving

Immerse the chickpeas in water several inches above the beans and soak for 3 to 4 hours or overnight.

In a food processor, combine the yellow onions, garlic, chile, parsley, and cilantro and pulse until you get a uniform green paste.

continued

Drain the beans, discarding the water, and gradually add them to the food processor, pulsing until the mixture is uniformly pale green and flecked with tiny specks of chickpeas. The texture is a matter of preference; I like mine the texture of fine bulgur. Proceed with care when blending; overblending can cause the herbs to oxidize and release water.

Test the bean mixture by forming a ball in your hands. The mixture should be moist enough to hold together but not so soft that it is difficult to shape. The liquid shouldn't be visible, but when you squeeze the mixture, water should leach out.

Transfer the mixture to a medium bowl and work the salt, coriander, cumin, ginger, cardamom, and baking powder into the mixture with your hands until well incorporated. Set the falafel mixture in the refrigerator for at least 30 minutes or the freezer for 10 minutes to chill.

To make the filling: While the falafel mixture is chilling, sauté the red onions in the oil over medium-low heat, until they become soft and slightly caramelized. Add the sumac, hot sauce, and salt and adjust to taste. Let the filling cool before using.

Use a falafel mold, ice cream scoop, or your hands to form fourteen balls (about 2 ounces each). Lay the balls on a sheet tray and chill in the freezer for 10 minutes.

When the falafel mixture is chilled, press each ball into a 3-inch patty in the palm of your hand. Place a teaspoon of filling in the middle and cup your palm to enclose the filling. Smooth the seam with your other hand and then gently roll the ball between both hands to form a uniform ball.

Place the falafel balls on a sheet tray and let the pan rest in the freezer for 10 minutes.

Line a sheet tray or plate with paper towels and place a cooling rack on top.

Heat 2 inches of oil in a deep pot over high heat until a probe or instant-read thermometer reads about 350°F.

Put the sesame seeds in a small bowl. Roll the balls in the seeds and, using a slotted spoon, gently lower them into the oil. Fry in batches of three to five, allowing room for them to bounce around. Coat the next set of balls as each batch fries. When the falafel float to the surface, flip them to ensure all sides cook evenly. Each batch should fry for 4 to 5 minutes.

With the slotted spoon, transfer the stuffed falafel to the prepared rack. Repeat the process until all the balls have been fried.

Serve with the hot sauce and flatbread.

SHAKSHUKA · شكشوكة
Eggs in Purgatory

Makes 4 to 6 servings

SHAKSHUKA, WHICH IN Arabic means "a mixture," builds a spicy base of charred red bell peppers and tomatoes for a crown of delicately poached eggs. This iconic Palestinian breakfast likely traces back to the Ottoman Empire, although the exact origin is disputed: Morocco, Tunisia, Turkey, and Yemen all lay claim to its inception.

Traditionally served directly from the hearth in a cast-iron skillet or clay pot, shakshuka is eaten piping hot, scooped up with Khobz Arabi (page 71), a yeasted flatbread.

As I often do, I upped the ratio of roasted red pepper in mine to balance the tomato's acidity and sweeten the base for the spices. Simple flavorful ingredients cooked down to their essence make all the difference in this dish.

4 Roma tomatoes, halved lengthwise

4 red bell peppers (about 1½ pounds)

2 tablespoons extra-virgin olive oil, plus more for drizzling

2½ cups medium-diced onions (about 1 large onion)

1 tablespoon finely minced garlic (about 4 cloves)

1 teaspoon ground cumin

1 teaspoon ground coriander

1 teaspoon paprika

1 teaspoon kosher salt, plus more for seasoning the eggs

½ teaspoon freshly ground black pepper

1 teaspoon Aleppo pepper or Chile-Spice Mix (page 27)

1 teaspoon honey

4 to 6 eggs

¼ cup crumbled feta (optional)

2 tablespoons coarsely chopped parsley

Arab Bread (page 71) for serving

Preheat the oven to 400°F.

Place the tomatoes cut side down in a roasting pan along with the peppers, leaving plenty of space between them. Coat them evenly with the oil. Roast until charred, about 40 minutes.

Remove the peppers from the pan once they have collapsed, are charred, and are bubbling. Transfer them to a large bowl and cover with plastic wrap. Leave the tomatoes to cool in the pan. Once the peppers are cool, peel away the skins and pull out the seeds and veins.

In a shallow saucepan over medium-high heat, sauté the onions until translucent. Add the garlic and cook for a minute more. Add the cumin, coriander, paprika, salt, black pepper, and Aleppo pepper and cook for another minute. Transfer the charred tomatoes, with skins, and any pan juices along with the peppers to the saucepan and simmer on medium heat for about 20 minutes, stirring frequently. Add up to ½ cup of water as needed to keep the sauce from burning.

Transfer the mixture to a food processor and mix to smooth before returning to the saucepan or blend the mixture in the saucepan with an immersion blender. Add the honey. The sauce should be thick. Make evenly spaced wells in the sauce and crack an egg into each well. Sprinkle with salt, cover, and simmer over medium heat for 5 to 10 minutes, until the whites are firm and the yolks are to your liking.

When ready to serve, take off the heat, drizzle with oil, top with the feta and parsley, and serve immediately with the bread.

Spicy Garlic-Smashed Potatoes with Spicy Red Pepper Aioli

Makes 4 to 6 servings on a mezze table or as a side

BATATA HARRA, WHICH translates to "spicy potatoes," goes on any large mezze spread. It's perfect for breakfast, lunch, and dinner. I made it my mission in this recipe to maximize the crispy outer edges while keeping the inside light and airy. The secret is to poach the potatoes in salted water before frying; this allows them to release some of their starch, keeping them moist and fluffy in the center. A solid smash before frying breaks the skin to create crispier edges.

Potatoes

1½ pounds fingerling or Yukon gold potatoes

1 tablespoon whole coriander seeds

2 tablespoons kosher salt, plus more as needed

Aioli

2 tablespoons Spicy Red Pepper Paste (page 38) or store-bought harissa paste

2 egg yolks

2 garlic cloves

2 tablespoons lemon juice (about 1 lemon)

½ teaspoon honey, plus more as needed

¾ teaspoon kosher salt, plus more as needed

¾ cup extra-virgin olive oil

1 tablespoon ice water

2 cups neutral oil, such as sunflower or canola, for frying

1½ teaspoons minced garlic (about 3 cloves)

¼ cup coarsely chopped cilantro

2 teaspoons Aleppo pepper or Chile-Spice Mix (page 27), plus more as needed

½ teaspoon kosher salt

2 teaspoons extra-virgin olive oil

Add the potatoes to a pot with enough water to cover by about 2 inches. Season with the coriander and salt. Bring to a low simmer and cook until tender; a knife should pierce with little to no resistance, 15 to 25 minutes, depending on the size of the potatoes. Drain the potatoes and allow to cool slightly.

To make the aioli: While the potatoes are cooking, combine the red pepper paste, egg yolks, garlic, lemon juice, honey, and salt in a blender or food processor and blend until well incorporated. Then slowly drizzle in half of the olive oil and continue blending, until the sauce is thickened. Add the ice water to help stabilize the sauce and keep it from breaking. Drizzle in the remaining oil until thickened a bit more. The sauce should resemble a loose, runny mayonnaise. Adjust the salt to taste. If using store-bought harissa, it can have some bitterness; balance the flavor by adding more honey if needed. Set aside.

When the potatoes are cool enough to touch, use your palm or the bottom of a bowl or coffee mug to smash the potatoes, just enough to break the skin and expose the insides. Give larger smashed potatoes a rough chop into bite-size pieces.

When ready to serve, heat the neutral oil until a probe or instant-read thermometer reads about 375°F. Fry the potato pieces until crispy and golden brown, about 2 minutes.

To finish: Immediately transfer the potatoes to a bowl, toss in the garlic, cilantro, Aleppo pepper, salt, and olive oil until evenly coated. Drizzle the aioli over the potatoes or serve alongside as a dipping sauce.

TAAJIN LUBNANI · طاجن لبناني
Smoked Fish, Caramelized Onions, and Tahini Spread

Makes 1 cup

THIS DELICACY, FLAKY white fish in creamy tahini with caramelized onions, is dedicated to my ride-or-die work wife, Zaynah, who helped me build Reem's from the ground up. Like me, one of her parents is a Palestinian-Beiruti transplant. Though it's mostly unspoken, we both claim our identities through food.

Her knowledge of Arab cuisine is so expansive that when customers hear her speak about our menu, they often ask if she, herself, is Reem. I laugh when I hear this, hoping she'll say "Yes"; to me, we could be interchangeable (if I were just a little more comfortable in public). Zaynah's comforting spirit embodies Reem's as a place to experience the warmth of Arab hospitality. She spent time living in Beirut and often reminisces about the food there. Having never lived there myself, I relish her stories, and whenever I have the next "big idea" for a menu item, no matter how silly, we experiment together until it's perfect.

Tajine Lubnani appears on many of the mezze spreads Zaynah sampled in Lebanon. Traditionally, the dish is made with baked fish, but it reminded me of the smoked mackerel salads I have tasted in Jewish delis, and that inspired us to substitute cured fish.

Cured fish is available at most local and chain grocery stores. I prefer mackerel or mullet, fattier fishes that absorb more smoke flavor. Cured fish varies in salinity, so taste the mix before adding salt to see if it needs any at all.

1 large onion, thinly sliced

¼ cup water

¼ cup tahini

2 tablespoons lemon juice (about 1 lemon)

¼ teaspoon ground cumin

8 ounces smoked white fish, deboned and broken into small chunks (about ½ cup of flaked fish)

Kosher salt (optional)

2 tablespoons extra-virgin olive oil for drizzling

1 tablespoon lemon zest

2 tablespoons chopped chives (optional)

¼ cup pine nuts or slivered almonds, toasted

In a medium pan over medium heat, add the onion slices and caramelize until they are soft and dark brown, 15 to 20 minutes, stirring frequently toward the end so they don't burn. Set the pan aside to cool.

While the onions are caramelizing, in a medium bowl, combine the water and tahini and whisk until no lumps remain. Add the lemon juice and whisk vigorously until the mixture starts to thicken, then add the cumin. Set aside.

Once the onions have cooled, fold them and the fish into the tahini mixture, creating a nice thick dip. Add salt to taste.

When ready to serve, spread the dip in a shallow bowl and press with the back of a spoon to form small wells. Drizzle with the oil and top with lemon zest, chives, and pine nuts.

FATTET LAHME WA HUMMUS · فتة لحم وحمص
Savory Bread Pudding with Short Ribs and Chickpeas

Makes 4 to 6 servings

ONE OF MY favorite memories from visits to Beirut was listening to the sizzle of fried pine nuts in hot clarified butter hit the top of a fatteh at street corner stalls, where vendors were making this dish to order for hungry crowds.

It takes only one bite to understand the magic of fatteh, the ultimate breakfast and brunch mezze dish and a perfect cure for a hangover. Fattet simply means "a fatteh composed of . . . [fill in the blank]." That could include a layered dish of chickpeas and any other ingredients your heart desires, spooned atop a bed of crispy pita chips and blanketed by a rich yogurt-tahini sauce, then rounded out with herbs, toasted nuts, and the delicious tart notes of pomegranate. I've opted here for the addition of an aromatic short rib braise. Left to sit for a while, the fried bread soaks in the rich broth and yogurt to resemble a savory bread pudding.

This recipe is also great for potlucks and can be doubled to create a larger casserole to share with friends or neighbors. It can be covered in plastic wrap and stored in the refrigerator for up to a week and reheats nicely in the oven, right in the same baking dish.

1½ pounds bone-in beef short ribs

1½ teaspoons kosher salt, plus more as needed

1½ teaspoons Seven-Spice Mix (page 26)

½ teaspoon Aleppo pepper or Chile-Spice Mix (page 27)

¼ teaspoon ground cardamom

¾ cup dried chickpeas, soaked overnight, or one 15-ounce can chickpeas, drained and rinsed

Pinch of baking soda (for dried chickpeas only)

2 tablespoons neutral oil, such as sunflower or canola

1 yellow onion, cut into large wedges

½ fennel bulb, cut into large wedges

3 garlic cloves, halved

½ teaspoon fennel seeds

5 cardamom pods

1 bay leaf

½ teaspoon ground cumin

Sauce

¾ cup whole milk yogurt

1 tablespoon tahini

1 tablespoon lemon juice (about ½ lemon)

1 teaspoon minced or grated garlic (about 1 clove)

½ teaspoon kosher salt

4 cups store-bought pita chips or 2-inch pieces of pita bread, fried

¼ cup pine nuts

2 tablespoons Clarified Butter (page 96) or extra-virgin olive oil

2 tablespoons coarsely chopped parsley

1 tablespoon pomegranate molasses, and/or ¼ cup pomegranate seeds

In a large bowl, rub the short ribs with the salt, spice mix, Aleppo pepper, and cardamom, then cover and refrigerate overnight or for at least 4 hours ahead of time. Set the ribs out at room temperature 90 minutes before cooking.

If you are using dried chickpeas, place them in a small pot with a pinch of baking soda and cover the beans with about 6 inches of water. Bring to a boil,

continued

skim, discard the residue from the water's surface, and decrease the heat to a simmer over medium heat. Cook, uncovered, until the beans soften, about 30 minutes. Test for doneness by squeezing a bean between your thumb and forefinger. If you are using canned chickpeas, skip this step.

Preheat the oven to 325°F.

Warm the oil in a Dutch oven over medium-high heat. Sear the short ribs, cooking to a nice crusty brown before flipping, about 3 minutes per side. Remove and set aside. In the same pot, char the onion, fennel bulb, and garlic on medium-high heat. Return the meat to the Dutch oven and add about 3 cups hot water or just enough to barely cover the ribs. Add the fennel seeds, cardamom pods, and bay leaf. Cover and braise until the meat easily pulls away from the bone, 2½ to 3 hours. If you do not have a Dutch oven, sear the meat and vegetables in a cast-iron or heavy skillet and transfer to a roasting pan, add water and spices, and cover with aluminum foil before cooking. Set the meat aside and allow to cool slightly if time permits.

Strain the braising liquid into a small saucepan. Discard the remaining braising vegetables and bones. Bring the liquid to a boil over medium heat and then decrease the heat to a simmer. Add the cumin and chickpeas and simmer until the chickpeas are tender but not mushy, about 10 minutes. Adjust the salt to taste.

Tear the meat to your liking, into shreds or small chunks.

To make the sauce: Combine the yogurt, tahini, lemon juice, garlic, and salt in a medium bowl and whisk until incorporated.

When ready to assemble, spread the pita chips in a base layer of a serving bowl or a casserole dish. Spoon the warm shredded meat over the top, then ladle the broth and chickpeas over the meat and chips. Next, drizzle on an even layer of the yogurt sauce.

When ready to serve, sauté the pine nuts in the butter over medium-low heat, stirring continuously until golden brown, about 3 minutes. Drizzle the sizzling butter and pine nuts over the dish. Top with the parsley and molasses.

Ground Meat and Bulgur Patties Stuffed with Herbed Ghee

Makes 24 patties

KIBBEH IS CONSIDERED the national dish of Syria. Aleppo alone has more than seventeen varieties. They are fried, grilled, and baked in an array of shapes and sizes. Some are filled by the piece, while others are pressed into large trays. We grew up receiving care packages from an aunt in Chicago, who shipped frozen ones to us overnight. She was the kibbeh master. Anytime we wanted, we could just pop them in the toaster oven.

This recipe is based on a variety I ate while visiting northern Syria with my youngest sister, Manal. Qraas, which translates to "disk" in Arabic, is used to describe this kibbeh. They look like small flying saucers and are traditionally grilled on an outdoor fire rather than fried or baked. We had never seen kibbeh shaped or cooked like that, and there was a surprisingly luxurious taste inside each disk that we only realized was tallow after eating one too many. I wanted to re-create that luxurious taste but make it a little lighter.

The filling can be made with any solid animal fat. If you're using butter, be sure to take the extra step of clarifying it (see page 96) to remove the moisture and milk solids.

You can make these patties and freeze them in resealable bags for up to 6 months. They're great to pull out for mezze spreads and late-night snacks.

Dough

¾ cup bulgur #1 (fine size)

1 pound lean ground beef or lamb (or a mixture of both)

2 cups diced yellow onions (about 1 onion)

1½ teaspoons Seven-Spice Mix (page 26) or ground allspice

2 teaspoons kosher salt

½ teaspoon freshly ground black pepper

½ teaspoon ground cinnamon

Filling

⅔ cup Clarified Butter (page 96), softened

1 cup chopped mint leaves (about ½ bunch)

1½ cups finely diced red onions (about 1 small onion)

1 teaspoon kosher salt

½ teaspoon Aleppo pepper or Chile-Spice Mix (page 27); optional

Olive oil for greasing the pan

To make the dough: Line a tray or a plate with paper towels.

In a small bowl, cover the bulgur with boiling water and allow to soak for 1 hour. After soaking, press the bulgur with your hands or with the back of a spoon and squeeze out the last remaining moisture. Make sure the bulgur is completely cool before mixing with the beef.

Combine the meat, onions, spice mix, salt, black pepper, and cinnamon and mix on high speed in a food processor, about 2 minutes, until the meat resembles a sticky dough; don't overmix or the meat will become grainy.

Add the hydrated bulgur and pulse just until the bulgur disappears. Knead the mixture in a bowl until it is uniform and homogenous and resembles a slightly sticky dough. Place a piece of plastic wrap directly on top of the meat and set the bowl in the refrigerator to chill.

To make the filling: Combine the butter, mint, red onions, salt, and Aleppo pepper in a food processor and blend until it forms a smooth paste. (If you don't have a food processor, chop everything very finely and paddle with a spoon.)

To make the patties: Prepare an ice water bath to chill your fingers and prevent the dough from sticking to your hands. Divide the dough into 24 pieces, about the size of golf balls (about 38 grams each). You may have a bit of dough left over; this is great to use for patching any holes if needed.

Place one ball of the meat dough in the palm of your hand and pat it into an even 3-inch disk.

Place a heaping teaspoon (about 11 grams) of the filling in the center of the disk. Cup the dough in your hand around the filling to create a sphere. Gently pinch and smooth the seam to seal. Pat gently into a 2-inch disk, making sure to smooth the sides so the filling doesn't burst out when cooking. Set aside and repeat until all of the dough balls have been filled and sealed.

Heat a cast-iron or heavy skillet over medium-high heat. Brush the pan with the oil and lay down four or five kibbeh at a time, depending on the size of your pan. Decrease the heat to medium-low and cook the patties for about 5 minutes, until they are crispy and brown; then turn over and cook for another 5 minutes, until they are cooked through and the stuffing has melted. Repeat the process until you cook all of your patties.

Alternatively, preheat the oven to 400°F. Bake the patties on a sheet tray for 25 to 30 minutes or until crisped and brown. Crisp under the broiler for a minute or two if needed. Serve hot on a mezze spread or as a finger food for a party.

Chapter Six

Suhoun · Main Plates

Spiced Rice with Fried Vermicelli

Makes 4 to 6 servings

FOUR THINGS SET Arab rice apart from all others: first, the confetti of toasty golden vermicelli noodle threads wrapped between white grains of rice; second, the sweetness of spices; third, the textural crunch of roasted almond slivers; and fourth, the bright visual contrast of forest green parsley.

My mom used to make this dish in huge mounds, topped with fried nuts, spiced ground meat, and parsley for dramatic effect. With the addition of the meat, it could make a main dish, although it rarely stands alone in Arab homes. This is feast food, whether around the family dinner table, at a wedding, a potluck, or anywhere in between.

My mom always had a stash of vermicelli from the Arab grocer in her pantry, dried into little fist-size nests, perfectly portioned to crush single-handedly into warm oil in the bottom of the rice pot. The thin noodles also come already fragmented, or you can break noodles from a supermarket box of vermicelli. All sources work equally well.

Cooking rice is as much an art in the Arab world as it is in every rice-eating culture. To produce loose, individual grains that roll off each other instead of sticking, ensure every morsel is coated in oil before adding water.

¼ cup neutral oil, such as sunflower or canola

1 cup Italian vermicelli (semolina based), broken into small fragments no larger than 1 inch (angel hair pasta makes a fine substitute)

1 cup basmati rice, rinsed

2 teaspoons Seven-Spice Mix (page 26)

1 teaspoon kosher salt

2½ cups water

½ cup fried or toasted slivered almonds or pine nuts

2 tablespoons coarsely chopped parsley (optional)

Heat the oil in a medium pot over medium heat. Once the oil is warm, fry the vermicelli a minute or two until golden. Add the rice, stir to coat, and fry, stirring frequently until the rice smells toasty, about 3 minutes. Add the spice mix, salt, and water and bring to a boil over medium heat. Turn down the heat to the lowest setting, cover the pot, and continue cooking, until all the water is absorbed, about 15 minutes. Do not to stir in the meantime—something I'm always tempted to do.

Fluff the rice with a fork and serve on a platter topped with the nuts and parsley. Serve alongside a main dish or use as a stuffing for poultry or vegetables.

The rice can be stored in an airtight container in the refrigerator for up to 5 days.

MUJADDARRA · مجدرة

Onion-Studded Lentil and Rice Pilaf

Makes 4 to 6 servings

THIS LENTIL AND rice dish is delicious, deeply satisfying, and easy to pull together. It's ironic to see this subsistence staple fancified on restaurant menus.

Although my family never used turmeric in this dish, I learned to love it made this way. Its musky hint gives the dish a biryani feel. Traditionally, the rice and lentils together are soft—even softer than rice alone. For more texture, I top mine with crunchy things such as seeds or nuts. Together with the Khyar bil Laban (page 218), a yogurt-mint salad, it's a quick and incredibly satisfying meal in a bowl.

⅔ cup brown lentils, rinsed

½ teaspoon kosher salt, plus more for sprinkling the onions

½ cup neutral oil, such as sunflower or canola

2½ cups thinly sliced onions (about 1 large onion)

1 cup basmati rice, rinsed

1 teaspoon ground cumin

½ teaspoon ground coriander

¼ teaspoon ground allspice

¼ teaspoon ground turmeric

Whole milk yogurt for serving

In a medium pot, immerse the lentils in water, about an inch above the lentils. Dissolve the salt in the water and bring to a boil. Turn down the heat to simmer and cook, uncovered, for about 15 minutes, until the lentils are al dente—soft outside and slightly firm in the center. Strain and reserve the liquid.

While the lentils are cooking, warm ¼ cup of the oil in a medium pan over medium heat. Add 1 cup of the onions and fry to a deep golden brown, stirring more frequently toward the end. The onions should be soft in the center, crispy at the tips, and deep brown in color. Sprinkle lightly with salt. Set the finished onions aside.

In a medium pot, warm the remaining ¼ cup oil over medium heat and sweat the remaining 1½ cups onions until translucent, about 5 minutes. Add the rice and stir to coat. Sauté the rice in the onion-oil mixture for about 5 minutes, stirring frequently, then add the cumin, coriander, allspice, and turmeric. Pour in 1½ cups of the reserved lentil water (if your lentils did not yield enough liquid, add water to make up the difference). Bring to a boil, cover, and turn down the heat to low. Simmer for 15 minutes. When most of the water has been absorbed, fold in the lentils, cover, and cook for 5 minutes more.

When ready to serve, spoon onto a serving platter and top with the fried onions.

The pilaf can be stored in an airtight container in the refrigerator for up to 1 week.

Cracked Green Wheat and Chicken Porridge

Makes 4 to 6 servings

EVERY CULTURE HAS a version of chicken soup, and ours has many. The one I love best is my mother's freekeh soup, a creamy porridgelike chicken stew made with cracked wheat, cooked to a risotto-like consistency in classic Arab spices. Beyond the warming spices of the chicken stock, this soup is unique for its freekeh, a green durum wheat, fire-roasted and smoky. I love the chewiness of freekeh, which turns soups into savory porridge.

2½ pounds bone-in, skin-on chicken thighs

4 teaspoons kosher salt, plus more for seasoning the chicken skins

2 tablespoons extra-virgin olive oil

2 cups medium-diced onions (about 1 onion)

1½ tablespoons minced garlic (about 6 cloves)

2 tablespoons minced fresh ginger

½ teaspoon freshly ground black pepper

1 tablespoon Seven-Spice Mix (page 26)

5 cardamom pods

6 cups water

1 bay leaf

1 cup freekeh, rinsed

2 tablespoons neutral oil, such as sunflower or canola

1 lemon, cut into wedges

2 tablespoons coarsely chopped parsley (optional)

Season the chicken with 2 teaspoons of the salt. Warm the olive oil in a stockpot over medium-high heat. Sear the chicken for 3 to 5 minutes on each side, until the skin crisps and turns dark golden brown and the fat from the bird releases into the cooking oil. Remove the chicken from the pot and set aside.

In the same pot, add the onions, garlic, and ginger and sauté for 5 minutes or until the onions are translucent. Add the remaining 2 teaspoons salt, pepper, spice mix, and cardamom pods, sautéing until fragrant. Return the chicken to the pot, add the water and bay leaf, and bring to a boil. Skim and discard any foam from the surface. Turn down the heat to simmer, cover, and cook for 20 minutes. The chicken should be cooked through but not falling apart. Remove the chicken from the stock and set aside.

While the chicken is cooking, stir the freekeh into the cooking stock and return to a boil, then simmer, uncovered, for 25 minutes. The soup should thicken, and the freekeh should be tender.

When the meat is cool enough to handle, pull it from the bones and reserve the skins. Place the skins on a paper towel to pat dry, then chop into ¼-inch pieces. Set aside.

Tear the chicken into bite-size pieces, about the width of your forefinger. I often save the bones to make a second broth for other uses. Return the chicken pieces to the pot and keep on low heat until ready to serve.

In a small pan on high heat, add the neutral oil and fry the chicken skins until crispy. Set aside on paper towels to drain and season generously with salt.

When ready to serve, remove the cardamom pods and bay leaf. Spoon the freekeh into bowls, crumble the crispy chicken skins over the tops, and add a squeeze of fresh lemon along with the parsley.

The freekeh can be stored in an airtight container in the refrigerator for up to a week or in the freezer for up to 3 months.

D'JAJ MAHSHI · دجاج محشي
Chicken Stuffed with Spiced Rice

Makes 4 servings

MAKING THIS DISH reminds me of my grandmother and my connection to family around the world. Every summer, my mother, sisters, and I would visit my grandparents' home in the San Fernando Valley of California—along with our extended family, who came all the way from Greece and the Arab Gulf. The festivities always commenced with a pool party, followed by stuffed Cornish hens for lunch. The rich, meaty stuffing, perfumed with cinnamon, allspice, and pine nuts, was the perfect match for the spice-rubbed birds.

Dry-brining—which is a fancy way of saying seasoning in advance—is an important step. It tenderizes and enhances the overall flavor of the otherwise mild chicken, while speeding up the browning process on the exterior, giving it a perfectly crispy skin. If you are short on time, you can let your seasoned chicken sit at room temperature for an hour before baking.

1 tablespoon kosher salt, plus more as needed

1 tablespoon Seven-Spice Mix (page 26)

1 teaspoon sumac

One 3- to 4-pound chicken

Stuffing

1 cup jasmine rice, rinsed

¼ cup extra-virgin olive oil

1 yellow onion, finely diced

10 ounces ground lamb or beef

2½ teaspoons Seven-Spice Mix (page 26)

½ teaspoon ground turmeric

¼ teaspoon freshly ground black pepper

1 teaspoon kosher salt, plus more to taste

1¾ cups water

½ cup pine nuts or slivered almonds, toasted, plus ¼ cup for garnish

2 tablespoons extra-virgin olive oil

¼ cup fresh dill (optional) for garnish

In a small bowl, combine the salt, spice mix, and sumac and rub it all over the chicken, both inside and out. Let the chicken sit, uncovered, in the refrigerator overnight or at room temperature for an hour.

To make the stuffing: Put the rice in a medium bowl, cover with cold water, and let it soak for 15 minutes. Drain and set aside.

In a large pot over medium heat, warm the ¼ cup olive oil until it shimmers, then add the onions and sauté for about 5 minutes until translucent; don't let them brown. Add the ground meat, spice mix, turmeric, black pepper, and ½ teaspoon of the salt. Cook, breaking up the meat with a spoon, until just barely browned, about 2 minutes.

Add the rice and mix thoroughly with the spiced meat mixture. Pour the water into the pot, season with the remaining ½ teaspoon salt, and bring to a boil. Decrease the heat, cover, and simmer until the rice is just tender and the water has been absorbed, about 10 minutes. Remove the pot from the heat and mix in ½ cup of the nuts. Adjust the salt to taste. Transfer the stuffing to a bowl and set aside to cool.

Bring the chicken to room temperature an hour before you're ready to bake it.

Preheat the oven to 350°F.

Stuff the cavity of the chicken loosely with 2 cups of the rice mixture. Reserve the remaining rice to reheat and serve alongside the cooked chicken. Tie the drumsticks together at the bottom with cooking twine to close the cavity.

continued

Drizzle the chicken with olive oil and set inside a Dutch oven or roasting pan, breast side up. Cover the pan with a lid or aluminum foil and roast for 1 hour. Remove the lid, increase the temperature to 400°F and continue to roast for another 30 minutes or until the chicken has browned on the outside and cooked through (a meat thermometer should read 165°F at the thickest part of the leg, near but not touching the bone). Remove the pan from the oven and set aside to rest for 15 minutes before serving.

Serve whole on a platter, surrounded by the reserved stuffing. Garnish with the remaining ¼ cup nuts and the dill.

The chicken can be stored in an airtight container in the refrigerator for up to 3 days.

MUSAKHAN · مسخّن
Sumac-Spiced Chicken Wraps

Makes 16 mini wraps or 4 full wraps

MUSAKHAN IS PERHAPS the most iconic of all Palestinian chicken dishes. I often joke that while we don't have a nation-state, we most certainly have a national dish. Extravagant and communal, the chicken is traditionally served whole, steeped in olive oil and reddish-purple sumac. It is mounded over caramelized onions atop a hearth-baked flatbread called taboon and soaked with the cooking juices. People sit around a table, using bite-size pieces of the bread to tear off bites of chicken.

I didn't grow up eating it that way. Ever. My mother, like lots of Arab mothers in the United States, adapted the chicken-onion combo into tortilla rolls. Eating this wrap with sumac and onion juices drizzling down your arms is part of the experience and a sign of a good juicy braise. It's equally great at room temperature and can be served as a party appetizer wrap.

This home recipe is adapted from my restaurant's most popular wrap called the Pali-Cali, since it brings together Palestinian musakhan with arugula, producing something deeply satisfying and easier for non-Arabic speakers to pronounce. I like to add avocado for some extra California love. I think my family in Gaza would approve.

1 pound skinless, boneless chicken thighs (about 4 thighs)

2½ teaspoons kosher salt, plus more as needed

3 tablespoons sumac

½ teaspoon Seven-Spice Mix (page 26) or ground allspice

5 tablespoons extra-virgin olive oil, plus more for drizzling

6 cups thinly sliced onions (about 2 onions)

¼ teaspoon freshly ground black pepper, plus more as needed

1 tablespoon pomegranate molasses

4 pieces Saj Bread (page 73) or your favorite brand of 12-inch flour tortillas

4 cups trimmed arugula

½ cup pomegranate seeds (optional)

1 avocado, sliced (optional)

In a medium bowl, rub the chicken thighs with 1 teaspoon of the salt, 2 tablespoons of the sumac, and the spice mix and let them sit for 2 hours at room temperature or refrigerate overnight.

Preheat the oven to 300°F.

In a medium pan, heat 3 tablespoons of the oil over medium-high heat. Add the onions and ½ teaspoon of the salt and sauté until the onions are soft and translucent and slightly browned.

Transfer 1 cup of the onions to an 8 by 8-inch baking dish and set aside.

Continue to caramelize the remaining onions on low heat.

Arrange the seasoned chicken in a single layer over the onions in the baking dish and drizzle with the remaining 2 tablespoons oil. Cover the pan tightly with aluminum foil and bake until the chicken is cooked through and breaks apart easily with a fork, 55 to 65 minutes.

continued

While the chicken is baking, continue to caramelize the onions on low heat, stirring often, until they're very soft and deep golden brown, 20 to 25 minutes. It's important to cook the onions slowly to reduce their liquid and bring out the sweetness. Remove the pan from the heat, add the remaining 1 tablespoon sumac, the remaining 1 teaspoon salt, and the pepper and drizzle with the molasses. Adjust the salt and pepper to taste. Let cool slightly.

Using two forks, pull apart the cooked chicken into bite-size shreds and fold the caramelized onion mixture into the cooked chicken.

Lay out the flatbreads on a dry work surface and distribute the pulled chicken and onion mixture in a nice straight line down the center of each bread. Top with the arugula, pomegranate seeds, and avocado. Fold in the sides and roll up each flatbread, burrito-style, going from the bottom to the top. Drizzle the flatbreads with a little oil and give them a quick toast in a cast-iron skillet or heavy pan for some color.

Serve whole as a meal or sliced into quarters for the perfect party bite.

The rolls can be stored covered or in an airtight container in the refrigerator for up to 3 days and reheated or enjoyed at room temperature.

Ode to the Olive Tree

Musakhan is an ode to the fellaheen—the farmers, harvesters, and cultivators of Palestinian land—and a tribute to the olive tree, which has a special place in our cuisine and heritage.

Under Israeli occupation, authorities have uprooted more than 800,000 olive trees, some centuries old, and taken the land beneath them, politicizing the very ingredient that makes this dish so special. According to the charity organization Oxfam, this has resulted in a loss of more than $12 million a year for those families who rely on the olive harvest for their livelihood. It can take forty years for a tree to produce consistently mature olives, making the razing of trees an even greater affront to Palestinian history and survival.

This, in addition to the displacement of Palestinians from their homes and farms in 1948 and the closure of Gaza from the rest of Palestine, has meant that millions of Palestinians can no longer access or afford olive oil. In fact, many Palestinians in Gaza no longer use olive oil to make their musakhan, instead substituting United Nations rations of canola oil.

The rituals surrounding the olive harvest are a rite of passage, and fresh, properly harvested oil is a delicacy unto itself. It's one I don't take for granted as a Palestinian. I've witnessed the harvest in Lodi, California, with my good friends at Corto Olive Oil, and I am deeply thankful for participating in the magic of its cultivation in a way that my family back home cannot.

SHAWARMA MEXICIYYA · شاورما مكسيكية
Al Pastor–Style Red-Spiced Chicken

Makes 4 to 6 servings

I LOVE FOLLOWING the tracks of Arabs who have arrived in different corners of the world, influencing and being influenced by the cuisine in their new homes. In the early 1900s, Levantine Arabs, mostly from Lebanon and Syria, fled to Mexico to avoid Ottoman rule. They brought along with them their love of marinated meats, grilled on outdoor spits, sliced thin, and served with pickled toppings and fresh herbs.

Al pastor, it turns out, is something that Mexicans took from the Lebanese and made even better, but I didn't learn that until after I had left Boston, since my family did not eat pork when I was growing up. The first time I tried al pastor, sweetened with pineapple juice and spiced with chiles, was in California. Later, in Mexico City, when I saw the masters deftly turning meat to crispy perfection on a trompo, a spit, I felt a great affinity, since that is exactly how we eat shawarma.

Although it's less common to see chicken bathed in the beautiful red spices of shawarma in the United States, chicken shawarma is actually quite popular back in the homeland. I remember one special occasion when my mom, coaxing me back to health when I was bedridden with mono at a young age, magically procured some and smuggled it into the hospital for me. It's a reminder of the ways that food, especially bright, beautiful, flavorful food, is such an important part of healing.

Here, I've brought shawarma indoors, so I can enjoy it no matter the weather, marinating thin slabs of thigh meat overnight and sizzling the pieces quickly on a hot griddle or heavy pan.

This meat goes to the next level when it is paired with a healthy dose of the tangy spread Toum (page 41). This doubles as a taco night special and can be enjoyed with fixings such as hot sauce, Quick-Pickled Red Onions (see page 43), fresh veggies, and avocados.

Marinade
6 dried guajillo chiles
4 garlic cloves
¼ cup extra-virgin olive oil
¼ cup lemon juice (about 2 lemons)
¼ cup apple cider vinegar
¾ cup pineapple juice
1 tablespoon Aleppo pepper or Chile-Spice Mix (page 27)
1 tablespoon ground coriander
1½ teaspoons ground cumin
2 teaspoons Wild Thyme, Sumac, and Sesame Mix (page 24) or oregano
1 teaspoon ground chipotle chile (optional)
½ teaspoon ground cardamom
½ teaspoon paprika
1 tablespoon plus 1 teaspoon kosher salt

4 pounds boneless, skinless chicken thighs, trimmed of fat
1 onion, sliced into ¾-inch wedges (with the core, so the onion doesn't fall apart)
Kosher salt for seasoning the onions, plus more as needed
½ bunch parsley, coarsely chopped (optional)
½ bunch cilantro, coarsely chopped (optional)
1 recipe Saj Bread (page 73) or your favorite brand of 12-inch flour tortillas for serving

continued

To make the marinade: Cover the guajillo chiles in hot water and allow to sit for 15 minutes or until soft. Remove the stems and seeds and chop into 1-inch pieces.

Combine all of the remaining marinade ingredients in a blender and mix until well incorporated. Add the chiles and blend until everything is smooth.

Bisect each chicken thigh widthwise to make thin slabs. This can be done by pressing your palm onto the thigh and making a lateral cut with small side-to-side sawing motions.

Place the chicken in a medium bowl or in a resealable bag, add the marinade, and marinate for at least 4 hours or overnight in the refrigerator.

Warm a cast-iron or flat heavy griddle over high heat. Making sure not to crowd the pan, sear the marinated chicken in batches, until both sides are nicely charred and cooked through, 3 to 4 minutes per side.

Set the chicken pieces aside as they come off the pan and cover to allow the meat to rest and reabsorb its juices. Once all the chicken is cooked, add just enough water to the pan to deglaze the juices and then drizzle over the chicken while it rests.

Wipe out the griddle and, while the chicken is resting, grill the onion wedges over medium-high heat. Season with the salt and continue cooking over medium heat until tender, about 10 minutes.

Chop the chicken lengthwise into ½-inch strips and place into a serving bowl or on a platter. Fold the onion wedges into the cut meat and stir to incorporate. Adjust the salt and heat to taste.

Sprinkle with the parsley and cilantro and serve with flatbreads.

Meat can be stored in an airtight container in the refrigerator for up to 3 days.

A Delicious Exchange

My Oakland and San Francisco restaurants are both nestled in the beating heart of the cities' Latinx districts. Many long, lean-staffed nights hustling to keep my restaurants open have ended with a late meal and a cold beer at a neighboring Mexican restaurant. Over time, the smells and tastes of the neighborhood have fed my imagination with menu ideas that play at the connection points between our cuisines.

I love traveling through Mexico City, not only for its amazing food but also for the deep familiarity of the city's century of Arab cultural influences from the different waves of Arab immigrants over the course of the twenty-first century. In many ways, the city resembles Beirut, a city of paradox, where rich and poor live side by side with the same propensity to enjoy a good life.

After fleeing Ottoman rule, an influx of Lebanese immigrants imported spices and marinating methods across the Yucatan Peninsula, Puebla, and Mexico City in the early 1900s; a half-century later, in 1948, there was another influx to Veracruz of Palestinians fleeing the takeover of Palestine. In many of these areas today, Arab culture is visible and vibrant. Although Arab dishes have been given different Spanish names (labneh to joceques, for instance), they still retain a distinctly Arab identity. On the other hand, some foods have melded into Mexican cuisine, from the addition of sweet acidic pineapple and pork to transform shawarma into al pastor, to the introduction of tacos arabes, delicious marinated carne asada on leavened bread. I am inspired by this exchange, which has made the food even more delicious across both cultures.

KAFTA · كفتة
Arab-Spiced Burger Patties

Makes 6 patties

NO FOOD BETTER represents my upbringing than this Arab-spiced ground lamb mix. Bursting with sweet onions and flecks of fresh parsley, infused with the spices of the Levant, my mom used this mix to make a variety of dishes: grilled patties, meatloaf wedged between grilled vegetables, or Kafta bil Bandoura (page 181), meatballs in tomato sauce. Simple to prepare, kafta makes the ultimate weeknight comfort food; with a little practice, it can go from fridge to table in about 20 minutes.

I love using kafta to make lamb burgers, a fan favorite at Reem's. Although traditionally made with lamb alone, kafta has been adapted into a more economical mix of beef and lamb. For people sensitive to lamb's gaminess, this can be a good option. Enjoy these burgers with your favorite buns or make your own Ka'ak (page 85) if you're feeling ambitious. Enjoy with all your favorite burger fixings.

TIP • To get the caramelized edges that elevate the patties to a sublime crisp, the cooking temperature is key. Drop a pea-size morsel of meat into the pan to see if it sizzles. If the pan is not sufficiently hot, the meat will release its water and boil instead of fry. If it's too hot, the meat will scorch before fully cooking inside. You want the oil shimmering but not smoking.

1 cup coarsely chopped onions
(about 1 onion)
½ cup finely chopped parsley
2 teaspoons ground allspice
1 teaspoon ground cinnamon
1 teaspoon freshly ground black pepper
2 teaspoons sumac
½ teaspoon ground nutmeg
4 teaspoons kosher salt
2 pounds ground lamb or beef
(or mixture of both)
2 tablespoons neutral oil, such as
sunflower or canola

Grate or pulse the onions in a food processor until they are finely mashed. Line a colander with cheese-cloth to drain the onions or squeeze out the liquid by hand.

In a large bowl, combine the onions, parsley, all-spice, cinnamon, pepper, 1 teaspoon of the sumac, nutmeg, and salt. Add the meat and, using your hands, knead the meat into the onion-spice mixture. To keep the meet tender, avoid overmixing.

Divide the meat into 6 even portions, roll into balls about the size of tennis balls (about 166 grams each). Using the flat side of your index and middle fingers, press down on the meatballs to create several shallow ridges in the surface of the meat while patting into ½-inch-thick, 4-inch-diameter patties. The ridges will crisp up and char while cooking.

Heat an electric griddle to 400°F or a cast-iron or heavy skillet on medium-high heat. Drizzle a thin coat of the oil onto the griddle or skillet and grill the patties for 3 to 5 minutes on each side.

Sprinkle with the remaining 1 teaspoon sumac. Serve immediately.

SHISH BARAK · شيشبرك
Lamb Dumplings in Yogurt Sauce with Mint Oil

Makes 4 to 6 servings

WHILE MY MOTHER favored expedience in the kitchen, there was one notable exception: when she was in an especially good mood or just wanted to spoil us, she'd set aside the demands of her job and spend an afternoon contentedly rolling out pasta for shish barak, tortellini-shaped meat-filled dumplings. She learned how to make this recipe from her best friend, Khadijah, a dumpling pro, who, like her, worked in the field of genetics.

Bathed in a garlic-yogurt sauce, these dumplings deliver a burst of juicy spiced lamb, enrobed in fresh pasta, and brightened with a drizzle of minty oil.

You can scale up and make even more of these to freeze. They're just as good and easy to dress up with sauce when you feel like a fancy meal. Shish barak are shaped into small rings, like tortellini, except with a delicious lamb filling. We used to call them elephants' ears because of their shape.

Any or all of the elements of this dish can be made up to several days ahead to be cooked and assembled just before serving.

Dough

3 cups all-purpose flour, plus more for dusting

1½ teaspoons kosher salt

¼ cup neutral oil, such as sunflower or canola

¾ cup warm water (about 100°F), plus more as needed

Filling

12 ounces ground beef or lamb (or mixture of both)

1 cup finely diced red onions (about 1 small onion)

1 teaspoon Seven-Spice Mix (page 26) or ground allspice

1 teaspoon kosher salt

½ teaspoon freshly ground black pepper

1½ teaspoons pomegranate molasses

2 tablespoons whole milk yogurt

Mint Oil

1½ cups mint leaves (about 1 bunch)

⅔ cup neutral oil, such as sunflower or canola

Sauce

2 cups full-fat Greek yogurt or labneh

1 tablespoon finely minced or grated garlic (about 4 cloves)

2 tablespoons cornstarch

1 teaspoon kosher salt, plus more as needed

2 cups cold water

12 cups water

Garnish (optional)

¼ cup toasted pine nuts

2 tablespoons mint chiffonade (sliced thin, crosswise)

½ teaspoon Aleppo pepper or Chile-Spice Mix (page 27)

½ teaspoon sumac

continued

To make the dough: In the bowl of a stand mixer or in a large bowl, combine the flour and salt.

To mix by hand: Using your hands, drizzle in the oil and incorporate, until the flour forms a fine crumble. Form a well inside the center, pour in the warm water, and slowly incorporate the flour from the inside of the well to bring the dough together. Turn out the dough on a flat work surface, dusted with flour as needed, and knead until the dough forms a smooth, elastic ball, about 5 minutes.

To mix in a stand mixer: Using the paddle attachment on slow speed, drizzle in the oil until the flour forms a fine crumble. Switch to the dough hook and slowly add the warm water. Drizzle in 1 more teaspoon of water at a time if needed to make the dough come together. Once the dough forms, remove the dough from the bowl and place on a flat work surface, dusted with flour as needed, and knead by hand until the dough forms a smooth, elastic ball, about 3 minutes.

Seal the ball in plastic wrap and let it rest in the refrigerator for at least 30 minutes.

To make the filling: While the dough is resting, in a large bowl combine the meat, onions, spice mix, salt, pepper, molasses, and yogurt and knead the mixture like a dough, until it is thoroughly mixed. Alternatively, you can use a food processor. Set aside.

To make the mint oil: Prepare a small bowl of ice water and set aside. Submerge the mint in boiling water for 30 seconds, remove from the heat, and plunge it into the ice water to stop the cooking. Remove the mint from the water and pat dry with paper towels.

In a small food processor or blender at medium speed, blend the mint with the oil until as smooth as possible, about 30 seconds. Set aside.

On a floured work surface, roll out the dough to 1/16-inch thickness, flouring the rolling pin and dough liberally, if needed, to prevent sticking. Let the dough relax for 5 minutes or so after rolling. With a dough cutter or the rim of a cup, cut out 3-inch circles. Cover the circles with a dish towel while you roll and cut out the rest of the dough. Set the scraps aside to rest, then knead them into a ball, roll into a sheet, and repeat the cutting process.

To make the dumplings: Put a tablespoon of the filling in the center of each dough round. Using your finger or a pastry brush, moisten the edges with water. Gently fold the dough in half and press the edges with your fingers to seal, expelling any air bubbles before closing the last portion. Pull the corners of each half-moon around the index finger of one hand and pinch together with your other hand to bind, forming a cupped outer edge and dimpled belly center. Place the dumplings on a lightly floured sheet tray. Repeat the process, shaping all of the dumplings. Refrigerate, uncovered, if not cooking right away.

To make the yogurt sauce: In a small saucepan, combine the yogurt, garlic, cornstarch, salt, and cold water and whisk to incorporate. Bring the sauce to a gentle simmer over low heat. Use a spatula or wooden spoon and scrape the bottom of the pan to make sure the sauce doesn't burn. Adjust the salt to taste. Remove the saucepan from the heat and set aside until the dumplings are cooked.

When you are ready to cook the dumplings, bring the 12 cups water to a boil in a large pot. Add the dumplings to form a single layer (about twelve at a time). The dumplings should float and cook for 3 to 4 minutes. Use a slotted spoon to transfer them into the yogurt sauce, gently tilting the pan from side to side to coat the dumplings evenly. Return the pan to low heat to make sure the dumplings

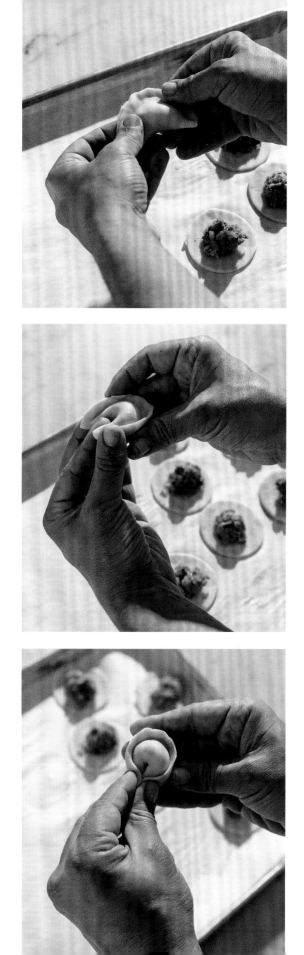

are warmed through. If your sauce has gotten too thick, you can drizzle in some of your dumpling water to thin it. Repeat the process until all of the dumplings are cooked and coated in sauce.

Spoon into shallow bowls to serve and drizzle with the mint oil. Top with the pine nuts, mint, Aleppo pepper, and sumac.

The dumplings can be stored frozen for up to 6 months. To keep their shape, freeze them first on a parchment-lined tray, then transfer to an airtight container or resealable bag for easy storage.

Lamb and Yogurt Stew

Makes 4 to 6 servings

THIS GORGEOUS LAMB never fails to impress with its tender hunks of shank perched atop a broth-enriched yogurt sauce and crowned with a bright mash of fresh herbs, lemon, and garlic.

Served to guests on a huge platter over Ruz Arabi (page 166), or Arab rice, this is a dish for special occasions. Its meaning is built right into the name: the root word for shakriyah is *ushkur*, meaning "to thank."

Maybe it was its collective, celebratory nature that appealed to my Amtu (the Arabic title for an aunt on your father's side) Elham, who came all the way from Syria, not once but three times to help take care of us, staying months at a time. Amtu, my father's elder sister who had helped raise him, had lost her husband early on, so it makes sense he would call on her to help take care of us when my mother decided to go back to school. Amtu's visits featured plenty of shakriyah, a caretaking dish for her. After her departure, it would become a comfort dish for my mother to carry on her tradition, and it has now become mine as well.

TIP • This is a yogurt-based broth that requires a lot of whisking to keep the base thick and emulsified. If the sauce breaks while it's cooking, add a dollop of yogurt and mix with an immersion blender (or transfer to a blender) to bring it back together.

4 pounds lamb shanks (2 or 3 shanks)
2 tablespoons extra-virgin olive oil
1½ tablespoons kosher salt
¼ cup Seven-Spice Mix (page 26)
2 large yellow onions, quartered
4 garlic cloves, smashed
¼ cup neutral oil, such as sunflower or canola
5 to 6 cups of water, plus more if needed

Sauce
1 cup whole milk yogurt
2 teaspoons minced garlic (about 2 cloves)
2 tablespoons cornstarch
¼ teaspoon kosher salt

Garnish
1 bunch parsley, coarsely chopped
Zest of 1 lemon
¼ cup toasted sliced almonds

Spiced Rice with Fried Vermicelli (page 166) for serving

Rub the lamb with the oil, salt, and spice mix. Cover and let sit for 2 hours at room temperature or refrigerate overnight. If refrigerated, let the meat sit for 1 hour at room temperature before cooking.

In a Dutch oven or a stockpot, heat the oil and sear the lamb and onions over medium-high heat until the lamb has browned and begins to caramelize, about 5 minutes on each side, and the onions are charred on the edges. If the pot is large enough for both the lamb and the onions to make contact with the pot's hot surface, this step can be done all at once.

Add the garlic and enough water to just barely cover the lamb and onion mixture. Bring to a boil, turn down the heat to a simmer, cover, and braise for about 2 hours or until the lamb is tender and pulls away easily from the bone. Remove the lamb and onions from the pot. Pour over a strainer into a small saucepot and then reduce the braising juices to about 1 cup liquid over medium-high heat.

While the liquid is reducing, pull the meat from the shank bones in large pieces, discarding the bones.

To make the sauce: In a medium pot, combine the yogurt, garlic, cornstarch, and salt and whisk until incorporated. Over low heat, warm the yogurt mixture and drizzle in the hot reduced liquid, whisking constantly to prevent the sauce from breaking. Let the sauce simmer gently for about 2 minutes. When the sauce has thickened enough to coat the back of a spoon (similar to the texture of hollandaise sauce), remove the pot from the heat.

When ready to serve, place the hunks of meat and the onions on a rimmed serving platter and then pour on the sauce.

Garnish with the parsley, lemon zest, and almonds. Serve with the spiced rice.

Stuffed Squid in Arak-Spiked Tomato Sauce

Makes 4 to 6 servings

SEARED INTO GOLDEN torpedoes, topped with squiggly tentacles, and nested in bright red sauce, these stuffed squid pack a lot of wow on the plate. The squid's immersion in arak-spiked tomato sauce is at once a tribute to my family's coastal roots on the shores of Gaza and entirely my own creation.

Growing up, I thought calamari came as a crispy first course in an Italian restaurant. As I threw myself into the art of Palestinian cuisine, I came across Joudie Kalla's stuffed squid in her book *Palestine on a Plate*. A light bulb went off for me: of course, we have squid, and, of course, we stuff it just like everything else.

This is my take on a popular Spanish dish of squid stuffed with breadcrumbs and chorizo. I stuff mine with bulgur and sujuk, a dry spicy, fermented East Asian sausage similar to chorizo, made beautifully by Armenians and common in Arab dishes. This fennel-tomato seafood combo draws inspiration from flavors, doused with arak, our anise-infused liquor, to give it an extra kick. While you have the bottle out, you might exercise the cook's prerogative: pour a splash over a cube of ice and watch the clear arak transform to a misty fog.

Sauce

2 tablespoons extra-virgin olive oil

1 fennel bulb, quartered lengthwise, with fronds reserved for garnish

1 tablespoon finely chopped garlic (about 4 garlic cloves)

½ cup arak, ouzo, Pernod, aguardiente, or any anise-flavored liquor

One 15-ounce can crushed tomatoes

2 cups Fish Stock (page 37), store-bought fish stock, or water

1 teaspoon kosher salt

1 teaspoon Seven-Spice Mix (page 26)

1 teaspoon Aleppo pepper or Chile-Spice Mix (page 27)

1 teaspoon saffron threads (optional)

½ cup fine bulgur #1 (fine size)

2 pounds squid or calamari, cleaned (about 1½ pounds cleaned)

Stuffing

1 serrano chile, stems, seeds, and veins removed, finely chopped

1 cup finely chopped red onions (about 1 small onion)

½ pound sujuk or chorizo, finely chopped

2 tablespoons finely chopped dill (about 5 sprigs), plus more for garnish

1 teaspoon kosher salt

1 tablespoon minced garlic (about 4 cloves)

2 tablespoons olive oil

Kosher salt for seasoning the tentacles

1 lemon, cut into quarters for serving

continued

To make the sauce: Warm the oil in a wide pot over medium-high heat. Add the fennel and sear, turning until the cut and rounded sides are golden brown. Add the garlic and cook for 1 minute more. Add the arak and scrape any cooked bits from the bottom of the pan into the bubbling liquor. Cook until the arak is almost evaporated. Add the tomatoes, stock, salt, spice mix, Aleppo pepper, and saffron. Bring to a boil. Then turn off the heat and set aside until ready to cook the squid.

In a small bowl, immerse the bulgur in cold water and soak for 10 minutes. Drain in a fine-mesh strainer, press out the water, and set aside.

To clean the squid: Cut just below the eyes to remove the tentacles, being careful to remove the sharp beak between the eyes and the tentacles. Set the tentacles aside.

Remove the hard cartilage by gripping the end tightly and slowly twisting and pulling until the whole thing slides out. Tug on the eye section of the squid, and the guts should also come out cleanly from the body. Using a sharp knife or your fingers, slice or pull away the winglike portions from the tip of the body. The skin should easily pull away as well. Give everything a rinse and pat dry.

To make the stuffing: In a large bowl, combine the chile, onions, sujuk, dill, salt, and garlic. Add the bulgur and mix until incorporated.

Stuff each squid two-thirds full, leaving room for the bulgur to expand, and thread the closure with a toothpick.

When you're ready to cook the squid, warm the oil in a heavy pan over high heat. Season the stuffed squid with a pinch of salt and sear until golden brown on both sides. Transfer each squid to the pot with the tomato sauce and fennel; tuck them in to make sure they are covered by the sauce. Bring the sauce to a simmer, cover, and cook for 10 minutes.

Remove the cover and cook for 20 more minutes to allow the sauce to reduce slightly.

Season the tentacles with a pinch of salt. In the same heavy pan, sauté the tentacles until just done, about 5 minutes. Set aside.

To serve, transfer the squid and sauce to a serving tray. Sprinkle with the tentacles and garnish with the dill and fennel fronds. Serve with lemon wedges on the side.

The Tomato's Twisted Route to the Arab World

Many of my recipes use tomatoes—sweet, acidic, and juicy. The Arab World's dry heat allows for a longer growing season than here in the United States, extending its availability and thus its popularity. But how did this fruit of the Americas make its way into so many foundational dishes of Arab Levantine cuisine?

Food documentarians trace one point of entry to the British, who arrived in Aleppo for the bustling trade of the Ottoman Empire toward the end of the eighteenth century. They brought tomato seeds they had likely received from the Spaniards, who centuries before had seized more than gold from the Aztecs and Incas, whose civilizations they eventually wiped out in South America. They also pilfered seeds, including those of the tomato. The vine did not receive a warm welcome in Europe. It was considered a "devil's fruit," from the family of poisonous nightshades. The colonists had no interest in learning about the plant from its Indigenous cultivators, and it languished.

Eventually, farmers in warmer countries like Spain and southern Italy recognized the tomato's versatility and overcame their fears; it soon became a staple of Mediterranean cuisine. The tomato went on to become among the Levant's largest crops, both for domestic use and export, securing its place as an important ingredient for the economy and the cuisine, becoming an affordable source of acidity to replace increasingly expensive traditional ingredients such as tamarinds and sour plums.

Gazan Clay Pot Shrimp

Makes 4 to 6 servings

I HAD NO idea my people ate shrimp until I came across a version of this dish in Laila El-Haddad's *The Gaza Kitchen*. My memories of shrimp dishes are limited to eating shrimp scampi with my family at TGI Fridays on occasional weekends. I was searching for shrimp in a sauce, and this is a *magnificent* sauce. The restaurant industry has taught me a few seafood techniques, including the secret to making a rich shrimp sauce: sear and then slow-cook the shrimp heads and shells. You can get shrimp heads from a butcher or buy whole shrimp and reserve the heads.

Laila's dish is tomato-based, but I have added red bell peppers to sweeten it, and I evoke its Gazan roots with a touch of dillseed and hot pepper. This dish is traditionally cooked in a clay pot in a high-heat hearth, allowing the shrimp to poach and the natural sugars in the sauce to caramelize and char, giving it a nice depth of flavor. Since most of us don't have clay pots at home, I created that flavor by charring the base vegetables and getting a nice caramelization on the shrimp shells before adding the liquid.

You can make this sauce ahead of time. Rewarm and poach the shrimp in the sauce just before serving.

3 pounds large shrimp, with heads and shells on (U-10 size if you can find them)

1 thinly sliced yellow onion

2 red bell peppers, thinly sliced

1 fennel bulb, thinly sliced, with fronds reserved for garnish

Sauce

¼ cup extra-virgin olive oil, plus more for drizzling

5 garlic cloves, coarsely chopped

½ teaspoon paprika

½ teaspoon ground cumin

½ teaspoon ground coriander

¼ teaspoon fennel seeds

¼ teaspoon dillseed (optional)

½ teaspoon Aleppo pepper or Chile-Spice Mix (page 27)

1 teaspoon kosher salt, plus more as needed

One 28-ounce can whole or crushed tomatoes

1 bay leaf

1 cup Fish Stock (page 37), store-bought fish stock, or water

2 tablespoons lemon juice (about 1 lemon)

Arab Bread (page 71) or rice for serving

Remove the heads and shells from the shrimp. Set the heads and shells aside for making the tomato-pepper sauce.

Devein the shrimp tails. Cover and refrigerate until ready to use.

continued

In a stockpot over medium heat, char the onions, bell peppers, and fennel bulb for about 5 minutes or until they have a bit of color. Set aside.

To make the sauce: In the same pot, sauté the shrimp heads and shells in the oil until caramelized, about 5 minutes. Add back half of the charred onion-fennel mixture to the pot, along with the garlic, paprika, cumin, coriander, fennel seeds, dillseed, Aleppo pepper, and salt. Stir and continue to cook to soften and use the juices from the vegetables to scrape up any bits from the bottom of the pan. Add the tomatoes, bay leaf, and stock and bring to a boil. Turn down the heat to medium-low and simmer for 30 to 40 minutes or until the sauce develops flavor and sweetness. Using a slotted spoon for scooping, discard the bay leaf and shrimp heads and shells.

In a food processor or food mill, blend the sauce and then push through a fine-mesh strainer. If you prefer a stronger seafood flavor, puree the heads and shells in the sauce before straining. (This makes about 2 cups of sauce for cooking the shrimp and 1 cup of solids to discard.)

Return the sauce to the pot with the remaining onion-fennel mixture and bring to a simmer over medium heat.

When ready to serve, season the shrimp tails with a sprinkle of salt and add to the sauce. Gently warm until the shrimp turn pink, 3 to 5 minutes. Remove from the heat immediately and scoop onto a serving platter. Squeeze lemon juice over the mixture to add some brightness and drizzle with the oil. Garnish with fennel fronds and serve with the bread or rice.

SAYADIYAH · صيادية
Fish in Caramelized Onion Rice

Makes 4 to 6 servings

NO DISH TRANSPORTS me to my Gazan roots quicker than sayadiyah. Translated to "the catch," this dish is traditionally made with fried fish scraps and rice, laced with caramelized onions and warming spices. Sayadiyah is prepared around the Arabian Gulf and the shores of the Mediterranean Sea. In Gaza, the dish cannot be separated from the reality of Israeli occupation. Fishermen, who for generations have made their living selling fish, now risk bullets when they take to the waters. In a culture that once subsisted on fish, seafood has become a luxury.

I think the women in my family instinctively keep this dish alive not just for nostalgia but also to maintain continuity with our heritage. My mom often turns to this dish to impress someone new. It's the dish she chose to make on the day I first brought my husband home to meet the family. He was hooked. To this day, whenever we visit my mother, he asks, "Is she making us sayadiyah?"

I substitute a braise for the fry, inspired by the sweet-savory umami flavors in my favorite Vietnamese clay pot dish called cá kho. Where cá kho uses a burnt sugar and fish sauce, I create an intensely aromatic fish broth, naturally sweetened with caramelized onions. Then I reduce it to braise the fish and cook the rice.

This recipe makes a lot of rice, probably more rice than you need, but it gets more delicious by the day, so save any leftover rice to pair with future meals during the week.

1 tablespoon coriander seeds

1 tablespoon cumin seeds

½ cup neutral oil, such as sunflower or canola

3 sweet or yellow onions, sliced lengthwise into ¼-inch crescents (about 7 cups)

3½ teaspoons kosher salt, plus more as needed

2 garlic cloves, minced

1-inch piece ginger, grated (about 1 tablespoon)

1 cinnamon stick

8 cups Fish Stock (page 37) or store-bought fish stock

2 cups basmati rice

1 tablespoon honey

½ teaspoon ground turmeric

Fish

2 pounds halibut or cod fillets, cut into 4- to 6-ounce pieces

2 tablespoons neutral oil, such as sunflower or canola

Coarsely chopped parsley for garnish

2 lemons, cut into wedges for garnish

Toast and crush the coriander and cumin seeds and mix. Reserve 2 teaspoons for the broth and 2 teaspoons for coating the fish.

In a medium pot, warm ¼ cup of the oil over medium-high heat and add the onions. Turn down the heat to medium and season with ½ teaspoon of the salt, stirring with increasing frequency toward the end, until the onions turn a deep mahogany brown, about 35 minutes.

continued

In the same pot, add the 2 teaspoons of crushed spices, garlic, and ginger. Cook for a minute or two or until the garlic and ginger are aromatic. Add the cinnamon stick and the fish stock. Bring to a boil, then turn down the heat to a simmer and cook for about 45 minutes or until the broth has taken on the rich brown hue of the onions, which are now mostly dissolved, and the broth has reduced to about 4 cups of liquid. Pour the darkened stock through a fine-mesh strainer and reserve any onions for the rice.

In a separate pot, over medium-high heat, add the remaining ¼ cup oil and rice and stir until the rice is coated. Stir in the reserved onions and add 3 cups of the enriched broth plus 1 teaspoon of the salt. Bring to a boil, turn down the temperature to low, cover, and cook for 20 minutes or until all the stock is absorbed. Fluff and adjust the salt to taste.

Keep remaining cup of broth simmering on low heat and stir in honey and turmeric. Adjust salt to taste.

To prepare the fish: While the rice is cooking and broth remains hot, season the fish with the remaining 2 teaspoons salt and add the remaining 2 teaspoons of the reserved crushed spices.

Heat the oil in a large pan or cast-iron skillet over high heat and sear (don't cook all the way) the fish on both sides, until the spices form a light crust, 30 to 45 seconds on each side. It's important to use high heat so that you give color and crust to the spices, although the fish will remain mostly uncooked in the center. If your pan isn't large enough to fit all of the fish at one time, sear the pieces in batches, moving them to a plate while you sear the rest. Return all fish pieces together in a single layer back into the pan and pour in the reserved seasoned broth. Simmer gently on low heat for 3 to 5 minutes or until the fish flakes easily and a cake tester or toothpick goes through the fish with no resistance.

When ready to serve, spoon the rice onto a serving platter, place the fish on top of the rice, and add the remaining broth. Garnish with the parsley and lemon wedges.

TIPS FOR FINDING AND CLEANING THE FRESHEST FISH

Purchasing a whole fish can help ensure you get the freshest fish available. There are a few ways to tell if your fish is fresh. The eyes should be shiny and bright. The gills should be pink with no slime. When you press the flesh of the fish, it should bounce back with a firm texture. You can ask your fishmonger to make sure the fish is cleaned, meaning that the scales, guts, gills, and fins have been removed. Leave the head and the tail attached.

To clean a whole fish yourself: Lay the fish flat against a cutting board and, using a sharp knife, make a shallow slit from the hole on the underside of the belly near the tail toward the head. Gently pull out the guts and rinse the fish clean under cold water. Pat dry and lay the fish down again to remove the scales. Holding the tail, pull the knife blade in the opposite direction of the scales to remove them. Doing this under a gentle stream of cold water can help with the mess. Another trick is to do this inside a large bag to keep the scales from flying around. Once scaled, use kitchen shears to cut away all of the fins, except for the tail. You can also clip out the gills using shears. Give your fish one more rinse and pat dry.

Roasted Whole Chile-Spiced Fish with Citrus-Tahini Sauce

Makes 4 to 6 servings

MY GRANDMOTHER WAS serious about citrus and fish. You can't have one without the other. Every time I pull these gorgeous stuffed fish from the oven, sizzling with spice rub and popping with the scent of citrus, I am transported for a moment back to her kitchen and even further back to her childhood in Yaffa, a Palestinian city known the world over for its oranges. I created this dish based on stories extracted from my mother's foggy memory of her mother's cooking in Gaza. It was my grandmother's own version, or so my mother told me, of a dish more commonly made with lemons.

I never got the chance to confirm this version of the dish. As my grandmother's health deteriorated so, too, did the memories. I honored her by sharing this dish at the James Beard House's culinary celebration, as an homage to my grandmother's journey and the way in which she brought family back together with each uprooting. This dish reminds me that her life carries on, through me.

Don't be intimidated by the long ingredients list. This is simply spice-rubbed fish stuffed with herbs, then baked and served in tahini-orange sauce and topped with more fresh herbs. I love citrus season when the sour variety of Seville and bergamot oranges come on the market.

3 whole branzino or trout (about 1½ pounds each)

Filling
3 garlic cloves, minced
2 serrano chiles, stems, seeds, and veins removed, minced (for more heat, do not remove the seeds)

⅓ cup minced parsley, with stems (about ½ bunch)

⅓ cup minced cilantro, with stems (about ½ bunch)

3 tablespoons lemon juice (about 2 lemons)

1 tablespoon lemon zest

2 tablespoons extra-virgin olive oil

1½ teaspoons kosher salt

Rub
1 tablespoon Aleppo pepper or Chile-Spice Mix (page 27)

1½ teaspoons ground ginger

2 teaspoons ground coriander

2 tablespoons kosher salt

2 tablespoons extra-virgin olive oil

Sauce
2 garlic cloves

¼ cup freshly squeezed orange juice (about 1 orange)

¼ cup tahini, at room temperature

1½ tablespoons lemon juice (about 1 lemon)

Zest of 1 lemon

Garnish
1 fennel bulb, shaved across the grain into thin slices, with ¼ cup fronds reserved for garnish

½ cup picked parsley leaves

½ cup picked cilantro leaves

½ cup mint leaves (about ½ bunch)

2 tablespoons extra-virgin olive oil

1 tablespoon orange zest

Pinch of kosher salt

continued

Lay the fish flat on their sides and, using a sharp knife, make three shallow horizontal slits (from the heads to the tails) about ¼ inch deep into the fillet of each fish. (See Tips for Finding and Cleaning the Freshest Fish on page 196.) Set aside.

To make the filling: In a small bowl, combine all of the ingredients and mix until incorporated.

To make the rub: In a small bowl, combine all of the ingredients and mix until they form a paste.

Preheat the oven to 400°F. Arrange one oven rack in the center and another at the top of the oven. Line a sheet tray with parchment paper.

Coat the outside and inside of each fish with the rub, making sure to get into the slits in the belly of the fish. Divide the filling into 3 portions and stuff the cavity of each fish. Set the fish on the prepared sheet tray and set aside, unrefrigerated, to temper while the oven is heating.

To make the sauce: While the fish is tempering, grate the garlic directly into a small bowl to preserve the juices. Add the orange juice, tahini, lemon juice, and zest and whisk to combine. The sauce should be just thin enough to pour off the tip of a spoon in a steady drizzle without clumping. If needed, thin by whisking in cold water, 1 teaspoon at a time. If you dip a spoon into the sauce and let the excess drip away, you should be able to run your finger down the back of the spoon, leaving a line where your finger touched. Set aside.

Cook the fish on the center oven rack for 20 minutes. Set the oven to broil, move the fish to the top oven rack, and cook on broil until sizzling and golden brown, 2 to 3 minutes. Flip the fish to crisp on the other side and broil for another 2 to 3 minutes.

Just before serving, combine the fennel, parsley, cilantro, and mint in a small bowl. Add the oil, orange zest, and salt and mix to incorporate. Set aside to garnish the fish.

When ready to serve, spread half of the sauce on a serving platter, lay the fish across it, and sprinkle the garnish on top. Serve the remaining sauce alongside.

Part Four

AN ARAB FINDS HER
Vegetable Roots

One blistering cold night, home for winter break during my sophomore year of college, I startled myself awake with the realization that I would not be returning to school for the following semester. Shivering and exhausted, I made my way to the bathroom and took a hard look in the mirror. I was hollow cheeked, with fraying hair and sallow skin. I'd turned into someone I no longer recognized, and I hated the person I saw. I was tired of trying to disguise my decline with makeup, tired of straightening my curls to appear composed. My clothes drooped and sagged off my frame.

I'd dropped to a skeletal 113 pounds, a weight dangerously below what was healthy for me. With no fat cells to shelter me and no emotional reserves for coping, doctors warned that my body had begun drawing from its organs to fuel its basic survival functions, taxing my kidney, liver, and heart. I had hit rock bottom.

Unable to eat, I could feel the urgency of my decline. The only way to escape it, I realized, was to leave Massachusetts, leave school, leave my parents, and find a new course. Despite the illness, the thought of leaving school made me feel as if I were a failure. As a daughter of immigrants, leaving seemed unthinkable.

I don't remember when I first felt as if I were falling into darkness. What I do remember is that I had often thought of college as a ticket away from escalating fights between my parents and my stressed-out teen (and preteen) sisters and toward a welcoming fold of students with backgrounds as varied as mine. At college, I planned to join the Arab Students Association and begin building community. I would find a place where I could finally belong.

However, it did not pan out that way. One Tuesday morning, my second week in college, I turned on the TV to see footage of one plane, and then another, flying into the Twin Towers in New York City. Panic overtook my body. I inhaled until my chest was full, sending up a silent prayer: "Please, God, let the hijackers be anything but Arab."

Not long after that, American flags were being unfurled on every street corner, in front of homes, and on trees—they seemed to be everywhere, as far as the eye could see. Locked in my car for my daily one-and-a-half-hour commute between my family home and school, the twang of "Proud to Be an American" greeted me on every radio station.

This was not the Yankee Doodle patriotism of my childhood. It was jingoism, masking violent aggression that trickled down even to my liberal arts school. Later, during the war to come, two students from a nearby fraternity would accost my dear friend, an Arab Trinidadian, one night on campus, leaving him bloody and unconscious and taunting him as a "Saddam-loving sand n***er." The university declined to call it a hate crime.

A few of the planes' hijackers had been Lebanese, and curious classmates asked, "Aren't your parents from Lebanon?" followed by, "I'm so sorry," when I explained my family's origins. Today, I wonder about that apology. Were they sorry for the backlash against Arabs in America? Sorry for my affiliation with an identity they now saw as negative? Sorry I'd drawn what they thought was a short stick, to be born Arab? I'm still not sure, but whatever their motive, receiving pity made me feel even more exposed. Even if I had still wanted to, blending in was no longer an option.

That same week, I found out my mother had filed for divorce. Over glazed holes at our local Dunkin' Donuts, my father and I had a heated argument about who was at fault for the difficulties between him and my mother. I had internalized, as many children of divorce do, that I could somehow have helped keep the family together and that I had failed. It was years before he and I would talk openly again.

As anti-Arab sentiments, war rhetoric, death, and grief exploded in the world around me, my inner world imploded. I tried to find refuge by visiting family in Lebanon, Syria, and Greece during the summer of my freshman year. Even while there, amid beautiful settings, inhaling cedar in the mountains of Lebanon, or sitting down to a platter of perfectly charred octopus on a Greek Island, I was unable to loosen the anxiety that gripped my body.

I returned to school in the fall to learn that many of my Arab and Iranian classmates were stranded outside the country, banned from reentry. I would soon find out that the FBI had infiltrated our mosque, entrapping a childhood friend, who had been openly critical of the US government, in a surveillance sting operation, sentencing him to seventeen years' imprisonment. One day, government officials intercepted my father on his way to work and revoked his security clearance, ending a thirty-year engineering career on the premise that his familial ties to Syria posed a threat to America.

My stomach continued to feel worse and worse. The nausea would not go away. My body developed a muscle reflex, sending the food I swallowed back up. Even small meals felt like a Vegas buffet line dinner. Eating became a chore, and I relied on saltines and water to keep me going.

For months, doctors struggled to diagnose my mystery illness. As my weight dropped, classmates became suspicious that I was purposely denying myself food. Neither they nor I knew how to deal with my condition. Afraid of being judged, I kept to myself. My mother believed I'd picked up a parasite on my travels. The gastroenterologist called it severe acid reflux, and more tests showed damage to my esophagus. A nurse politely told me that she'd only ever seen these symptoms in people three times my age.

Angry with my body for betraying me, angry with a country uniting against me and my community, and angry with my parents who were waging an acrimonious divorce, I detached. In my detachment, I began overexercising to numb the pain and the loneliness. I remember the perverse pleasure I felt as my feet beat against the pavement and my muscles struggled against fatigue. In hindsight, I'm not sure if that pleasure came from punishing my body or feeling that I could control something in the midst of my helplessness.

When Ramadan rolled around that year, I stopped fasting for the first time since I'd begun a decade before. Even God, I felt, had betrayed me. Gradually, the rage turned inward and dissolved into depression.

I wanted to go away, the farther the better. My mother made a few calls, and soon, I was San Francisco–bound, taking the semester off to recuperate with my aunt Emily and uncle Eyad.

My uncle Eyad is my mother's youngest brother. When I was three and he was sixteen, he arrived at the University of Massachusetts in Amherst to study electrical engineering. As a child who had dodged snipers on his way to school in Lebanon, he already had a vivid sense of which side of justice he was on.

One Thanksgiving Day, Eyad headed to Plymouth to express solidarity with Native Americans participating in a protest called Against the Mayflower, acknowledging that the Mayflower's arrival had been the beginning of a brutal end for the Wampanoag Tribe of Massachusetts. When my school took a field trip to Plymouth Rock to celebrate the pilgrims, my uncle pointed out that these same pilgrims had gifted the local tribes with smallpox-infected blankets in an act of germ warfare, seeding an early awareness of settler colonialism.

My aunt Emily is Jewish. She studied at Hampshire College, just up the road from Amherst, where she met my uncle, cooped up in the lobby of a building they'd taken over with a group protesting the university's involvement in weapons research. Her activism extended to teach-ins she helped to organize in support of the Palestinian intifada and in opposition to Israel's political ideology, Zionism, which denies Palestinians rights and excludes them from their own land. Her commitment to justice for Palestinians grew from the legacy of resistance to persecution on one side of her family and her dedication to challenging the history of Zionism on the other side of her family. Until meeting Emily, I had never met a Jewish person whose worldview transcended their ethnic identity. Through her, I began to consider that our identities could be composed of more than one thing. The stories of my aunt and uncle's first years together involved protests, paddy wagons, and rollicking debates at their local pizza hangout.

Emily grew up off the grid in California's rural northern Humboldt County; my uncle, under Beirut's bombardment. Her grandparents survived Russian pogroms (violent anti-Jewish riots); his fended off Jewish Zionist militia. And yet, the two found themselves more alike than different. Both came alive beneath the majesty of the redwoods and along the craggy bluffs of the Pacific. Both had a commitment to justice and gave their nights to political organizing, and both loved planning, preparing, eating, and sharing fresh, flavorful food. Their unlikely relationship and their shared love of cooking, activism, and nature turned out to be the perfect ingredients for my healing.

I should have been happy as I stepped off the plane in California; instead, wrapped in my heavy wool peacoat under the bright winter sun, I felt nothing. I answered my uncle's greetings sullenly, with a yes or a no. "Yes, I'm okay." "No, there's nothing I want." Sensing that I needed something to remind me of life's pleasures, he headed straight to North Beach, San Francisco's Italian neighborhood, for a taste of his favorite amoretti pignoli cookies, little pine nut–studded almond macaroons from Stella Pastry & Café. Taking in the surrounding streets and shops, I felt as if I had stepped into an alternate universe: a glance was met with a smile or even a "Hello. How are you?" from strangers. Although it was still too painful for me to eat Stella's cookies, I remember that spot every time I walk by it as the sweet start of my rebirth.

On the day after I arrived, my aunt asked if I'd like to go with her to Muir Woods, a legendary redwood grove north of San Francisco.

Confused, I asked her, "For what?"

"Just to walk around," she said.

Walking in the woods eventually helped me become safe with my thoughts. Even though I had grown up next to Thoreau's fabled woods, I had overlooked the "art of walking," but now here, I came to love it. A steep trail connecting the woods to the beach along California's wild craggy bluffs became a place my uncle and I would hike together, back when we were in shape. As we climbed Cardiac Hill, on the trail connecting the woods to the sea below, my uncle, a half-generation above me, treated me as an adult and his equal.

This meant that he challenged me often, and lovingly, with whys. Why did I use the term "we" to discuss US policy? Why did I avoid using "Arab" to describe myself? He worried that I had internalized a sense of inferiority while growing up in America, and he helped me explore my conflicting feelings. He introduced me to revolutionary psychiatrist Frantz Fanon, known for his work explaining the effects of colonization on our psyche. I kept Fanon's book *The Wretched of the Earth* within arm's reach for several years, as I worked to unwind the fear and hostility that I felt toward myself and the world.

Soon, hiking turned into backpacking or, in the words of my aunt and uncle's friends, "frontpacking" trips. A good outing, they joked, meant that we'd consumed more than we burned. My aunt and uncle spent as much time planning and preparing food for these trips as they did on the trails themselves. Although still waif-thin and cautious, it was impossible not to get swept along in their food adventures. As my body started to ease into the pleasures of fresh air and tree canopies, I began to trust it more and ingest the medicine I so deeply needed—za'atar deviled eggs, fresh loaves of fougasse from a local bakery, sheep milk cheese, summer peaches, and homemade maple-sweetened granola bars, packed with toasted almonds and pumpkin seeds. My healing had begun.

My aunt and uncle ran with a posse of South Asian transplants: activists, academics, and engineers like them. Amid the meals and riotous political talk, this was the first time I'd seen people so passionate about food. They were happy devoting a day or more to produce perfectly fragrant biryanis, coconut-laced vegetables, and delicate shrimp curries. In a twist that appealed to my feminist heart, it was the men in their circle, Jayanth, Shabi, and Ashok, who commandeered the kitchen while we women relaxed. On other evenings, my aunt and uncle and I met up with teams of activists in an effort to head off the country's march toward war with Iraq. After the meetings, we'd gather for meals in San Francisco's Mission District, the neighborhood where many years later I would open my second Reem's location. We made the rounds to all of their favorite restaurants, and I finally recovered enough to feast with them long into the night on Pakwan's Pakistani curries and Pancho Villa's legendary burritos. Around the corner from our meeting place, Truly Mediterranean's tiny walk-up counter churned out falafel and shawarma, layering in their trademark grilled eggplant and potato fries, grilled to crispy perfection in thin lavash wraps.

The day after George W. Bush declared war on Iraq, I attended my first high-risk direct action. My aunt and uncle coached me: "Take only your ID. Dress warmly. Jot the number of a lawyer on your arm with a Sharpie." We ran ahead of the police, up an on-ramp to the Bay Bridge, blocking traffic between San Francisco and Oakland. As I took my first blow from a billy club, I remember feeling not only fear and pain but also the rush of being face-to-face with the might of the police. The power of our collective strength coursed through me. I was hooked. That evening, as my aunt boiled ravioli to

toss over our salad, we talked about the energy we'd felt in the streets and, for the first time in a long time, I knew I would be okay.

I began to see a role for myself in the world, and, as my view widened, the cloud of sadness began to lift. I almost forgot what had brought me to San Francisco in the first place. I started to observe my uncle, who spent hours in the kitchen, obsessed with perfecting his technique for focaccia. He tested all the variables. Did the fog outside slow its rise? What might happen if he upped the salt and reduced the water slightly? Looking back, I realize that his science-inspired approach to cooking sparked my curiosity, and that, in and of itself, was new. I was no longer avoiding the kitchen. I wanted to hang out, smelling, tasting, and trying new things.

While my uncle was methodical, my aunt loved to improvise with seasonal vegetables. She was a Californian through and through. Their home was perched on a hillside in Daly City, where their kitchen faced the Pacific. A bookcase filled one wall, crammed with my aunt's collection of cookbooks. Her go-to was Deborah Madison's treatise on fresh simplicity: *Vegetarian Cooking for Everyone*. My aunt was an expert salad maker. She would wilt spinach by tossing it with sizzling seared mushrooms or substitute candied citrus peels and fried cheeses, when she ran out of fresh options. On weekends at a nearby farmers' market, the city's oldest, she would search for the first fava beans of the season, encased in silky fuzz. Where my mom's beans had always endured a rigorous tumble in the pressure cooker to serve stewed, my aunt and I shed the fava's outer pods, blanched the delicate, slightly sweet beans in a quick bath of salty water, and tossed them into salads—in the same way as I do now in Salatet Amah wa Ful Akhdar (page 217), my wheatberry-fava bean salad.

What a departure from the tomato-cucumber salads I had grown up with, no matter the season. The unorthodox combinations were intriguing enough to spark my appetite and light enough to digest without discomfort. Every week, a new vegetable made its way into a marinade to toss over a salad or to chop into a stir-fry, soup, or omelet. My aunt's sense of adventure and openness inspired me. To this day, despite a flicker of doubt I might feel about buying produce I don't recognize, I still get a jolt of excitement when I see a new vegetable.

My aunt gently lured me into her cooking experiments. One day, while perusing bookstores on San Francisco's Haight Street, the one-time center of the city's counterculture movement, my aunt pulled from a shelf a slim volume of recipes that spanned from Turkey to Saudi Arabia and brought it to the register. When it came to Arab cooking, my aunt and I were equally lost, and we often turned to the book's glossy photos of grilled, stewed, and roasted meats and vegetables for inspiration. Our first experiment was making a handsome dish from the Arabian Gulf: meat-stuffed onions in tamarind broth that was neither Californian nor Palestinian.

While the recipe we chose now seems random, it was a gateway to the wonder I began to experience each time I thumbed through a new cookbook. The more I learned about food in California, the closer it tracked the foods of my ancestors. Both Arab and Californian cuisine are all about seasonality. That spring, stalks of purslane, a small purply-green leafed vegetable, appeared in farmers' markets. Purslane is the English word for *baqla*, an Arabic name I'd often heard spoken with nostalgia while growing up. Purslane, it turns out, is a traditional ingredient in Salatet Fattoush (page 211), an Arab-style version of panzanella salad, and I now use it whenever it comes into season.

Poring over Deborah Madison's collection, I gained a greater sense of my own origins, recognizing that I come from a people who live off the land. Gradually, I came to understand why many of the Arabs I know have to brave US Customs to smuggle in za'atar seeds for their home gardens. Through our food, we create home wherever we are. Discovering the parallels between foods in my new California home and the foods of my family's past, as winter rolled into spring and eventually into summer, by experimenting with taste and texture, I tended to more than just my health: the process connected me with my roots.

I discovered that my own roots, although buried under years of distress, were still intact. Food not only reconnected me to my body but also connected me to the land on which I live. I now know that food can heal the traumas we experience collectively and the depression they cause. Being able to grow, eat, and share the foods connected to our land and ancestry repairs the parts of us that wither in the darkness. It makes us whole.

A perennial presence, the height of my depression returns each fall and stays with me throughout winter. With time, I've learned to befriend my depression. It is, after all, what led me to California. I rely on its inward pull, the shutting down I feel, to tell me when something is not right in my life. I now know that I am not alone. In my food and activist worlds, I've communed with others who share this path and who accept, rather than fight, the body's response to the hurt we see in the world. As with the land we live on, it takes work to tend to our being. This work cannot be done alone. When we support one another to be our truest, fullest selves, we make the ground fertile for our liberation.

Chapter Seven

Khodrawat · Veggies

California Fattoush Salad

Makes 4 to 6 servings

IN MY EARLIEST food memories, my mom is frying leftover bread into an addictive crunchy snack, a topping for soups or, more often than not, croutons for fattoush. Although I loved the chips, I fault the tasteless trucked-in tomatoes for my childhood aversion to the salad, an aversion I abandoned the first time I tasted field-fresh tomatoes in California. There's no need to forgo this staple of the Palestinian dinner table when tomatoes fall out of season, since citrus makes a great winter substitute.

The medley of vegetables is what makes fattoush so special. If you're not a purist, you can make it a medley of anything. Mine has all the elements of a delicious balanced salad: mustardy arugula, Little Gem or romaine lettuce for crunch, tomatoes, cucumbers, red onions, spicy radishes, and fresh herbs. This base welcomes seasonal additions. In the summer, I add corn—grilled or raw—pomegranate seeds, pickled cherries, or fresh purslane. In the winter, I swap segments of Cara Cara oranges and other citrus and fried sunchokes in place of tomatoes. In the spring, I look for varieties of radishes, including Easter Egg, Ninja, and French Breakfast to mix things up a little.

Dressing
1 garlic clove, crushed
2 tablespoons lemon juice (about 1 lemon)
1 tablespoon pomegranate molasses
½ teaspoon kosher salt
¼ teaspoon freshly ground black pepper
¼ cup extra-virgin olive oil

Salad
3 cups store-bought pita chips or 2-inch pieces of pita bread, fried
2 cups halved cherry tomatoes
1 Persian cucumber, halved lengthwise and cut into ⅛-inch crescents (about 1 cup)
4 radishes, sliced into thin rounds
¼ red onion, halved stem to root and thinly sliced into crescents (about 1 cup)
2 cups Little Gem lettuce or chopped Romaine
2 cups loosely packed arugula
Leaves from 2 sprigs of parsley
Leaves from 2 sprigs of mint
1 tablespoon sumac

To make the dressing: Combine all of the ingredients in a blender or a bowl and mix or whisk to incorporate. Make sure to whisk well again before using, since the oil will separate.

To assemble the salad: In a medium bowl, toss half the chips with the tomatoes, cucumber, radishes, onion, Little Gem, and ¼ cup of the dressing.

Lay the arugula on a serving platter and cover evenly with the dressed veggies and chips. Tuck the remaining half of the pita chips into the salad to fill in any gaps. Drizzle the remaining dressing over the salad. Sprinkle the parsley and mint over the dish and top with the sumac.

Beet and Kishk Salad

Makes 4 to 6 servings

I LOVE THE way the funk of kishk, fermented yogurt and bulgur, offsets a beet's natural sugars in the same way gorgonzola or blue cheese might but with the added bonus of yogurt's sour notes. It can be served warm or chilled.

Kishk is versatile. It can be made a day in advance for a headier mix or a few hours ahead for a milder, crumbly goat cheese–like flavor. With a dash more salt, it can be made to resemble feta.

While recipe testing for this book, my dear friend and talented chef Michelle Minori was inspired to give this salad even more of an Arab flair and developed a brilliant recipe for the spiced candied walnuts.

3 or 4 beets (about 1 pound)
1 tablespoon extra-virgin olive oil
Kosher salt for seasoning the beets

Candied Walnuts
1 cup walnut halves or pieces
6 tablespoons sugar
1 tablespoon unsalted butter
¼ teaspoon sumac
¼ teaspoon Aleppo pepper or Chile-Spice Mix (page 27)
¼ teaspoon ground coriander
¾ teaspoon kosher salt

Vinaigrette
¼ cup finely diced shallot (about ½ shallot)
½ cup finely chopped cilantro
½ cup finely chopped parsley
½ teaspoon finely diced garlic (about 1 clove)
½ cup champagne vinegar
½ cup extra-virgin olive oil
1 teaspoon kosher salt
½ teaspoon freshly ground black pepper

8 cups arugula (about 6 ounces)
⅔ cup Fermented Yogurt and Bulgur (page 47) or crumbly cheese, such as chevre, feta, or ricotta salata

Preheat the oven to 350°F.

Coat the beets with the oil and season heavily with the salt. Place the beets in a baking pan and fill with 1 inch of water. Cover the pan with aluminum foil and roast the beets for about 1½ hours or until they can easily be pierced with a knife. Set aside to cool. When the beets are cool enough to handle, rub away the skins with gloved hands or peel with a paring knife. Cut into ¼-inch wedges.

To make the candied walnuts: While the beets are roasting, in a small pan, toss the walnuts in the sugar over low heat, until the sugar begins to turn golden brown and coats the nuts. Keep tossing to encourage the nuts to take on an even golden-brown color. Once the sugar begins to harden and stick to the nuts, add the butter and immediately sprinkle on the sumac, Aleppo pepper, coriander, and salt. Mix with a wooden spoon over low heat for 3 to 5 minutes. Remove from the heat and allow to cool before serving on the salad.

To make the vinaigrette: Whisk together all of the ingredients in a bowl. Alternately, pulse them together in a food processor or blender.

To assemble: Spread the arugula on the bottom of a broad, shallow serving bowl, layer on the beet wedges, sprinkle with the fermented yogurt and bulgur and walnuts, and drizzle with the vinaigrette.

DAA'A GHAZAWEEYA · دقة غزاوية
Gazan Tomato Salsa

Makes 4 to 6 servings

SPICY, HERBY, TOMATOEY, and fresh, fresh, fresh—those are the hallmarks of a daa'a Ghazaweeya, the salsa-like salad I used to eat with every breakfast, back when we could still get across the border to see our family in Gaza. I remember scooping it up with bread, along with the many other breakfast mezze dishes on my family's table, while watching the 1994 World Cup on TV, playing, ironically, in cities across the United States. To this day, I associate the dish with Brazil's cherished place in the hearts of Arab soccer lovers.

Daa'a, which in Arabic means "pounded," is traditionally mashed in a mortar and pestle to infuse the flavors quickly and effectively, but you can easily get the same effect by mixing all of the prepared ingredients and letting them sit for a few hours in the fridge.

Since daa'a is eaten with Arab meals mostly as a condiment, the portions are fairly small.

2 heaping cups finely diced tomatoes
(about 4 tomatoes)

2 tablespoons finely chopped fresh dill
(about 5 sprigs)

¼ cup extra-virgin olive oil

2 tablespoons lemon juice (about 1 lemon)

2 heaping teaspoons minced garlic
(about 4 cloves)

2 heaping teaspoons minced serrano chile
(about 1 chile)

2 teaspoons dill seeds

1½ teaspoons kosher salt

Combine all of the ingredients in a small bowl.

Serve immediately or store, covered, in the refrigerator for a few hours and serve when the flavors have melded into a salsa-like consistency.

Gaza after the Peace Accord

In 1994, as the world celebrated the road map for peace that was negotiated under the Oslo Accords, my mom saw a window of opportunity and packed us off to meet our family in Gaza. All around our family's neighborhood, the farm fields, roadways, and buildings bore the marks of bombings and military occupation. I could see people's relief at being able to walk the streets without bumping into the butts of rifles and the Israeli soldiers who carried them, but there was also a lingering sadness because people recognized that their leaders' concessions had left them in a kind of purgatory with little hope for a free Palestine.

Behind the rubble of home fronts smashed in by tanks, families hosted us with lavish meals. I'm not sure how they managed this, given the food shortages at the time. Even water had to be purchased from Israel, since bombardments had taken out Gaza's water treatment plants. At the age of eleven, I felt both comforted and self-conscious at the same time, realizing deeply that I was not just an American kid but a child of refugees. I was a stranger yearning to belong, and yet even a dose of my family's day-to-day reality under military rule was enough to send me back home to the States, never wanting to return there until Gaza was once again free.

TABBOULET SHITTA · تبولة الشتاء
Winter Tabbouli with Orange and Fennel

Serves 4 to 6

MULTICOLORED, HERB-RICH tabbouli is a mainstay of the Arab American plate both at home and in eateries. If you've sampled various tabbouli, you know that they are not all created equal. Two things set this bright, vibrant tabbouli apart from other contenders. First and most importantly, herbs must be handled like royalty.

My earliest memories of tabbouli involve my grandmother—carefully supervising my younger sister Dalyah as they prepared for the day's main afternoon meal. She showed her tricks that I would later learn as a chef: bunch the herbs together under the weight of your knuckles, easing them back in tiny increments, to guide a sharp blade in nice, clean, strokes to produce finely minced shards.

Second is texture: Tabbouli combines a soft fruit with a crunchy vegetable. I love fennel and citrus together, and so, too, I think, does Mother Nature, who gave us these two gifts in the winter months when tomatoes and cucumbers are out of season.

TIP • Thoroughly dry the herbs after washing; discard all of the stems and use only the leaves. As for the olive oil, this is an occasion to splurge on your fruitiest, highest-quality oil.

⅓ cup bulgur #1 (fine size)

2 medium oranges

1 small fennel bulb, small diced, with fronds reserved for garnish

½ cup finely chopped red onions (about ½ onion)

2 cups finely chopped parsley (about 1½ bunches)

1 cup finely chopped mint (about 1 bunch)

¼ cup lemon juice (about 2 lemons)

¼ cup extra-virgin olive oil

1 tablespoon pomegranate molasses

2 garlic cloves, finely minced

1 teaspoon sumac, plus a pinch for garnish

1 teaspoon kosher salt, plus more as needed

½ teaspoon freshly ground black pepper, plus more as needed

4 heads Little Gem lettuce or 1 head romaine

In a small bowl, cover the bulgur with hot water and set aside for 15 minutes or until doubled in size.

Meanwhile, zest the oranges and set aside for garnish.

Peel the oranges or use a sharp knife to cut away the peels. Use a sharp knife to cut the oranges into segments and dice the segments into bite-size pieces. Toss the diced segments into a large bowl and add the fennel, onions, parsley, and mint.

Using a fine-mesh strainer, drain the excess water from the bulgur and then add it to the bowl with the oranges, vegetables, and herbs.

Add in the lemon juice, oil, molasses, garlic, sumac, salt, and pepper and mix thoroughly. Adjust the salt and pepper to taste.

Serve in one large bowl, or individually, with the lettuce leaves wedged beneath the salad's perimeter. Garnish with the orange zest, fennel fronds, and more sumac.

سلطة القمح والفول الأخضر

Wheatberry–Fava Bean Salad

Makes 4 to 6 servings

THIS RECIPE IS inspired by my aunt Emily's love for seasonal salads. When I first went to live with her and my uncle in San Francisco, it was the prime season for fresh favas. She always found a way to incorporate them into dishes.

This salad does beautifully with an array of fresh herbs including parsley and minced chives. Fresh favas are delicious but laborious; choose your own adventure by substituting frozen soybeans or peas, depending on time and availability.

The length of time needed to cook fresh beans and peas increases as the season progresses. Early in the season, they cook beautifully in the heat of the grains, as they're draining in the colander. Later in the season, as the sugars convert to starches, the beans and peas need a quick boil to sweeten up; adjust accordingly.

1½ cups wheat berries or farro

½ cup walnuts

Neutral oil, such as sunflower or canola, for coating the pan

4 ounces Halloumi cheese, cut into ⅛-inch slices

¼ red onion, thinly sliced

3 tablespoons white vinegar

½ teaspoon kosher salt, plus more as needed

2 heaping cups fresh or frozen fava beans, soybeans, or peas

1 tablespoon minced preserved lemon peel (about ¼ of a preserved lemon); optional

2 tablespoons lemon juice (about 1 lemon)

Zest of 1 lemon

3 tablespoons extra-virgin olive oil

Freshly ground black pepper to taste

⅓ cup thinly sliced mint (about 4 sprigs)

Bring a medium pot of salted water to a boil. Once the water boils, add the wheat berries, turn down the heat to a simmer, and cook, uncovered, until tender, about 1 hour. (If you are using farro, cook for about 20 minutes.)

Meanwhile, toast the walnuts at 325°F for about 12 minutes or until lightly golden. Set aside to cool.

Warm a medium skillet over medium-high heat with enough oil to coat the pan. Gently slide the cheese slices into the skillet to minimize spatter. Cook for 1 minute on each side or until the cheese turns dark golden-brown and the surface crisps. Transfer the slices to a plate. Set aside to cool.

In a small bowl, toss the onion with the vinegar and the salt.

If the beans need cooking, add them to the pot with the grains a few minutes before they finish cooking. Otherwise, add them to the grains as they drain. Stir to disperse evenly and gently cook the beans. Drain in a colander and transfer to a medium bowl.

Drain the onion slices and place them in the bowl with the grains. Add the lemon peel, lemon juice and zest, olive oil, pepper, and mint and toss. Adjust the pepper to taste.

To serve, transfer the salad to a serving bowl. Using your hands, crush the walnuts, crumble the fried Halloumi, and sprinkle them on top of the salad. The cheese and onion add salinity; taste before adding more salt.

KHYAR BIL LABAN · خيار باللبن
Yogurt, Mint, and Cucumber Salad

Makes 4 to 6 servings

I LOVE WHIPPING up this salad with crunchy chunks of cucumber, a little garlic zing, and enough yogurt to have some left over as a condiment. It goes with just about everything.

Each element contributes a cooling effect, creating a nice balance with Arab food's warming spices, a relationship that I imagine might trace back to Ayurvedic practices and Indian raita, which is prepared in much the same way. Arabs love eating this salad with rice or meat dishes. After a long day, I sometimes wonder, is there anything better than a hearty bowl of Mujaddarra (page 167), topped with this salad?

Since khyar bi laban is eaten with Arab meals mostly as a condiment, the portions are fairly small. It can also serve as a condiment for sandwich fillings like Kafta (page 179) and Shawarma Mexiciyya (page 177).

4 unpeeled Persian cucumbers

2 or 3 garlic cloves

1 teaspoon kosher salt, plus more as needed

1 cup whole milk yogurt

1 tablespoon dried mint

½ cup chopped mint leaves (about 5 sprigs), plus more for garnish

1 tablespoon lemon juice (about ½ lemon)

1 teaspoon lemon zest (optional)

Cut the cucumbers lengthwise into sixths and then chop them into ¼-inch pieces.

Mince the garlic with the salt on a cutting board, until it releases its liquid or mash in a mortar and pestle until a paste forms.

Combine the cucumbers and garlic with the yogurt, dried mint, mint leaves, and lemon juice and zest in a serving bowl. Adjust the salt to taste. Garnish with additional chopped mint leaves.

Palestinian Braised Dandelion Greens

Makes 4 to 6 servings

HINDBEH, OUR TRADITIONAL dish of dandelion greens, is all about the perfect balance of candy-like caramelized onions, bitter greens, and bright fresh lemon juice. And therein lies the secret of Palestinian cuisine: make a complex dish with just a handful of ingredients. Throw in some heat, and you have a winner!

While I only discovered them in California at a farmers' market, it turns out dandelion greens, edible from root to flower, are a staple Palestinian ingredient, that is often foraged in the wild. When my mother revealed this to me, I almost felt deceived that I had been kept in the dark for that long about the traditions she had grown up with. Picking wild plants became political when the Israeli government began to ban foraging in the occupied territories under the pretext of conservation, separating Palestinians from their culinary traditions and modes of survival. I think about this whenever I see dandelion greens come into season. Cooking them helps connect me to the traditions of my people.

The key to this recipe is sweating the onions over medium-low heat so caramelization brings out their natural sugars. Blanching the braised greens prevents them from overcooking and preserves their gorgeous bright color. You want the greens wilted so you can bite through them easily but not so broken down that they lose their form and nutrition.

This dish works beautifully as a side, but it's meant to be eaten as a mezze, scooped with bread.

½ cup walnuts

4 cups sliced yellow onions (about 2 medium)

½ cup extra-virgin olive oil

8 cups dandelion greens, tough ends removed, chopped into 1-inch pieces (about 12 ounces)

1 teaspoon kosher salt, plus more for the cooking water

2 tablespoons lemon juice (about 1 lemon)

1 tablespoon extra-virgin olive oil

½ teaspoon Aleppo pepper or paprika

½ teaspoon sumac

Toast the walnuts at 300°F until fragrant and slightly darkened, about 12 minutes. Let cool and then coarsely chop. Set aside.

In a large pan, caramelize the onions in the oil over medium-low heat, until they're a deep golden color throughout, 15 to 20 minutes. Stir occasionally since the bottoms will brown.

Meanwhile, bring a pot of salted water to a boil. Blanch the greens in the water until they are wilted, about 2 minutes (less if early in the season when the greens are most tender and more when they toughen later in the season). Scoop the greens out of the water, draining well, and add to the cooked onions.

Stir until the greens have come together with the onions, about 3 minutes. Add the salt.

To serve, place the greens on a platter and top with the lemon juice, oil, and toasted walnuts. Sprinkle the top with the Aleppo pepper and sumac.

TIP • If dandelion greens are unavailable, substitute mustard or collard greens.

HALIYOON · هليون

Charred Asparagus with Soft Egg and Spiced Bread Crumbs

Makes 4 to 6 servings

THIS EGG-ADORNED ASPARAGUS, covered in spiced bread crumbs, is inspired by an Indian asparagus dish my friend chef Preeti Mistry served at my Oakland restaurant as part of a collaboration for La Cocina's annual Week of Women in Food in 2018. During the event, I was in prodromal labor: I'd begun and then stopped contractions weeks before and could no longer see my feet. It was time to have this baby, and I returned again and again for helpings of Preeti's spicy asparagus in an effort to induce labor. Four hours later, it did the trick, and baby Zain was born.

Rich, soft yolks complement this charred herby asparagus. Pita bread crumbs, pan-fried the traditional Italian way in olive oil, add a rich, deep flavor. It's perfect for a spring dinner side or mezze. Feel free to up the heat by swapping in a higher Scoville pepper for the Aleppo, whether you're trying to induce the birth of a reluctant baby or you just like things spicy.

This dish is also a great way to use up bread that's gone dry.

Garlic-Lemon Sauce

1 garlic head

2 tablespoons lemon juice (about 1 lemon)

1 teaspoon kosher salt, plus more as needed

2 tablespoons water

½ cup extra-virgin olive oil

Bread Crumbs

1 round of pita, toasted, or ½ cup bread crumbs

3 tablespoons extra-virgin olive oil, plus more as needed

Zest of 1 lemon

1 teaspoon Aleppo pepper or Chile-Spice Mix (page 27)

2 tablespoons finely chopped parsley (about 5 sprigs)

¼ teaspoon kosher salt

Freshly ground pepper to taste

2 eggs

1 pound asparagus (1 bunch), trimmed and cut on the bias into 3- to 4-inch pieces

1 tablespoon extra-virgin olive oil

1 teaspoon Za'atar (page 24)

½ teaspoon kosher salt

½ teaspoon freshly ground black pepper

To make the sauce: Separate the cloves from the garlic head and then peel. Place the cloves in a small pot, cover with water, bring to a boil, then drain. Repeat, blanching the garlic a second time.

In a blender, puree the garlic with the lemon juice, salt, and water until completely smooth. Drizzle in the oil, until the mixture is thick and emulsified (like a hollandaise sauce). Adjust the salt to taste. Set aside.

To make the bread crumbs: In a food processor or spice grinder, pulse the pita to a fine crumb. (If you already have bread crumbs, skip this step.)

Sauté the bread crumbs in the oil over medium heat until crunchy, about 5 minutes. You should add enough oil to lightly coat the bread crumbs.

In a small bowl, combine the bread crumbs with the lemon zest, Aleppo pepper, parsley, salt, and black pepper. Set aside.

Prepare a bowl of ice water and set aside.

In a small saucepan, bring water to a roaring boil. Use a spoon to gently lower the eggs into the water and cook for 6 minutes. Then plunge the boiled eggs immediately into the prepared ice water. Allow the eggs to cool, then peel and halve the eggs lengthwise. Let the eggs come to room temperature.

In a large bowl, toss the asparagus with the oil, za'atar, salt, and black pepper. In a medium cast-iron skillet or heavy pan, sauté the asparagus over high heat until tender and charred in spots, 3 to 5 minutes.

To serve, scatter the warm asparagus on a platter and drizzle with the sauce. Place the egg halves yolk side up decoratively across the plate and sprinkle with the bread crumbs. Serve immediately as a side or a mezze dish.

LOUBIEH · لوبيه
Green Beans in Tomato Reduction

Makes 4 to 6 servings

GREEN BEANS BATHED in Arab-spiced tomato sauce are a staple of my childhood. The dish is easy to make and works equally well as a mezze or vegetarian main dish.

Beans are the star of the show: tomato sauce, caramelized in its own natural sugars, makes the beans pop. When I moved to California, I discovered all kinds of beans, and I love to mix things up with seasonal varietals. In summer, I look for the reddest, sweetest Roma tomatoes, and in winter, canned whole tomatoes do nicely. A hit of lemon and drizzle of olive oil at the end ties this beautiful dish together.

My mom liked to stew canned tomatoes down, until most of the water had evaporated and a thick, sweet paste clung to the beans. If using canned tomatoes, skip the oven roasting and add them directly to the caramelized onion-garlic mixture. I like my sauce blended and strained, but you can keep it chunky, with all the goods, if you like.

TIP • When in season, substitute yellow wax beans for half the green beans to create a colorful effect.

5 cups ripe Roma tomatoes
(about 12 tomatoes), sliced lengthwise

1 serrano chile, stems, seeds, and veins removed (optional)

½ cup extra-virgin olive oil, plus more for drizzling

2 cups medium-diced yellow onions
(about 2 onions)

Kosher salt as needed

2 tablespoons minced garlic
(about 8 cloves)

1 tablespoon coriander seeds, toasted and ground, or ½ teaspoon ground

2 tablespoons neutral oil, like canola or sunflower

1 pound green beans, trimmed and halved lengthwise at a diagonal (about 4 cups)

½ teaspoon freshly ground black pepper, plus more for garnish

2 tablespoons lemon juice
(about 1 lemon)

Maldon salt (optional) for garnish

Preheat the oven to 450°F.

On a sheet tray, rub the tomatoes and chile with 2 tablespoons of the olive oil. Roast in the oven until the skins are black and blistered, 50 to 55 minutes.

Meanwhile, in a heavy saucepan, sauté the onions in the remaining ⅓ cup of olive oil along with a generous pinch of salt on medium-low heat, until the onions are lightly caramelized, 10 to 15 minutes. Add the garlic and continue to cook for another 5 minutes. As the onions darken, stir to keep from burning.

Once the garlic is fragrant and soft, add the coriander, charred tomatoes and chile, and another pinch of salt. If the tomatoes are dry, add enough water to barely cover (about 1 cup).

Raise the heat to bring the mixture to a simmer, then lower the heat to maintain the simmer. Cook, uncovered, for 25 to 35 minutes or until the tomatoes break down completely. I prefer a smooth sauce without fragments of tomato or pepper skins, so I run mine through a high-powered blender or strain it, but that's optional.

In a medium pan over medium-low heat, warm the neutral oil. When the oil shimmers, add the beans, another pinch of salt, and the pepper and cook for 7 to 10 minutes or until the beans are softened. Then add the tomato sauce and lemon juice and mix thoroughly.

To serve, transfer the beans to a serving plate. Drizzle with olive oil and top with Maldon salt and pepper.

KIBBET AL YAKTEEN · كبة الياقطين
Pumpkin-Bulgur Casserole

Makes about 20 pieces

IN THIS VEGETARIAN dish, spiced pumpkin and bulgur dough encases a filling of brightly flavored chard, red onions, sumac, and pomegranate molasses. *Kibbet* in Arabic simply means "kibbeh of [insert your favorite ingredient here]," and Arabs often switch up meat kibbeh with vegetarian alternatives such as potato, tomato, squash, or, in this case, pumpkin. Perfect for a snack, mezze, or main, kibbeh is delicious any time of the day.

My mother remembers Catholic friends and neighbors forgoing meat every Friday for the forty days of Lent. This dish makes a lovely main when accompanied with Taratoor (page 39) and Salatet Fattoush (page 211).

Most kibbeh recipes call for presoaking the bulgur before mixing it with the binder. I skip this step, since pumpkin puree has enough water content to hydrate the bulgur.

TIP · Your pumpkin or squash may come in various sizes, so you may have to adjust your bulgur ratios accordingly. My rule of thumb is 1.5:1 on the pulp-to-bulgur ratio in weight.

¾ cup dried chickpeas, soaked overnight, or one 15-ounce can chickpeas, drained and rinsed

Pinch of baking soda

1 small sugar pumpkin or acorn, kabocha, or butternut squash (about 2½ pounds)

2 tablespoons extra-virgin olive oil

½ teaspoon kosher salt

Filling

2 tablespoons neutral oil, such as sunflower or canola

2 cups finely chopped red onions (about 1 onion)

1 bunch rainbow chard, stems removed and coarsely chopped (about 4 cups packed leaves)

1 tablespoon sumac

¼ teaspoon Seven-Spice Mix (page 26) or ground allspice

½ teaspoon Aleppo pepper or Chile-Spice Mix (page 27); optional

½ teaspoon kosher salt, plus more to taste

¼ teaspoon freshly ground black pepper, plus more to taste

2 tablespoons pomegranate molasses

2 tablespoons pomegranate seeds (optional)

Dough

1 onion, grated

1 tablespoon lemon juice (about ½ lemon)

2 teaspoons kosher salt

¼ teaspoon freshly ground black pepper

2 teaspoons Seven-Spice Mix (page 26)

¼ teaspoon ground cinnamon

½ teaspoon Aleppo pepper or Chile-Spice Mix (page 27); optional

2 cups bulgur #1 (fine size)

3 tablespoons all-purpose flour

Neutral oil, such as sunflower or canola, for greasing the pan

Extra-virgin olive oil for drizzling

Lemon wedges for serving

If using dried chickpeas, place the chickpeas in a small pot with the baking soda and cover the beans with about 6 inches of clean water. Bring to a boil, skim, discard the residue from the water's surface, and decrease the heat to a simmer over medium heat. Cook, uncovered, until the beans soften, about 30 minutes. Test for doneness by squeezing a bean between your thumb and forefinger.

Preheat the oven to 400°F.

Halve the pumpkin from base to stem; scrape away and discard the seeds. Rub the inside with the olive oil and sprinkle with the salt. Place skin side down on a sheet tray, place in the oven, and roast for about an hour or until the flesh is soft when pierced with a fork and the skin peels away easily. Once the pumpkin is cool, scoop out the flesh.

To make the filling: While the pumpkin is cooking, warm the neutral oil over medium heat in a medium pan and sauté the onions, stirring them often, until they have softened and are slightly caramelized, 4 to 5 minutes. Stir in the chard, sumac, spice mix, Aleppo pepper, salt, and black pepper and cook until the chard has softened. Stir in the chickpeas, molasses, and pomegranate seeds and continue to sauté for another 5 minutes on medium heat until the flavors come together. Adjust the salt and pepper to taste. Let cool completely.

To make the dough: Soak the grated onion in the lemon juice while the filling cools.

In the bowl of a food processor, combine the pumpkin pulp, lemon-soaked onion, salt, pepper, spice mix, cinnamon, and Aleppo pepper and blend until smooth.

Add the bulgur to the mix and pulse until fully incorporated. Transfer to a medium bowl and refrigerate for 20 minutes.

Sprinkle the mix with the flour, 1 tablespoon at a time, and knead until it forms a wet-dough-like consistency. It should hold together when you squeeze it. (If your dough is not holding together, add more flour.)

Divide the dough into 2 equal portions. Generously grease a 10-inch springform pan or a 8-inch square casserole dish with the neutral oil and spread out 1 portion of dough, patting and smoothing it into an even layer about ¼ inch thick.

Spread the filling evenly across the dough.

Wet your palms with cold water and shape small handfuls of the remaining dough into ¼-inch-thick patties and distribute evenly across the filling. Patch any gaps with more dough, using your fingers to spread and smooth, until the entire surface is covered. Chill your fingers in cold water, as needed, to keep them from sticking to the dough. Chill the kibbeh for about 20 minutes.

With a sharp knife, score the kibbeh into parallelograms (four lines across and four lines diagonal), making sure to cut through all of the layers down to the bottom of the pan. Dipping your knife in cold water each time will help keep the knife from sticking. Drizzle with olive oil and brush evenly using a pastry brush.

Bake for 35 minutes or until the edges turn golden. Turn the heat to broil and watch carefully until the crust turns deep golden, about 5 minutes.

Serve warm or at room temperature, along with the lemon wedges to squeeze on top.

Spiced Rice Tower, Layered with Caramelized Veggies

Makes 8 to 10 servings as the main event

MA'LOUBA IS A layered Palestinian rice dish; its name means "upside down" in Arabic. Flipping the pot to reveal its contents is the moment of truth. Will it stand upright, revealing a tower of rice layered with mosaics of vegetables? If not, just remember the first spoonful will send it cascading into the serving tray anyway.

No two ma'loubas are alike. While I was growing up, we had it Gazan-style with eggplant and lamb. In California, Palestinians from the West Bank insist that chicken and carrots make the ultimate ma'louba. While disputes rage on the best proteins and veggies from village to village, family to family even, devotion to this dish unites all Palestinians, both within Palestine and in the diaspora.

I've opted for a version of this dish that places vegetables in the star role. You can use just about any vegetable.

I've offered a fairly traditional method of preparation, but there are several ways to simplify this dish. It may seem like a lot of frying, but it goes quickly, and it's the best way to get the caramelized flavor we're looking for. And if you fry hot enough, your veggies shouldn't feel or taste oily at all.

TIP • If you prefer not to fry, toss the vegetables in neutral cooking oil, such as sunflower or canola, add a sprinkle of salt, and roast at 425°F until sizzling and golden brown, about 30 minutes.

1½ cups basmati rice

1 large globe eggplant, sliced into ¼-inch rounds (about 1 pound)

2 tablespoons kosher salt

2 cups neutral oil, such as sunflower or canola

½ cup cornstarch

1 russet potato with skin, sliced into ¼-inch rounds

2 large carrots, cut on the bias into ¼-inch rounds (about 2 cups)

1 head cauliflower, broken into 1½-inch florets (about 4 cups)

2 red bell peppers or 3 or 4 small mixed bell peppers, sliced into ¼-inch strips

Cooking Liquid

4 cups water or vegetable stock, plus more as needed

2 tablespoons Seven-Spice Mix (page 26)

1 teaspoon ground turmeric

2 teaspoons kosher salt, plus more as needed

1 teaspoon freshly ground black pepper, plus more as needed

Neutral oil, such as sunflower or canola, for greasing

2 Roma tomatoes, sliced into ¼-inch rounds

4 garlic cloves, thinly sliced

¼ cup slivered almonds, toasted

¼ cup chopped parsley

2 cups plain whole-milk yogurt or Yogurt, Mint, and Cucumber Salad (page 218) for serving

Rinse the rice and soak for 30 minutes. Drain well.

Meanwhile, sprinkle the eggplant with 1 tablespoon of the salt and set aside for 5 minutes to release some of its water (and some bitterness along with it).

continued

Line two sheet trays with paper towels.

Pour the oil into a large pan, until the oil is deep enough to immerse a layer of the vegetables, about 2 inches, and warm over medium-high heat. The oil is the right temperature if the vegetables sizzle and swim around immediately and slowly brown while cooking. If using an instant-read thermometer, heat the oil to 350°F.

Place the cornstarch in a shallow bowl. Pat the rounds of eggplant dry with a paper towel, coat both sides in cornstarch, and gently lower them into the oil, filling a single layer. Fry in batches until golden, about a minute on each side. Set the rounds on the prepared sheet trays to drain.

Fry the potato, a single layer at a time, until brown. The potato rounds should be lightly golden and about halfway cooked; set aside to drain.

Fry the carrots, a single layer at a time, until the surface bubbles and browns slightly; set aside to drain.

Fry the cauliflower, a single layer at a time, until the florets are crispy and brown; set aside to drain.

Fry the bell peppers, a single layer at a time, until they curl and brown; set aside to drain. The carrots, cauliflower, and bell peppers need to take on a browned color but stay al dente.

Use the remaining 1 tablespoon salt to season the vegetables after they're fried.

To prepare the cooking liquid: Add the water to a small pot and bring to a simmer. Add the spice mix, turmeric, salt, and black pepper and maintain a simmer.

When ready to assemble, brush the bottom and sides of a large straight-sided pot (a 3-quart Dutch oven works great) with oil. In concentric circles, layer half the eggplant, carrots, potato, tomatoes, bell peppers, and cauliflower, in that order. Sprinkle half of the rice on the first vegetable layer. Repeat the layering with the second round of vegetables and sprinkle the remaining rice on top. Scatter the garlic across the top.

Gently pour in the spiced stock, taking care not to disturb the vegetables and rice; you want to keep the layers intact. Add more water if necessary to ensure the rice is at least ½ inch below the waterline. Over medium heat, return the pot to a simmer, taking care not to reach a vigorous boil, which might displace the layering. Turn down the heat to low, place a heavy plate smaller than the pot as a weight on top to keep the layered rice tower compact, and cover with a tightly fitted lid. Cook for 30 to 45 minutes or until the rice is fully cooked.

Turn off the heat and let the pot rest for 10 to 15 minutes, then remove the lid and plate and cover the pot with a large flat-bottomed platter. Using oven mitts, sandwich the pot with one hand on the platter and the other beneath the bottom and quickly flip the pot upside down so it rests on the platter.

Now comes a little luck and superstition: thump the bottom of the pot with the base of your palm or a wooden spoon and give the rice a few minutes to slide down to the platter. Carefully jimmy the pot directly upward and, if all goes well, the rice and vegetables will retain the shape of the pot to form a layered tower.

Sprinkle with the almonds and parsley. Serve warm with a side of plain yogurt or with the yogurt-cucumber salad.

Rice-Stuffed Grape Leaves

Makes 10 to 12 servings

THIS DISH IS spectacular: herbed and spiced rice is tightly enclosed in grape leaves, packed together in concentric rings, then topped with scalloped potatoes and held together with a thin layer of caramelized tomatoes.

When I think of stuffed grape leaves, I think immediately of my sister Dalyah. She was the master wrapper and my grandmother's right hand when it came to this labor of love. I, on the other hand, always found a way out of rolling the leaves into little rice-stuffed cigars. I lacked the patience. I even tried rolling the leaves using a little gadget my mom ordered off a late-night infomercial, but mine never came out as neatly wrapped as the ones my sister rolled by hand.

My mother made this dish for special occasions, steamed in a pressure cooker. Luckily, she was able to outsource much of the work to my sister.

This recipe works equally well with fresh or preserved grape leaves. For leaves from a jar, soak them in warm water for about 5 minutes and rinse well to remove the brine. My mother was an expert forager and could find fresh leaves as close as our neighbor's backyard in early spring. If using fresh leaves, submerge them in boiling water for 1 to 2 minutes until softened and then plunge them in ice water to prevent further cooking. Drain, stack, and cover the prepared grape leaves for assembly.

Filling

2 cups short- or medium-grain rice (a starchy rice like Arborio or carnaroli works well)

1 cup finely chopped parsley (¾ bunch)

4 cups finely diced yellow onions (about 2 onions)

3 cups finely diced vine-ripened or Roma tomatoes (about 4 tomatoes)

2½ teaspoons kosher salt, plus more as needed

1 tablespoon Aleppo pepper or Chile-Spice Mix (page 27), optional

1 tablespoon Seven-Spice Mix (page 26)

3 tablespoons pomegranate molasses

¼ cup extra-virgin olive oil

2 cups fresh grape leaves or one 500g jar preserved grape leaves

Base

2 tablespoons extra-virgin olive oil

1 large potato, sliced into ¼-inch rounds

1 large beefsteak tomato or 2 Roma tomatoes, cut into ¼-inch slices

1 teaspoon kosher salt

1 teaspoon paprika

1 teaspoon Aleppo pepper (optional)

3 to 3½ cups water or vegetable stock

1 tablespoon Seven-Spice Mix (page 26)

1 tablespoon pomegranate molasses

½ teaspoon kosher salt

1 tablespoon lemon juice (about ½ lemon)

Rinse the rice until the water runs clear, then immerse in water and soak for 30 minutes to an hour. Drain.

To make the filling: In a large bowl, combine the rice, parsley, onions, tomatoes, salt, Aleppo pepper, spice mix, molasses, and oil. Mix with a spoon or your hands. Adjust the salt to taste.

When ready to assemble the prepared grape leaves, grab a leaf that doesn't have too many tears or holes. Place it smooth side down (vein side up) with

continued

the tip pointing away from you. With a paring knife, make two slits around the stem and pull in the leaves to overlap so that you have a straight base.

Place 1 tablespoon of the filling in a thin horizontal line across the base of the leaf. Fold the bottom of the grape leaf over the filling and roll tightly to midway. Fold the right and left sides inward toward the middle, tightly encasing the stuffing; continue rolling upward until you have a tightly rolled cylinder. Repeat until you've used up all of the filling. You may need to strain away some of the liquid as you're filling, since the onions and tomatoes will release some liquid as you work. Reserve the liquid for cooking the grape leaves.

Drizzle the oil into a Dutch oven or a heavy pot and layer in all of the potatoes in concentric circles, followed by all of the tomatoes. Sprinkle the vegetable layer with salt, paprika, and Aleppo pepper.

Snugly pack the stuffed grape leaves in concentric circles on top of the layers of vegetables. Arrange each layer of stuffed grape leaves perpendicular to the one beneath it. Repeat until all are lined up in the pot.

In a separate medium pot, combine the reserved juice from the filling and water to make 3½ cups of liquid. Add the spice mix, molasses, and salt. Bring the mixture to a boil, then pour over the grape leaves and cover the Dutch oven or pot with its lid. Simmer on low heat for 1 to 1½ hours or until cooked through and very little liquid remains.

Remove the pot from the heat, then uncover and drizzle the grape leaves with the lemon juice.

To serve, flip the pot onto a serving platter and let it sit upside down for a minute or two while the grape leaves and vegetables ease out. Gently lift the pot to reveal a tower of stuffed grape leaves, topped with broth-infused tomatoes and potatoes.

Leftovers can be stored in an airtight container in the refrigerator for up to 1 week. Rewarm gently in a covered pot over low heat with a little water to prevent burning.

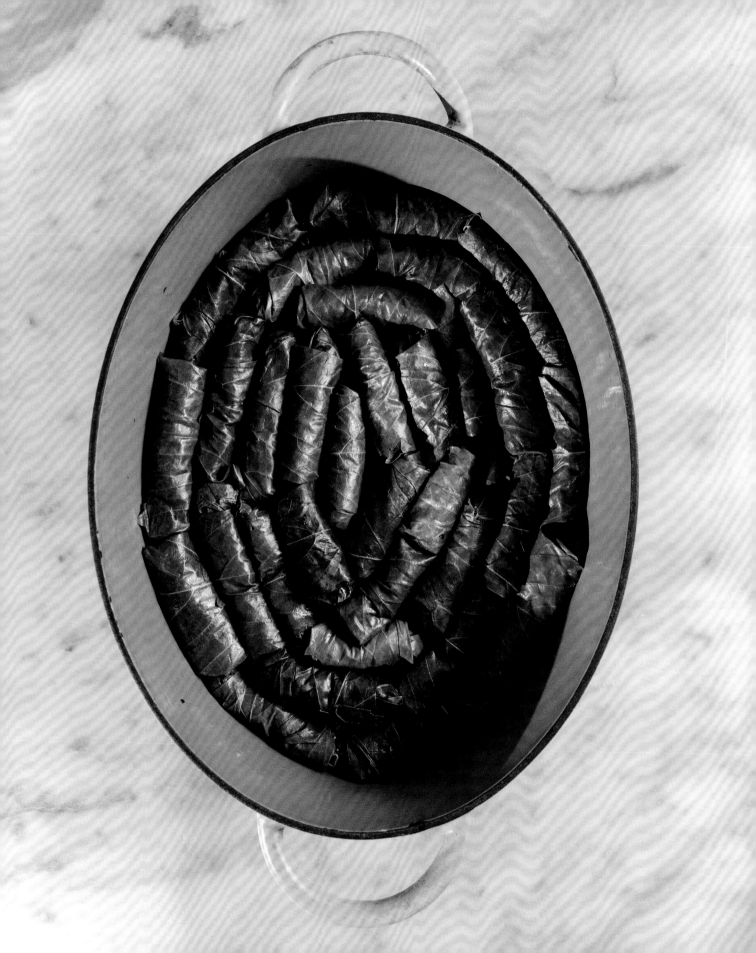

Chapter Eight

Mouneh · Pickles and Preserves

LIFIT · لفت

Magenta Pickled Turnip Spears

Makes 1 quart

IF EVER THERE was an iconic pickle of Levantine cuisine, it would be turnip. Delicious and a brilliant magenta, *lifit*, the Arabic word for "turnip," formed a kindling-shaped pyramid atop just about every mezze spread I ate growing up.

At Reem's, when I think of colors that scream California, I think of the hot pink and appealing green combo of pickled turnips and olives, served side by side as a mezze or in a Falafel Mahshi (page 153). Our restaurant menu calls them "pickled purple things," a feast for the eyes and the belly.

Lifit also brings back memories of Mid East–brand jars, hiding in the back of our refrigerator. My sister used to stash them out of sight to manage her pickle addiction. It's easy and inexpensive to keep high-quality fresh pickles on hand. These pickles are at their best the first month or two after pickling, but they're not likely to last that long, once you get the taste for their craveable, punchy pickle flavor. They're equally good for snacking and for serving alongside just about every mezze spread, savory bread, and meat or veggie main in this book.

NOTE • **You will need one 1-quart wide mouthed Mason jar with lid, sterilized.**

1 pound turnips
1 red beet (about 5 ounces)
1 cup apple cider vinegar
1 cup water
1 tablespoon kosher salt
2 heaping teaspoons black peppercorns
1 serrano chile, stem removed
5 garlic cloves, halved lengthwise

Peel the turnips, cut off the roots and stems, halve lengthwise, and with the flat sides down, slice each half lengthwise into ½-inch pieces. Slice the pieces into ½-inch-wide sticks. Do the same for the beet, except cut it half as thick. (Wear gloves, if you have them, to keep your hands from turning red.)

In a medium pot, combine the vinegar, water, salt, and peppercorns and warm over low heat until the salt dissolves, then remove from the heat.

Meanwhile, pierce the chile with the tip of a knife, making small incisions all over.

Line the jar with layers of turnips and beets and wedge in the chile and garlic pieces. Pour in the pickling brine, leaving a ½-inch gap at the top. If the veggies begin to float, press a nonreactive weight or a crumpled sheet of parchment paper or wax paper over the vegetables to keep them submerged.

Close the jar tightly and set aside at room temperature, out of direct sunlight, for 3 days. Gently tilt the jar from side to side each day to distribute the beet's trademark magenta hue into the turnips.

The turnip spears can be stored in the refrigerator for up to 3 months.

MAKDOUS · مقدوس
Stuffed and Cured Mini-Eggplants

Makes 2 quarts

TINY, SAVORY, SOUR, and spicy stuffed eggplants are a prized delicacy in Lebanon and Syria. When they come into season, they sell out faster than we can stuff them at my restaurant. It takes about two weeks to develop their je ne sais quoi magical tang. Makdous are traditionally eaten as part of a mezze spread with bread for breakfast or as a late-night snack.

My grandmother, like home cooks across the Arab world, knew from experience to expel the eggplant's water. Handling the peppers and garlic gently prevents them from leaching water. These tricks help differentiate flavorful, tender makdous from their soggy counterparts that risk spoilage.

NOTE • You will need one 2-quart wide mouthed Mason jar or two 1-quart wide mouthed Mason jars with lid(s), sterilized.

20 baby eggplants (the size of tennis balls), such as the Indian varietal (about 2 pounds)
2 tablespoons kosher salt

Stuffing
1 heaping cup walnuts
3 large red bell peppers, cut into large chunks (about 1 pound)
4 red Fresno chiles (about 4 ounces) or 2 green jalapeño chiles, stems, seeds, and veins removed
12 garlic cloves
2 teaspoons kosher salt
¼ teaspoon Aleppo pepper or Chile-Spice Mix (page 27); optional

4 cups extra-virgin olive oil, plus more for drizzling
Chopped parsley for serving
Toasted walnuts for serving

Fill a large pot three-quarters full with water and bring to a boil. Add the eggplants, then turn down the heat to medium and simmer for 30 to 40 minutes until the eggplants are just cooked through. The eggplants should preserve their vibrant color and be soft to the touch but not collapsing.

Remove the eggplants with a slotted spoon, dunk them in a pot of ice water to stop the cooking process, and then drain in a colander.

Cut or twist off each eggplant stem as close as possible to the top. At the midway point between the stem and the bottom, slit the side of the eggplant most of the way through, leaving the top, bottom, and opposite side intact. Squeeze each eggplant from top to bottom between your thumb and forefinger to open the slit, then rub about ¼ teaspoon of the salt (a generous pinch) into each cavity.

Lay the eggplants slit side down in a colander and weight them with a heavy object, such as a pot, to press out the moisture. Leave them to drain for 4 to 12 hours, or overnight, in order to cure the flesh. The less water they retain, the better the eggplant will keep.

To make the stuffing: Finely chop or pulse the walnuts in a food processor or blender and transfer to a large bowl.

Finely chop the bell peppers, chiles, and garlic or pulse them briefly in a food processor, taking care not to mash them, then add them to the walnuts along with the salt and Aleppo pepper.

continued

Once the eggplant has drained, use your fingers to stuff each cavity with the filling (about 2 tablespoons per eggplant), until just full but not overflowing.

Add the oil to the jar. Pack the eggplants against each other in the jar as tightly as possible, slit sides against the sides of the jar, immersing each layer in the oil as you go, ensuring every cranny is saturated.

When the eggplants are packed and completely submerged in oil, seal the jar tightly. Set the jar away from direct sunlight for 7 to 10 days. Serve as a mezze course, drizzled with fresh oil and sprinkled with chopped parsley and toasted walnuts.

Unopened, the eggplants can be stored at room temperature for up to 1 year. After opening, they will keep in the refrigerator for 6 months or longer. To avoid spoilage, add more oil and swirl it around the jar every time you take out makdous to eat.

ARNABEET M'KHALAL · قرنبيط مخلل
Sun-Colored Pickled Cauliflower

Makes 2 quarts

ARAB CUISINE IS as much a feast for the eyes as it is for the belly. I use turmeric to turn these cauliflower florets yellow, adding to the mosaic of colors in our mixed pickle spreads. Sun-colored cauliflower makes an excellent pairing in both color and flavor with the magenta Lifit (page 234).

NOTE • **You will need one ½-gallon Mason jar or two 1-quart wide mouthed Mason jars with lid(s), sterilized.**

1 cauliflower head (about 20 ounces)
2 cups white champagne vinegar
2 cups water
2 tablespoons sugar
2 tablespoons plus 1 teaspoon kosher salt
One 2-inch piece fresh turmeric, or 1 teaspoon ground turmeric

Cut away the stem and leaves of the cauliflower and reserve for another use. Carve away the stem's core, angling the knife toward the center of the cauliflower (the core and other scraps are great roasted or turned into soup). Break apart the florets and continue cutting the cauliflower until it's reduced to bite-size pieces, about ½ inch in size.

In a medium pot, combine the vinegar, water, sugar, salt, and turmeric over medium heat and warm just until the salt and sugar dissolve.

Fill the jar with the florets and pour in the pickling brine, leaving a ½-inch gap at the top. If the florets start to float, press a nonreactive weight or a crumpled sheet of parchment paper or wax paper over the florets to keep them submerged, then cover and refrigerate. The florets will be ready to use within 3 days.

The pickled florets can be stored in the refrigerator for up to 6 months.

BOMELU BIL SUKAR · بوميلوبالسكر
Sour Candied Pomelo Rinds

Makes 2 cups

PEOPLE WHO KNOW me best know that the quickest way to my heart involves sour candies. The minute I see a bag of sour gummies slipped onto my desk I know it's a bribe, and I gladly accept it.

Growing up, candy was hard to come by—my mom was a stickler when it came to sugar. I managed to feed my cravings by smuggling goods from my sister's job at the local penny candy store and cutting side deals with my dad for chocolates to feed both of our addictions.

This recipe is my sour-candy adaptation of a traditional recipe I used to enjoy at my Syrian piano teacher's house. She was known in the Boston music scene for playing her Arab classical music both on the piano and the oud, the traditional sitarlike instrument; she often played to sold-out shows. I always wanted to learn her greatest hits, but she insisted we stick to Western classical music to build my foundation. Despite the missed opportunity, I felt lucky to be welcomed into a home rich with Syrian traditions—the food especially—at my weekly piano lessons.

The secret sour ingredient in this candy is sumac, which perfectly pairs with the pomelo's blossomy fragrance, making a naturally sweet and sour candy. I add citric acid or dried lime for extra punch, but sumac works fine on its own if you don't have the other ingredients. Pomelos, which look like giant grapefruits, are often available in Asian shops. They're among the many fruits Arabs share in common with the rest of the Asian world. Grapefruits make a fine substitute if pomelos are unavailable.

This recipe uses the spongy pith. The pith absorbs the syrup, giving it a soft and luscious texture, almost like a gummy. Because the outer rind is bitter, especially in pomelos, the trick to this recipe is to remove the zest and leach out as much bitterness as possible.

Candying the pith and zest make a great way to use the extra parts of the pomelo fruit, saving the sweet fruit inside for snacking or to toss over salad. (See Candying Zest on page 242.)

1 pomelo or 2 grapefruits
2½ cups sugar
1 cup water
2 tablespoons lemon juice
(about 1 lemon)
1½ teaspoons dried lime
2 tablespoons sumac
½ teaspoon citric acid (optional)

Peel the zest from the pomelo rind using a vegetable peeler. Cut away the stem end of the pith. Use a paring knife to quarter the pith, scoring it down to the fruit. Peel away the pith and cut the pith lengthwise into strips of matching width and thickness.

In a medium pot, immerse the strips in just enough water to cover and use a lid smaller than the pot to hold the pith under the water. Bring to a boil for 5 minutes, then drain in a colander. Cover again with cold water. Repeat this step twice more, reducing the length of each boil to about 1 minute.

In a wide saucepan large enough to accommodate a single layer of strips, bring the pith, 2 cups of the sugar, and the water to a boil over medium heat. Add the lemon juice, then turn down the

continued

heat to a simmer and cook until the strips appear translucent, with an almost glass-like appearance, and have absorbed most of the syrup, about 20 minutes.

Set a wire rack over a large pan, remove the pith with a slotted spoon or tongs, and spread the slices on the rack to cool.

Grind the dried lime to a fine powder in a spice grinder or mortar and pestle. Then combine the ground lime, sumac, and citric acid with the remaining ½ cup sugar in a medium bowl.

Toss batches of the candied pith in the sweet-and-sour mixture. Set the pith slices back on the rack and leave for a few hours or overnight to firm up.

If you prefer the rinds a bit chewier, you can leave them in a 200°F oven for about 3 hours, then allow them to cool and harden slightly.

The rinds can be stored in an airtight container at room temperature for up to 2 weeks and in the refrigerator up to 1 month.

CANDYING ZEST

To candy the zest, begin by blanching the zest to remove some of its bitterness. Cover the zest in cold water and bring to a boil. Strain the water and cover again with cold water. You will need to blanch the zest a total of three times. After the final blanch, cover the zest with ½ cup sugar and 1 cup cold water. Bring to a simmer and slowly cook the zest in the syrup, until the zest is tender and sweet, about 20 minutes. Store the zest in an airtight container in the refrigerator for up to 3 months.

Sun-Dried Apricot Preserves

Makes 2 quarts

IN ARABIC, WE say "bukra fil mish mish," meaning "when the apricots are in season" to denote when something has little to no chance of happening. A precious staple of the Arab table, we keep an eye out for the few weeks—a very small window of time—when apricots are at their peak ripeness, so we can preserve them for the year ahead.

During peak season in Lebanon, my grandmother used to buy heaping buckets of apricots from her favorite growers, who strapped together their own makeshift farmers' markets and rolled their carts through the streets—the original farm-to-table entrepreneurs.

The pectin in apricots naturally thickens them into jam when they are heated with sugar. Traditionally, we spread the jam onto trays covered in a thin protective cloth and lay the trays in the sun, where fermentation and evaporation add a layer of complexity and intensify the flavor. If you do not have time for this process, you can skip straight to packing the jam into sterilized jars.

This jam can be laid out very thinly on parchment paper and baked at a low temperature. See the methodology for Dibs Safarjal (page 245), quince paste, to create amardeen, an apricot fruit leather that we dissolve into a nourishing Ramadan drink after a day of fasting to remind ourselves of the richness of life and to jump-start our blood sugar with electrolytes.

This sweet treat serves as an excellent addition to a brunch mezze spread to scoop onto bread with labneh, as a treat all on its own, or spooned up with almonds or hazelnuts.

NOTE • You will need one 2-quart or two 1-quart wide mouthed Mason jars with lid(s), sterilized.

4 pounds apricots, quartered and pitted
2½ cups sugar
3 tablespoons lemon juice (about 1½ lemons), plus more as needed

In a large pot, toss the apricots, sugar, and lemon juice together and allow to stand for 1 hour. The apricots should begin to release their juices.

Bring the pot to a boil over medium heat, then turn down the heat and simmer for 30 to 45 minutes or until the apricots are soft and falling apart. Stir frequently to prevent the fruit sugars from burning on the bottom. The lemon's acidity brings out the contrasting tart flavor that makes apricots so irresistible. Taste and add more lemon if your apricots are on the sweeter side.

Spread the mixture in a large 9 by 13-inch glass baking dish. Cover with a cheesecloth or dish towel and set the dish in the sun for 2 or 3 days, bringing the pan inside at night to prevent humidity from causing mold.

Taste daily. Once the preserve is to your liking, spoon it into the jar or jars and close tightly. The preserve can be stored in the refrigerator for up to 3 months.

Quince Paste

Makes sixteen ½-inch slabs

MY MOTHER WOULD often point out this bumpy fruit with its vibrant yellow color, when we passed trees on our trips to Lebanon and Palestine, where they grow abundantly. A distant relative of the pear and apple, quince is super fragrant, like guava, but confusingly, too astringent to eat raw. When activated by heat, the white flesh turns deep red and becomes delicately sweet. The magic is in the cooking. High in pectin content, quince makes a beautiful jam to be eaten with butter and bread on a morning mezze spread.

This is the Arab version of a popular Spanish delicacy called membrillo with a magical ingredient called mastic, otherwise known as Arabic gum, which gives it a subtle note of pine. It makes a good accompaniment to dry, aged cheese.

¼ cup lemon juice (about 2 lemons), plus more to prevent browning

8 quinces (about 2½ pounds)

2½ cups sugar

8 cardamom pods

2 mastic pods, smashed or ground to a powder (optional)

Zest of 2 lemons

Fill a medium bowl with cold water to hold the quinces after they are peeled and cut and add a generous squeeze of lemon.

Peel, core, and cut the quinces into 1-inch pieces and place the pieces in the prepared bowl to prevent the fruit from turning brown quickly.

Remove the quinces from the bowl and drain well before tossing with the sugar.

In a separate medium bowl, mix the quinces and sugar and let sit for a couple of hours or overnight, until the liquid releases. This will macerate the fruit and create a cooking liquid for the hard flesh.

Crack the cardamom pods, pressing them on a hard surface with the flat side of a knife.

In a medium pot, combine the quince-sugar mixture, cardamom pods, and mastic and cook over medium heat until mixture comes to a boil. Turn down the heat and simmer for 1 to 1½ hours, until the mixture has developed a deep brick color and becomes very soft. If you have an instant-read thermometer, the mixture should read 220°F. Remove from the heat and stir in the lemon juice and zest.

Preheat the oven to 200°F. Line an 8 by 8-inch baking dish with parchment paper.

Puree the quince mixture in a food processor or blender until smooth. There may be some little bits of black cardamom seeds, so if you'd like, you can press the paste through a fine-mesh sieve to remove them, but I leave mine inside.

Pour the mixture into the prepared baking dish and smooth the top with a spatula or the back of a spoon. Set the pan in the oven to dehydrate for 3 hours or until the jam firms into a paste. Remove the pan from the oven and cool at room temperature.

Once the quince cools completely, cover the dish with plastic wrap and refrigerate overnight. When ready to use, invert the paste onto a cutting board, remove the parchment, and slice into ½-inch slabs.

The paste can be stored in an airtight container in the refrigerator for up to 3 months.

AN ARAB FINDS HER
(Food) Way

Tuesdays at Reem's had been uneventful during the summer, our slow season, awaiting the return of students and professionals from vacation. But on one bittersweet Tuesday in mid-September, we found ourselves bumping up our usual hustle, stretching hundreds of sourdough rounds and braising waist-high vats of sumac-infused chicken in anticipation of a busy service.

We were preparing a farewell for our beloved leader, Rasmea Odeh, whose beaming smile greeted me as I arrived at work each morning from a lime green and hot pink technicolor mural on the biggest wall of my Oakland restaurant. In the year leading up to the opening of my restaurant, Rasmea had been singled out by US Immigration and Customs Enforcement (ICE) for deportation, based on immigration papers she had filed twenty years earlier. Rasmea's example as a soft-spoken, but relentless, community organizer had helped young Palestinian activists like me face our fear of speaking out. We could not let her go without celebrating her accomplishments, even as she languished in a Detroit women's prison.

That morning, I could no longer see my feet over my pregnant belly, even needing help tying my shoes. I reached back to cinch my apron, suiting up for battle, because for some months, I'd been the target of a campaign intended to drive me out of business for my Palestinian activism. Online trolls from as far away as Tel Aviv, activated by the far-right Breitbart News Network, were calling me a terrorist and filling Yelp with one-star reviews and hate speech.

The aggression had grown physical, coming right to our doorstep. Just the week before, I had engaged a handful of ragtag disruptors who had proven themselves willing to cross the line into violent confrontation, shoving, hitting, and, in one instance, using a motorized chair to ram a friend who'd put her body on the line to protect my staff and me. I knew they'd be coming.

I pulled hot trays of golden baklava from the oven, and, as the syrup hit the hot buttery phyllo, the scents of rose and orange blossom eased my nerves. I released a long breath, realizing my friends' imminent arrival would protect us.

My staff and I had worked around the clock, blending gallons of chickpeas into hummus and roasting and peeling crates of red bell peppers for our sweet-and-tart muhammara spread. With fragrant olive oil from California's hot Central Valley at the ready, we set up our stations to plate our mezze for the hundreds of guests we were expecting.

My comrade Lara was on her way, along with Arab youth from a program she'd built. She had also put out a call to many of the Black- and Brown-led organizations we had worked with to protest the Muslim ban at San Francisco International Airport and to end programs like Urban Shield, which equipped police with military gear and training. These were the same police forces that had killed Oscar Grant, the young Black man who'd

been celebrating New Year's Eve almost a decade before on the transit platform right above Reem's. And not coincidentally, these were the same forces who had cross-trained and shared intelligence and equipment with an Israeli military that had imprisoned and tortured Rasmea in her youth.

The first to arrive that day were Ellen and Sara, progressive Jewish community leaders who put olives on their Seder plates at Passover to invoke a free Palestine. They had spent months challenging fake reviews on Reem's Yelp page, fielding hate messages and writing op-eds about what Reem's meant to them—a safe space for people to come as they are, celebrate Palestinian culture, and draw strength from one another. I loaded freshly ground beans into the espresso machine to welcome them in the most Arab way possible, with hot cups of coffee to fortify us for the day ahead.

At opening time, a stream of customers formed at the register. It was only 11:00 a.m. I could feel the heat of our hearth on my back, as I started to fire orders for mana'eesh and salatet fattoush. In minutes, our ticket rail was full, and the room was starting to buzz.

By noon, Lara arrived along with fifteen rowdy youths, whose roots traced to Yemen, Egypt, and Palestine; they were sporting embroidered keffiyeh scarves over the latest denim and Nike kicks. My friend Eman, DJ Emancipation, who, years before, had welcomed me to Arab feminist protest lines, set up her turntables and cranked up Arab hip-hop tunes. My team had reserved tables for the youth, but they weren't about to sit still. They were riled up by a flyer they'd seen on the way in that called me "the butcher, the baker."

They didn't know that Lara, Ellen, Sara, and I had spent weeks learning de-escalation tactics from Black and Latinx experts in a technique called community safety, developed to keep people safe from the police and vigilantes. We had learned that when someone shouts in your face, you take a breath and plant your feet and call on the strength of your ancestors to face the violence with calm. You never meet aggression with the same. You use good old-fashioned jujitsu to redirect violence away from yourself and others at risk. Turha, our teacher, had assigned us the best possible security detail from his team for that day—Che, a six-foot Black vegan, who was happy to be paid in mana'eesh.

I tried to assure the youth that we could handle whatever might be coming our way that day. Still, no amount of training could hide a shudder of nerves that tightened my jaw.

Soon, the place was packed, and people were milling about in search of seats. My soccer crew, Left Wing Fútbol Club, whose politics were cleverly embedded right in the name, took up a whole rowdy section, excited about the feast and primed by years of activism and anti-war protests to offer us protection.

My husband, J (his name is a shortened version of his family nickname J. R.), arrived just in the nick of time. He and I had met on the soccer pitch. Sunday with our soccer team was our church day. Our love story had unfolded over potlucks with elaborate spreads, representing the cultures of our bunch, from Indonesian jackfruit stew to Mexican grilled corn, smothered in crema and Cotija cheese. J's and my love of food, hospitality, and making "good trouble" rooted us in our Arab and Filipino cultures. Tapping into those roots (and crowd-control skills he had honed from years spent in the kindergarten classroom), he let people know where to go and brought them snacks and drinks to ease the wait. By the time he'd moved through the restaurant, everybody was laughing and having so much fun that they had forgotten about the thirty-minute wait time for a man'oushe.

I made my way to the courtyard to take stock. I was raw from months of dread and fear, compulsively scrolling through social media to see what threats lay in store, shocked anew at lines like "A good Arab is a dead Arab." In the distance, I heard a familiar commotion, the sounds of disruptive shouting.

As if on cue, Eman upped the volume, and the speakers thumped out heavy bass notes. Arab youth spontaneously linked hands to start a dabke line, our traditional dance for special occasions but also a dance Palestinians had taken up during the intifada to assert our existence in the face of violent aggression from Israeli occupying forces. Dancing, much like food, feeds our spirit.

I smiled as the crowd clapped and cheered. People drawn from their commute stopped to watch. Even people I didn't recognize got in on the fun, finding a spot to slip into the line as it wound through the courtyard, gradually picking up the footwork. Our resistance became our joy. And those who wished us harm no longer mattered. It was hard to tell they were even there.

I threaded my way through the dining room to check on my cooks, who were busier than they had ever been, and I realized, at the sight of mezze platters and wraps growing cold, that our servers were busy bussing tables. Catching my worried gaze, several white lefties wearing "Jewish Voice for Peace" T-shirts, their gray hair pulled back in ponytails, approached the counter and offered to run our dishes to tables. Without hesitation, I replied, "Table 10, please."

I stepped back to take it all in and soon found myself backed all the way to the farthest nook of the kitchen. Tucked away among sacks of potatoes, relief and exhaustion coursing through me, I had a good, long cry.

People from many parts of my life—from my poker league to grassroots leaders on whose doors I had once knocked—came together that day to protect me like a force field. They weren't there just for me or for our sourdough man'oushe but rather to defend a place that had provided them with a sense of warmth and belonging, a feeling that extended even to people I didn't know. Customers were arriving not only by train from across the bay but even straight from the airport, luggage in tow, to experience Reem's. My community had grown larger than I had ever dreamed.

I gathered myself together and made my way to the mural that had ignited a new level of consciousness about the Palestinian struggle, and I looked up at Rasmea's reassuring smile. Just then, an elder tapped me on the shoulder, and, speaking in Arabic, he said, "Thanks for putting her on your wall. I wouldn't have had the guts." I nodded, reflecting on what his generation had endured and the path they had paved. I recognized that I was widening that path for the child kicking in my belly.

I turned around to look at all of the faces in the room, some familiar and some new, taking a moment to enjoy this refuge. My stand for justice had allowed me to create a space where each one of us could feel safe and whole, including myself. Here, where the man'oushe meets the movement, I had finally found my purpose.

Chapter Nine

Halaweyat Al Munasabat · Special Occasion Sweets

ASHTA · قشطة
Clotted Cream

Makes 1½ to 2 cups

ASHTA IS THE King Midas of Arab desserts: everything it touches turns to gold. Whether layered onto Layali Lubnan (page 259), a farina custard, or served on its own with a touch of honey and sprinkled with pistachio bits, it delivers a rich, mouthy goodness.

In Lebanon, entire factories are lined with giant shallow stainless-steel pans boiling fresh local milk over low heat to harvest the sticky film of protein that forms on top. In everyday life, however, it is not practical to wait for skin to develop and slowly skim it off layer by layer. I've sped up that process by using lemon and vinegar to force the fat to separate from the whey through curdling.

This recipe comes together in two steps: (1) collecting and reserving clots of cream formed by curdling a portion of the cream or milk with lemon; and (2) thickening the remaining cream with starch. The two parts are then whisked back together.

TIP • This recipe works using all milk if you don't have cream on hand, but I like the extra richness of the cream. Avoid using reduced-fat milk, since it will not curdle properly.

4 cups whole milk

2 tablespoons sugar

1½ teaspoons rose water

1½ teaspoons orange blossom water

1 tablespoon lemon juice (about ½ lemon), plus more as needed

1 tablespoon distilled white vinegar

2 cups heavy cream

2 tablespoons cornstarch

Line a colander or sieve with cheesecloth and set over a bowl.

In a medium saucepan over medium heat, heat the milk until just before a boil. Stir the bottom of the pot occasionally to make sure the milk isn't scalding. Just before the milk boils, stir in 1 tablespoon of the sugar, the rose and orange blossom waters, lemon juice, and vinegar. The milk should immediately begin forming clots. Turn down the heat to the lowest setting.

Using a slotted spoon, collect the clots of milk from the surface and place them into the prepared colander. Continue collecting the clots, until the milk that remains looks thin and pale and takes on a yellowish hue. If needed, add a few more teaspoons of lemon juice to induce further clotting.

Pour out and discard the whey (you could save this for another purpose, such as using it in a smoothie, but that's up to you). Remove the pot from the heat and add the cream, cornstarch, and the remaining 1 tablespoon sugar, then return the pot to the stove and bring to a boil on medium heat, whisking until the mixture thickens, about 5 minutes. Remove the pot from the heat. Allow to cool slightly, then add the strained clotted cream and whisk well, until it forms a thickened spread. If it's still clumpy, pass the clotted cream through a fine-mesh sieve. Put into a bowl and cover directly with plastic wrap to prevent a skin from forming. Chill for at least 1 hour before using.

If not using right away, the clotted cream can be stored in an airtight container in the refrigerator for up to 1 week.

MEGHLI · مغلي
Spiced Rice Flour Pudding

Makes 6 servings

IN THE ARAB world, each special occasion merits its own distinct sweet. Meghli, a smooth, cool, spice-steeped rice flour pudding, is made to celebrate the birth of a child in many Arab homes. It is believed that caraway helps increase milk for new moms, but that doesn't stop everyone else from savoring this mildly sweet, refreshing dessert. Elegant when served in chilled parfait glasses, it's also a festive dessert for Christmas, celebrating one of the world's most famous births.

Growing up, we must have had many births around us! It seemed my mother was always whisking and chilling meghli into delicate glasses that the Lebanese called demis, short for demitasse or half cups, and sprinkling them with blanched almonds and coconut.

I learned to love meghli served cold, as it is done in Lebanon. In Syria, it is called karawyah and served as a delicious warm winter pudding. A wheat version called snayniyeh is often made to celebrate a child's first tooth. This gluten-free, vegan version is sure to meet everyone's needs. If you don't have nut milk or oat milk, you can make it the traditional way with water.

½ cup rice flour

¾ cup sugar

1½ teaspoons ground caraway

1½ teaspoons ground anise

1 teaspoon ground cinnamon

4 cups almond or oat milk

¼ cup shredded unsweetened coconut

¼ cup ground pistachios

½ cup toasted sliced almonds

In a small bowl, mix together the flour, sugar, caraway, anise, and cinnamon.

Warm the milk in a medium saucepan over low heat. When the liquid just begins to simmer, gradually whisk in the flour mixture. Continue to cook over medium-low heat, whisking for 5 to 7 minutes or until the milk thickens. Test for doneness by running your finger down the back of a coated spoon. When it leaves a clear streak, remove the pan from the heat and pour the mixture into six small serving dishes (6- to 8-ounce ramekins work well) to cool. Once the meghli reaches room temperature, refrigerate, uncovered, to chill for at least 2 hours.

To serve, sprinkle each cup with layers of coconut, pistachios, and sliced almonds. The meghli can be stored, covered, in the refrigerator for up to 5 days.

MAHALABIYA · مهلبية
Arab Milk Custard and Strawberry Compote

Makes 4 servings

MAHALABIYA IS THE custardy cousin or, I would argue, maybe the original Italian dessert panna cotta. In my search for a simple but elegant dessert, I became obsessed with learning about this delicacy. It has roots in seventh-century Persia and was introduced to Arabs in tenth-century Baghdad, but it must have influenced custards beyond the region. Mahalabiya is not much different from blancmange in Europe and maja blanca in the Philippines.

Mahalabiya is the ideal canvas for showcasing seasonal fruit. When it's apricot season, I incorporate a thin layer of M'rabaa Mish Mish (page 243) on top. When it's summer, this chilled dessert gets a crown of berries, as it does in this recipe. Strawberries in this recipe can be swapped for 8 ounces of any seasonal fruit, so feel free to be creative!

This custard firms up beautifully in small glasses or ramekins. The trick to perfecting this fragrant treat is to frequently whisk the custard as it cooks, so as not to scald the milk.

Custard

2 cups whole milk

1 cup sugar

1 tablespoon gently cracked cardamom pods (about 18 pods)

¼ cup cornstarch

1 cup cold heavy cream

2 teaspoons rose water

Topping

8 ounces strawberries, hulled and quartered or sliced

1 tablespoon rose water

1 tablespoon sugar, plus more as needed

¼ teaspoon ground cardamom

1 tablespoon lemon juice (about ½ lemon)

¼ cup crushed pistachios, toasted

2 tablespoons dried rose petals (optional)

To make the custard: In a medium saucepan over medium-low heat, combine the milk, sugar, and cardamom pods and bring to a slow simmer. When bubbles start to form, turn down the heat to low and simmer for 10 minutes to steep the cardamom pods.

In a medium bowl, whisk the cornstarch into the cream until fully incorporated. Slowly whisk the cornstarch mixture into the hot milk, until it's thickened. When the mixture holds the imprint of the whisk's loops, remove it from the heat after about 5 minutes.

Add the rose water and then pour the warm mixture through a fine-mesh strainer. Transfer into four 6-ounce serving glasses or ramekins. Refrigerate, uncovered, for 4 to 6 hours to firm and chill.

To make the topping: In a medium saucepan, combine the strawberries, rose water, sugar, and ground cardamom and bring to a boil over high heat. Then turn down to low, cover the pan, and simmer for about 10 minutes to release the fruit's juices. Uncover the pan and simmer until the liquid thickens and the strawberries soften, intensify in color, and start to shrink, another 10 to 15 minutes. Add the lemon juice. Adjust the sugar to taste. Let cool.

Just before serving, spoon the compote onto each chilled custard and sprinkle with the pistachios and rose petals.

The custard can be stored, covered, in the refrigerator for up to 3 days.

LAYALI LUBNAN · ليالي لبنان
Farina Custard and Cream Trifle

Makes 12 servings

LAYALI LUBNAN TRANSLATES to "Lebanese nights," but no one seems to know quite why. I believe, as many do, that the dessert's layers celebrate the colors of the Lebanese flag: white pudding, green pistachios, and red rose petals or pomegranate seeds.

Like all trifles, this one delivers an elegance that belies its easy assembly. If the ingredients are already in your pantry, it's easy to whip up on a moment's notice, as my mother did on many occasions. She always kept a tub of Cool Whip in the freezer just for this dish. I've upgraded, layering in clotted cream on the lower deck to create a decadent but light melt-in-your-mouth custard.

This recipe is portioned for a dinner party—made in a clear dish 9 by 13-inch—but it can be easily halved and served in goblet-shaped glasses or in a clear 8 by 8-inch dish.

½ cup sugar

7 cups whole milk

1¼ cups farina or Cream of Wheat

½ teaspoon kosher salt

1 tablespoon orange blossom water

1 tablespoon rose water

1 teaspoon vanilla extract

1 cup heavy cream

1 recipe Clotted Cream (page 254)

1 cup Blossom Syrup (page 97)

½ cup ground pistachios

¼ cup pomegranate seeds (optional)

In a medium saucepan, dissolve the sugar in the milk and bring to a simmer over medium heat. When the milk starts to bubble, sprinkle in the farina, whisking vigorously. Turn down the heat to low and switch to a spatula or wooden spoon so you can scrape the bottom of the pot. Use caution when stirring, since the cereal may bubble aggressively. Add the salt, orange blossom and rose waters, and vanilla. Continue to whisk until the custard is thick enough to make whisking tiring, about 5 minutes; it should look like thick mashed potatoes. When scraping the bottom of the pot, you should be able to see the bottom of the pot for just half a second before the cereal covers the bottom again. Turn off the heat and pour the custard into a 9 by 13-inch pan or other clear-sided serving dish. Refrigerate, uncovered, for at least 1 hour to cool.

While the custard is cooling, in a chilled medium bowl or in a stand mixer fitted with the whisk attachment, beat the cream until it forms soft peaks.

When ready to assemble, remove the custard from the refrigerator and spoon in the clotted cream over the farina base, then smooth it out with a spatula or the back of a large spoon. Next, spoon in the whipped cream and smooth. Cover and chill for another 3 to 4 hours before serving to allow the creams to set.

When ready to serve, drizzle the trifle with the syrup and sprinkle with the pistachios and seeds. Serve in squares from the pan or scoops from a bowl.

The trifle can be stored, covered in plastic wrap, in the refrigerator for up to 1 week. It makes a great midnight snack or afternoon pick-me-up.

Orange and Espresso Date Cookie Bars

Makes 24 pieces

MA'AMOUL IS A quintessential holiday cookie that is enjoyed for Eid, Christmas, and Easter. In its traditional form, it is made by pressing semolina cookie dough into circular molds and filling them with nut or date paste.

In our kitchen, when the holiday season rolled around, beautiful wooden molds, traditionally used for these cookies, would surface. My sisters and I would make these labor-intensive cookies with gusto. But my mother, ever efficient, often made a Fig Newton–form of cookie bar, rolling out two layers of dough to sandwich the date filling. For years, I thought this was her own invention but, it turns out, this is another form of ma'amoul called *med*, which literally translates to "spread."

The yeast in this recipe gives a little spring to the dough. As the dough rests, it becomes easier to handle and flavors develop more fully.

This recipe is my own rendition of a traditional date filling. Espresso adds depth to the date flavor, but if you are sensitive to caffeine, you can either omit it or substitute decaf espresso. The procedure here calls for soaking the dates to soften them. If your dates are already gooey and soft, you can skip this step.

I also offer an ashta cream filling variation, what many call the queen of ashta desserts in Lebanon. It is a softer, more cake-like version of the bar, since it's drenched in syrup, and equally divine.

Dough

1½ cups/245g semolina flour

1⅓ cups/187g all-purpose flour

½ teaspoon/2g kosher salt

½ cup/60g confectioners' sugar

1 teaspoon/3g ground mahlab (see page 21) or amaretto extract (optional)

½ teaspoon/2g active dry yeast

1 cup/200g melted Clarified Butter (page 96) or softened ghee

Filling

2 cups/225g pitted dates

1 tablespoon/15g softened Clarified Butter (page 96) or ghee

1 teaspoon/3g espresso powder

½ teaspoon/2g ground cinnamon

½ teaspoon/2g orange zest

¼ teaspoon/2g ground cardamom

½ cup/120ml whole milk

2 teaspoons/12ml orange blossom water

Confectioners' sugar for dusting

To make the dough: In a medium bowl, combine the flours, salt, sugar, mahlab, and yeast. Add the butter to the dry ingredients and mix by hand or in a mixer until it forms a paste. Cover with plastic wrap or a dish towel and set aside to rest for 30 minutes.

To make the filling: While the flour mixture rests, immerse the dates in hot tap water and allow them to soak for about 10 minutes or until softened. Once they are soft, drain thoroughly and pulse them in the bowl of a food processor along with the butter, espresso powder, cinnamon,

continued

Arabiyya

orange zest, and cardamom to form a sticky paste. Refrigerate until thoroughly chilled, about 15 minutes.

After 30 minutes, the dough will have hardened, so use a wooden spoon or other utensil such as a dough cutter to break up the dough a bit. Pour the milk and orange blossom water into the flour mixture and mix until smooth. Let stand at room temperature for another 30 minutes or up to 4 hours.

Preheat the oven to 300°F. Cut four sheets of parchment paper to fit an 8 by 11-inch sheet tray.

Form the dough into a ball and divide it into 2 equal parts.

Press half the dough onto one of the sheets of parchment. Layer a second piece of parchment on top and, using a rolling pin, roll an even ¼-inch crust to the paper's edges. Remove the top layer of parchment and flip the dough into the sheet tray. Re-use the sheets of parchment and roll out the second ball of dough. Set aside.

Sandwich the date filling between two new sheets of parchment and roll into an even ¼-inch layer, out to the paper's edges. Remove the top sheet and flip the date layer onto the dough. Remove the remaining parchment. Flip the remaining dough over the date filling and remove the final sheet of parchment.

Transfer the sheet tray to the oven and bake, rotating the tray once, until the bars are light golden brown on the edges, 30 to 35 minutes. Remove the tray from the oven and, when it is cool enough to touch, cut the bars into 2 by 2-inch squares. Transfer the tray to a wire rack to finish cooling. When the ma'amoul is completely cool, dust with the confectioners' sugar before serving.

The bars can be stored in an airtight container in the refrigerator for up to 1 week.

Variation: Ashta Cream Filling

1 recipe Clotted Cream (page 254)
½ cup Blossom Syrup (page 97)
¼ cup crushed pistachios

To replace the date filling with the cream filling, follow the same assembly procedure but spread the clotted cream on the bottom layer of dough. Top with a second layer of rolled dough. Press gently and bake. After removing the pan from the oven, immediately drizzle the syrup over the top and sprinkle with the pistachios. Allow to set for 15 minutes at room temperature. When it's cool enough to touch, cut the bars into 2-inch squares and serve.

The bars can be stored in an airtight container in the refrigerator for up to 1 week.

GHRAYBE · غريبة
Blossom-Scented Shortbread Cookies

Makes about 48 loops or 24 mounds

GHRAYBE IS THE shortbread cookie of the Arab World. Made with just five ingredients, it's light in texture, yet rich in flavor. For this recipe, clarified butter is essential. My fondest memory of ghraybe is of walking through Souq al-Midan, a section of Damascus, and seeing sweet shops packed with mounds of cookies, cakes, and baklava. I was mesmerized by the shapes and sizes of all of those sweets; it took mighty self-control not to purchase every kind.

I love the cookie with its traditional pistachio stud, but for holidays I dress it up: dipped in melted chocolate for Eid or in pastel-colored white chocolate coating for Easter and for Sham El-Nasim, which is the celebration of the spring equinox and Mother's Day in the Arab world.

Here, I offer two popular ways to shape the ghraybe: loops or mounds.

NOTE • Clarified butter is essential to minimize gluten formation and achieve melt-in-your-mouth lightness.

1 cup/100g sifted confectioners' sugar
1 cup/200g softened Clarified Butter (page 96)
1 tablespoon/13ml orange blossom water
or vanilla extract
½ teaspoon/2g kosher salt
2 cups/240g sifted all-purpose flour
¼ cup whole raw pistachios for garnish

Line 2 sheet trays with parchment paper.

In a stand mixer, fitted with the whisk attachment, cream the sugar and butter on medium speed, until the mixture is pale and fluffy, 3 to 5 minutes.

Switch to the paddle attachment and decrease the speed to low. Add the orange blossom water and

salt. Incorporate the flour ¼ cup at a time to keep it from spilling out of the bowl. Continue mixing for another 5 minutes on low, scraping down the sides of the bowl from time to time, until the mixture resembles hummus.

Preheat the oven to 300°F.

To make loops: Scoop the batter onto plastic wrap in a pan or on a work surface, press it into a 4-inch block, and chill it in the refrigerator until the block firms up, about 15 minutes. Divide the block into 4 equal parts.

Using your hands, roll each quarter into about ¼-inch-thick logs. Cut each log into 3-inch segments. Bring the ends of each segment together, overlapping slightly, and connect them with a pistachio to form a loop.

To make mounds: Chill the batter in its bowl for about 10 minutes. Use a small ice cream scoop or soupspoon to form rounds about the size of a whole walnut. Flatten each dough ball slightly and press a pistachio into the center.

Place the loops or mounds on the prepared sheet trays. Bake the ghraybe until the raw sheen is gone and the cookie is baked through without browning, turning the trays at the midway point to ensure the cookies bake evenly. (The loops will take about 13 minutes and the mounds about 16 minutes.)

Transfer the cookies to a wire rack to cool. Resist the temptation to snack—these cookies must be fully cool before they're eaten.

The cookies can be stored for up to 1 week in an airtight container at room temperature.

KNAFEH · كنافة
Shredded Phyllo-Crusted Sweet Cheese

Makes 10 to 12 servings

MY GRANDFATHER WAS a man of few words, but making knafeh became for him a language of love. Although my grandmother ruled the kitchen, this Palestinian delicacy was his pride and joy. For special occasions, he would create a golden-crusted masterpiece, enclosing hot gooey cheese and soaked with sweet syrup.

He cooked the knafeh over an open fire and knew by smell and sound just when the crust was perfect, gathering praise and appreciative murmurs from everyone around him.

There are many variations of knafeh, by country and personal preference. The Lebanese, for instance, have developed a fine bread crumb crust and clotted cream filling, while the Palestinians prefer a thinner stretchy cheese filling and a shredded phyllo crust. In the Palestinian city of Nablus, they make a variation called knafeh Nabulsiyeh, which uses orange food coloring, while the same-textured knafeh in Jordan and Syria is referred to as knafeh na'ameh (Arabic for "fine" to describe the texture of the crust), made without the orange food coloring. Over time, I've developed a preference for a finer crust and creamier filling, since the cheese that makes the purely cheesy version is hard to get. I mix melting cheese with Ashta (page 254), or ricotta. It's a perfect mix of my Lebanese, Syrian, and Palestinian identity.

Among the proudest moments in my cooking career was the day my grandfather came for his first visit to my restaurant. My grandmother had passed away the year before, and grief had dampened his appetite. He's a man of high standards, and I watched nervously, as he slowly scooped a piece of knafeh and savored it. He turned to my mother and told her that my knafeh was even better than his.

NOTE • To make this recipe, you'll need to soak the cheese for 4 hours or more to leach out its salt.

TIPS • Knafeh is best eaten right out of the oven. If you want to prepare knafeh earlier in the day to serve later, cut the cheese-bake step in half (baking just long enough for the cheeses to merge into one uniform layer). Later, you can complete the bake as you would at the bottom of the recipe.

This recipe is scaled to make use of one packet of shredded phyllo and serves a crowd, because what is knafeh, after all, without a party? If this is too much and you don't have the trays for it, you can easily halve the recipe and save the remaining shredded phyllo in your freezer.

Crust
1 packet shredded phyllo dough (about 1 pound)

½ cup melted Clarified Butter (page 96) or ghee, plus more for greasing the parchment

¼ cup Blossom Syrup (page 97), cold or at room temperature, plus more for topping

Zest of 1 lemon

Filling
1 pound low-moisture whole milk mozzarella or Oaxaca cheese

1 pound ricotta cheese, drained, or 1 recipe Clotted Cream (page 254)

½ cup finely ground raw pistachios for garnish

continued

Preheat the oven to 450°F. Line one 9 by 13-inch straight-sided sheet tray or two 10-inch cake pans with parchment paper, then grease the parchment.

To make the crust: Grind the phyllo in a food processor at high speed for 3 to 5 minutes, until a fine crumb forms. Add in the butter and syrup and continue mixing, until the crust comes together like a dough.

Press the crust into the large sheet tray or divide the crust evenly between the two cake pans. Use your fingers to press the crust into an even ¼-inch layer, allowing some of the crust to come up the sides of the tray or pans. Use the back of a soup-spoon to press and smooth the crust into an even, well-packed layer; it should resemble a graham cracker piecrust.

Bake for 10 to 15 minutes or until the crust is golden brown (take care not to let the crust burn, since it will be baking a second time with the cheese filling). Remove the tray or pans from the oven and sprinkle the lemon zest evenly over the crust. Decrease the oven temperature to 350°F.

To make the filling: While the crust is baking, taste the cheese; if it tastes salty, soak it in fresh water for up 30 minutes and drain.

In a food processor on low speed, grind the mozzarella if your cheese is not already grated. Add in the ricotta and blend until you get a spreadable cheese.

Spoon the cheese filling over the crust or divide it over the two crusts if you are using two pans. Return to the oven and bake for another 15 to 20 minutes, until the cheese mixture starts to form faint golden spots; you don't want to overbake the cheese.

Remove the pan or pans from the oven and run a knife around the edges. Cover with a serving plate and carefully flip, cheese side down. Top with the syrup and garnish with the pistachios. Serve piping hot.

Date-Walnut Pie

Makes 8 generous servings

I GREW UP loving pecan pie, and this mixture of walnuts, dates, and spices is my homage to the legendary walnut pies that Mission Pie used to make, my predecessor at the location of my San Francisco restaurant. Lines formed around the corner for them as Thanksgiving approached each year.

Before we even opened our doors, people came knocking, asking if we had pie. Our displays of spinach, cheese, and meat turnovers weren't quite what they had in mind. When the first holiday season rolled around, just as the pandemic was in full swing, we decided to find out what would happen if an Arab bakery provided a seasonal pie like the good ole days.

While we do not observe holidays tied to colonization, we felt some resonance with the beloved bakers at Mission Pie and with our own traditions growing up as Arabs, celebrating this odd holiday. This pie combines the spiced walnuts and dates of our holiday ma'amoul cookies, and the crust, with traces of mahlab, completes the parallel.

Crust

1¼ cups plus 2 tablespoons/177g all-purpose flour

1 teaspoon/10g ground mahlab (optional)

1 tablespoon/13g granulated sugar

1½ teaspoons/5g kosher salt

½ cup plus 2 tablespoons/142g chilled unsalted butter, cut into ¼-inch pieces

¼ cup/60ml cold orange blossom water

Filling

2¼ cups/225g walnut halves

½ cup/120ml Blossom Syrup (page 97)

2 tablespoons/50g melted unsalted butter

1 teaspoon/5ml vanilla extract

3 eggs

¾ cup/150g lightly packed brown sugar

1½ teaspoons/5g kosher salt

1 teaspoon/2g ground cinnamon

½ teaspoon/1g ground cardamom

1 cup/200g medjool dates, finely chopped

Unsalted butter for greasing the pie tin

All-purpose flour for dusting

1 cup/240g cold heavy cream

2 tablespoons/125g sugar

1 tablespoon/15ml orange blossom water

To make the crust: In a food processor, combine the flour, mahlab, granulated sugar, and salt and pulse with the butter until just crumbly (about ten pulses). Slowly drizzle in the orange blossom water, pulsing until the dough just begins to come together, two or three 2-second pulses. Scrape the moistened dough crumble onto a floured surface and use your hands to bring the dough together. Flatten the dough into a 6-inch disk, about 1 inch thick, and wrap in plastic wrap. Chill the dough in the refrigerator for at least an hour or up to 3 days.

To make the filling: While the dough is chilling, toast the walnuts at 300°F for about 25 minutes or until they are golden and fragrant. Set aside to cool.

In a medium bowl, combine the syrup, butter, vanilla, and eggs, then whisk together with the brown sugar, salt, cinnamon, and cardamom. Fold in the walnuts and dates and set aside.

continued

Butter a 10-inch pie tin and set aside.

On a lightly floured surface, roll out the chilled dough, starting from the center, moving gently and evenly in each direction. Continue rotating the dough in quarter turns, sprinkling flour on top and beneath at each turn. Roll out the dough, until the disk is about 12 inches in diameter and ⅛ inch thick. It is important not to overwork the dough, so the fewer the touches and the faster you work, the better. You want your dough to remain cold.

Drape the dough over the rolling pin and ease it onto the prepared pie tin. Gently press the dough onto the surface of the pan, starting at the center and working out to the rim. If the dough becomes sticky, cool it in the refrigerator for 5 to 10 minutes. Using a sharp knife, trim the excess dough away from the rim. To create a rippled rim, crimp the edge of the crust using the index finger from one hand to push the edges out into the groove between the index finger and thumb of the other hand.

Preheat the oven to 325°F.

Chill the dough for another 15 minutes, then line the dough with parchment paper and weight with pie weights or dried beans. This will prevent the crust from expanding when the butter creates air pockets. Bake for 30 to 40 minutes or until the bottom crust appears completely dry. Remove the pie tin from the oven and cool to room temperature on a wire rack.

Preheat the oven to 350°F.

Pour the filling into the crust and bake for 40 to 45 minutes, until the edges are golden brown and the filling is set (when it doesn't jiggle). If your crust is getting too brown, decrease the oven temperature to 300°F or cover the edges of the crust with aluminum foil.

While the pie is baking, whip the cream with the granulated sugar and orange blossom water by hand or in a stand mixer, fitted with the whisk attachment, until the cream is thick and fluffy. Keep the cream in the refrigerator until serving.

Let the pie cool completely. Slice and serve, topped with a dollop of the whipped cream.

The pie can be stored, covered, in the refrigerator for up to 1 week.

Nut-Filled or Clotted Cream–Filled Pancakes

**Makes 16 nut-stuffed pancakes
or 32 cream-stuffed pancakes**

WHATEVER ELSE MAY have been happening in our lives, when it came time to celebrate the holy month of Ramadan, we could always count on having these festive little pancake treats. We made them two ways: stuffed with nuts, folded, fried, and served hot; pinched into cone-shaped pockets for Ashta (page 254) and pistachios and served cold. Unless, that is, my youngest sister, Manal, happened to be nearby. She loved to pull them straight from the pan and pop them into her mouth before they could even reach the pot of oil for frying or the fridge for cooling.

Making atayef is fun, and we usually got to help mix the batter and pinch them closed. When I exchange stories with other Arabs from the Levant, this dish, more than any other, represents Ramadan for us. Cooked only on one side, and porous with perfect, tiny, crumpet-like bubble pockets, atayef are velvety-soft receptacles for the filling and syrup to come.

At age seven, wanting to enter the world of adults around me, I took up fasting half days. Every once in a while, I'd forget I was fasting and pop a half-assembled atayef from my hand straight into my mouth. I'd be mortified at breaking my fast, but my mom, who thought I was too young to fast anyway, told me, "That's okay. God made you forget to give you a break; your fast is not broken."

Recipe and technique are equally important here: it's all about getting a good seal by keeping the pancakes moist and pinching them closed. The components can each be prepared ahead of time for quick assembly before serving. I recommend making the ashta using the recipe in this book (see page 254), since store-bought ashta tends to be too runny and does not hold as well in the pancakes.

Pancakes
1½ teaspoons active dry yeast
1½ cups warm water (about 100°F)
4 cups all-purpose flour
⅔ cup semolina flour
1 tablespoon plus 1 teaspoon sugar
2 teaspoons baking powder
1 teaspoon kosher salt
2 cups whole milk
2 eggs

Walnut Filling
2 cups walnuts
¼ cup sugar
¼ cup shredded unsweetened coconut
1 teaspoon ground cinnamon
1 tablespoon orange blossom water
1 tablespoon rose water

2 cups neutral oil, such as sunflower or canola, for frying, plus more for greasing the pan
1 cup Blossom Syrup (page 97), plus more for drizzling
½ cup finely ground pistachios

Cream Filling
2 recipes Clotted Cream (page 254)

To make the pancakes: Dissolve the yeast in warm water and set aside.

While the yeast is blooming, in a large bowl, combine the flours, sugar, baking powder, and salt and mix.

Once the yeast is frothy, combine it with the milk and eggs and whisk thoroughly. Pour the wet

continued

ingredients into the dry and whisk vigorously until incorporated. Let sit for at least 30 minutes at room temperature or store in the refrigerator, up to 1 day until ready to use.

To make the walnut filling: In a food processor, combine the walnuts, sugar, coconut, and cinnamon and pulse until the walnuts form a fine crumble. Drizzle in the orange blossom and rose waters and pulse until just damp (two pulses should do it). Avoid overprocessing or a paste will form.

To fry the pancakes: Set a sheet tray next to the stove along with a clean dish towel to cover the pancakes as they come out of the pan; keeping the pancakes moist enables the next step, sealing them.

Lightly oil a nonstick pan or pancake griddle and preheat the pan over medium-low heat.

For large pancakes, ladle ¼ cup batter onto the pan and swirl to form a 6-inch pancake. Remove the pancake from the heat as soon as the bottom browns, bubbles form on top, and the gloss on the batter disappears; it should be barely cooked.

For smaller pancakes, use 2 tablespoons batter and follow the same process as above to form 3-inch pancakes.

Place the pancakes cooked side down on the prepared tray and cover with the dish towel. Once the pancakes are cool, they can be stacked.

To assemble the walnut atayefs: Bring the edges of a pancake together to form a half-moon shape and pinch into a cone. Repeat, shaping and pinching all of the pancakes.

Spoon 2 tablespoons walnut filling into each cone. Tamp with a finger or spoon to fill the bottom crevice. Pinch to seal the closure around the bulging center. Repeat until all of the pancakes are filled. Cover and store until ready to fry and serve.

Set a wire rack over a sheet tray. Fill a small bowl with the syrup and another smaller bowl with the pistachios.

Fill a medium pot two-thirds full with the oil and heat until the temperature reaches 325°F on an instant-read thermometer or until a droplet of batter sizzles on contact. Fry two half-moons at a time. When the bottoms are brown and crisp, they should float to the surface. Flip and continue to fry until both sides are done, about 4 minutes total. Remove and place on a paper towel to dab away oil.

While the next batch is frying, dunk the warm atayef in the syrup. Transfer to the wire rack and sprinkle with the pistachios. Serve hot or at room temperature.

To assemble the cream atayef: Pinch the edges of a pancake halfway up, until it forms a cone. Once all the shells are formed, fill each one with the clotted cream. Keep cold until ready to serve.

When ready to serve, pour the pistachios on a small plate and press each cream mound into the nuts to form a crust. Then drizzle with the syrup. Serve cold or at room temperature.

Chapter Ten

Mashrubat · Drinks

AHWA ARABI · قهوة عربي
Arab Coffee

Makes 4 to 6 servings

IT COULD BE argued that at the very center of Arab hospitality lies a small steaming pot of coffee, inspiring a moment of shared appreciation for its complex roasted flavor compounds.

Coffee was my grandmother's ultimate gesture of generosity. When she poured it, she'd offer each person extra sugar, and the requests would come in fractional increments: one teaspoon for this aunt, a half teaspoon for that one, until everyone had their coffee just the way they liked it. The lion's share of the delicate crema—the fine foam formed from coffee's soluble oils on the surface—would usually go into the first cup. She'd hand that cup to whomever she wanted to make feel special that day. Or, if it were a routine morning, she might distribute the crema with a small pour into each cup, followed by a larger pour to bring it to the top.

Each cup had to be filled to the brim, to be lifted by the saucer and gingerly sipped to avoid spillage. I am passing along her method in the hope you will find what works for you and make it your own.

The storytelling that comes at the end might be my favorite part of drinking coffee the Arab way. Coffee reading is a ritual passed down over many centuries through the family. We use the Rorschach-like patterns in the grounds at the bottom of an inverted cup to tell the future of the person who'd drunk it. My mother is a pro. When she finishes her coffee, she flips the cup onto her saucer and lets the liquid slide away. Reading the swirling patterns in the sediment, she tells stories to friends and family. The moral for men always seems to be that a husband's role is to make his wife's life a little easier. I love the way she uses our traditional rituals to subvert patriarchy.

3 or 4 cardamom pods
2 cups water
2 heaping tablespoons finely ground Arabic or Turkish coffee beans
1 teaspoon sugar (optional), plus more to taste

Crack the cardamom pods, pressing them on a hard surface with the flat side of a knife.

Fill the rakweh or small saucepan with water. Add the cardamom pods and bring to a boil, then remove from the heat.

Spoon the coffee into the pot. The coffee will rest on top of the water. Spoon the sugar on top of the coffee.

Turn down the heat to low and ease one edge of the pot over the heat. As the water begins to boil, it will pull clumps of coffee down and start to bubble. When you see this happen, remove the pot from the heat to quiet the bubbles, rotate the pot a quarter turn, and then ease it back over the heat to bubble up a new side. Continue pulling from the heat, rotating, and returning, until all of the coffee has been incorporated. Resist the temptation to stir. Do not overboil (or boil over, for that matter)! The entire process goes pretty quickly—around 10 minutes from start to finish, depending on the size of the pot and the strength of the burner.

Remove the pot from the heat, cover with a small saucer, and set aside to rest for 3 to 5 minutes. Doing this will allow the grounds to settle and produces a frothy head of crema on top.

Pour each serving to the very brim of a small espresso cup or teacup. Add sugar to taste.

SAHLAB CHOCOLATA · سحلب شوكولاتة
Thickened Hot Chocolate

Makes 4 servings

SAHLAB IS A really delicate pudding in liquid form. The addition of chocolate to this traditional Ottoman beverage makes the ultimate winter comfort drink. Sahlab's milkiness is traditionally thickened with orchid root. (Its namesake comes from the Turkish word *salep*, which means "orchid root.")

But mass consumption has made this root harder to find, and people, including me, have turned to alternate thickening agents. If you're lucky enough to find sahlab, its floral fragrance will add something special, but I love mine just the way it is.

Sahlab reminds me of atole, an indigenous corn based–thickened drink from Mexico that becomes champurrado when spiked with chocolate. I'm not the only one who thinks so! One day, in our restaurant kitchen, while stirring a pot of sahlab, one of the cooks suggested it would be good with chocolate, and she was absolutely right. Now I always make mine with chocolate.

Sahlab can easily become vegan by swapping in almond milk for the dairy.

4 cups whole milk

3 tablespoons plus 1 teaspoon cornstarch

2 tablespoons sugar

1 tablespoon unsweetened Dutch-processed cocoa powder

1 teaspoon vanilla extract

1 tablespoon orange blossom water

½ teaspoon ground cinnamon

¼ cup chopped pistachios, walnuts, and/or almonds

2 tablespoons shredded unsweetened coconut

1 teaspoon orange zest (optional)

In a large saucepan, combine the milk, cornstarch, and sugar and whisk until smooth. Bring to a simmer over medium heat, stirring until the mixture begins to bubble, about 5 minutes. Add the cocoa, turn down the heat to low, and continue to simmer, stirring frequently until the mixture thickens considerably, about 10 minutes. It should resemble a runny pudding, forming a thick ribbon when drizzled from a spoon back into the pot.

Remove the pan from the heat and add the vanilla and orange blossom water.

Divide evenly among 4 mugs, top with the cinnamon, nuts, coconut, and orange zest, and serve immediately.

POLO · بولو
Damascus Lemonade

Makes about 8 servings

IN MY RESTAURANTS, I call this drink Damascus lemonade to give it a sense of place. Spiked with orange blossom water, it's our most popular drink, no matter the time of year.

Whenever we used to walk into the homes of friends and family in Syria and Lebanon, the first thing we'd usually hear is, "Let me get you a lemonade." Except there, they called it polo. I did a little sleuthing to try to find out why this lemonade has a distinctly non-Arab name (we don't even have the letter *P* in Arabic). The theory that I favor traces the name to a British breath mint called Polo. This adds up. The drink is distinctly minty, and it's even green in color. Calling it that is consistent with the Syrian habit of giving names to foods that make little sense but that nonetheless catch on, and before you know it, everyone's using that name.

The sweet-and-sour combo with blossom notes also makes an outstanding gin cocktail for a hot day or at any time of the year, whenever you're craving a bright, sparkling drink.

1½ cups sugar
4 cups water
2½ cups lemon juice
2 tablespoons orange blossom water
2 cups mint leaves (about 2 bunches)

In a medium pot, combine the sugar and water and heat until the sugar dissolves. Remove from the heat. Add the lemon juice and orange blossom water. Blend the mint with a small amount of the liquid and strain back in. Allow the lemonade to cool and serve over ice.

Variation: Lemonade and Gin Cocktail

Makes 1 serving

2 ounces gin
3 ounces Damascus Lemonade (recipe above)
Sparkling water to taste

Fill a glass with ice. Add the gin and lemonade. Top with the sparkling water. Stir.

KARKADEH · كركديه
Hibiscus-Rose Cooler

Makes about 8 servings

HIBISCUS'S TART, BRIGHT flavor and deep crimson color make it a favorite for punch mixes from the Latino neighborhoods of my restaurants to the swirling drink mixers on the counters of street-side eateries in Egypt. There's no denying it; this is a fun drink. I cap the animated flavors of the hibiscus flowers with a dose of rose water to turn the drink into a floral bouquet.

1¼ cups sugar
8 cups water
2 cups hibiscus flowers
2 tablespoons rose water

In a large pot, combine the sugar and water and heat until the sugar dissolves. Add the flowers and bring the mixture to a boil. Turn down the heat to the lowest setting and simmer for 15 minutes. Strain out the flowers and add the rose water. Allow to cool and serve over ice.

The drink can be stored in an airtight container in the refrigerator for up to 3 weeks.

Lebanese-Style Smoothie Parfait

Makes 4 servings

SOMEWHERE BETWEEN A drink and a dessert, these fruit refreshments are served by street corner vendors and in cafés all over Lebanon. They are a perfect treat, made with tart berries, hunks of fruit, velvety sweet avocados, blossomy Ashta (page 254), and sweet nuttiness with the honey-almond topping.

In the summer, these are loaded with up to seven different fruits, from strawberries and kiwis to mangos and bananas. Any seasonal fruit will work.

When I don't have time to make my own, I get my fix on hot afternoons by picking up tall cups of chile-lime Mexican mangonadas in the neighborhoods around my cafés or creamy avocado Vietnamese sinh tố bò in Chinatown. It's the Vietnamese version that inspired the addition of condensed milk with avocado puree to mine.

Differing densities and colors layer together into an art piece; in this case, representing the Lebanese flag. With the addition of a few black-berries on top of the fruit mix, that flag can easily become Palestinian!

2 avocados, pitted, scooped, and the flesh frozen

½ cup whole milk

2 tablespoons condensed milk

1 pound frozen strawberries or mixed berries

½ cup water, plus more as needed

1 cup fruit of your choice, cut into 1-inch cubes and/or slices (optional)

½ recipe Clotted Cream (page 254)

½ cup sliced almonds

1 tablespoon honey

In a blender, combine the avocado, whole milk, and condensed milk and puree until smooth. Pour the mixture through a fine-mesh strainer (if you want a smoother mix) and set aside.

Rinse the blender and puree the frozen berries with ½ cup water to the desired consistency.

To assemble, divide the avocado puree evenly among four tall glasses. Next divide the berry puree among the glasses, followed by the fruit cubes. Add a dollop of clotted cream on top of each glass. Sprinkle each glass with the nuts and drizzle with the honey for the final touch.

Enjoy with a spoon or a straw.

Epilogue
Arab Hospitality Is Not for Sale

IN THE SUMMER of 2018, I touched down in Aspen, Colorado, on a small jet packed with culinary celebrities whose accomplishments I had followed for years. I was about to showcase my cuisine at the Food & Wine Classic, a destination for the highest echelon of fine dining. In the wake of a vicious political backlash I'd experienced the year prior, Reem's had been named one of the Top 10 New Restaurants by *Food & Wine* magazine, which is based in Birmingham, Alabama—not exactly a hotbed of radicalism.

Despite the thrill of being honored, I hadn't wanted to go. With a three-month-old baby in tow, I was exhausted and miserable with raging postpartum depression. Still, an old, familiar doubt kept nagging at me, insisting that this might be my only shot; I might never be invited again. And so, I decided to go.

By the time I entered the showroom, my heart was racing with worry that my food would not be good enough for people who'd paid thousands of dollars for entry. My mouth turned dry at the thought of what I might say to people, many of them white and rich and with whom I felt I had little in common. Would they even know where Oakland was on a map? How would they react when I say the word *Arab* to describe my food?

The first guest to my table picked up a round of my hot grilled flatbread, spread with muhammara and sprinkled with arugula, and she immediately asked whether it was red pepper hummus. Before

I could even form my words, she grabbed another plate, raving about it, and then walked away. Learning about Arab food traditions was not on her agenda.

It had been a long time since I'd been tempted to hold my tongue just to get through an uncomfortable event, but there I was, a James Beard semifinalist for Best Chef West with a dozen other accolades behind my name worrying that I was underserving. I couldn't shake the feeling that this attention had been staged by media, hungry for a rags-to-riches story to prove that even a Brown girl like me could make it in the food world.

I had worked hard to bring the different parts of myself together at Reem's. Although the press had called my rise meteoric, I had never felt so fragmented. Was I becoming a sellout? Could I afford to say "No" to the stream of invitations arriving each month? Despite my misgivings, I kept accepting one uncompensated gig after another, hoping these opportunities would further my career. So, when Daniel Patterson, a Michelin-starred chef, offered me a waterfront restaurant partnership with no financial strings attached, it was hard to say "No." After all, I had a family to feed, and I'd put everything on the line for my bakery—every cent I'd hustled at farmers' markets, the thousands of hard-earned dollars I'd borrowed from friends and family, and the loans I'd taken from the only organizations that would lend to a first-time restaurateur. Even with all of that, it still wasn't enough to make ends meet in my single-income family.

After a series of meetings, it became official: Daniel would handle the capital and the back end of the business, and I would help him launch a restaurant called Dyafa, the Arabic word for "hospitality," and introduce my vision for Arab food and culture to Bay Area fine dining.

Daniel had built a reputation for collaborations to boost chefs of color like me, who had come from outside the mainstream of the American culinary establishment. He clearly must not have Googled me since I caught him by surprise when I asked if he considered the backlash against me a liability. He said he did not. Instead, he expressed solidarity with Palestinians. I suddenly felt more at ease.

Since I couldn't afford a maternity leave, only two weeks after my child was born, I launched a busy restaurant, leaving me no time to recuperate. In the subtext, however, the hardest challenge came not from external forces but from within. Increasingly, my brain space was taken up figuring out the power dynamics in my new partnership. It turns out, the subtext is everything.

It was not uncommon for customers to approach me at Dyafa and ask to meet the chef. I was, of course, not the person they had imagined. I tried to get comfortable in my role, but I found myself beholden to standards and etiquette I'd had no part in shaping and little power to change. I did not know how to sharpen my knife correctly or fold my hand towels properly. I didn't even like being called "the chef." In this setting, being chef meant I could walk in and say, "This sauce has to be changed." But my organizer self knew that it was the training and the systems that went into making the sauce that needed changing. The democratic values I had manifested for my bakery seemed to be going nowhere. Even the food itself seemed

to be getting away from me. When I was told my musakhan was too one-note, I could feel the blood rushing to my face, my feet tingling. Musakhan, a sweet and sour onion-sumac umami wonder, was our best-seller at Reem's. I knew better.

The headlines had turned me into a protégé, a chef whose cuisine was being "elevated," when I knew that Arab food needed no elevating. At Reem's, creating recipes with different twists had always brought me joy, but at Dyafa, as I watched my own personal recipes—those of my ancestors—undergo adaptation through a European aesthetic, it did the opposite. I realized that Arab hospitality could not be subcontracted.

Hitching my star to Daniel's had seemed like being handed the keys to the kingdom, but now, it was that very kingdom I wanted to overthrow. Its founding myth was one I had internalized, despite my training and beliefs: that wealth equals knowledge, and an accomplished white male chef knows secrets about running a successful restaurant that I didn't. It wasn't long before my doubts caught up with reality.

I came to understand that serving as a figurehead, without any real power, was turning me into a token. I knew I needed to return to the fringes, where, yes, I'd find fewer dollars but also more support. So I decided to leave the partnership and invest directly in myself and in my employees.

By the time I opened my third restaurant, in March of 2020, I had enough experience behind me to know what really mattered. I'd learned to inspire employees around my values, and I had built a dedicated, cross-trained, mission-oriented team. I'd opened one restaurant to death threats and another through an ill-fated partnership. I felt ready to open a bakery on my own terms, in San Francisco's Mission District, in the very same neighborhood where we had launched our first farmers' market stand five years earlier.

But on opening day, I found myself holed up in the bunkerlike basement of my restaurant, flipping through an order from the mayor, reading the term *social distancing* for the first time. With bills mounting, payroll looming, and new debt, I wondered how I could stay open. But also, I wondered, how could I afford to close? Later that same afternoon, the governor issued shelter-in-place orders and mandated the closure of all restaurants.

The next day, I lay in bed, feeling once again that it was all over. Maybe it was not possible, after all, to revolutionize the food system. Maybe the time had come to shutter my doors and walk away.

The fourth night of the shutdown marked a watershed moment in my experience as an organizer and business owner. My employees summoned their courage and sent me a letter demanding answers. I had none. What would be my plan? And what would become of them? The prospect of failing my workers felt devastating, but their collective action also inspired me.

Grief has a way of clarifying purpose and values. I did not start Reem's to own a restaurant but rather to build a transformative space, where everyone has a voice; for my employees, my customers, my community, and, not least of all, for myself. I did it to build a strong, resilient community, using the foods of my heritage as a tool. On a perfect day, I would walk through my kitchen and see Nino, who could only speak Tagalog when he first joined Reem's, patiently teaching Angela, newly arrived from El Salvador with no kitchen experience, solid knife skills. I would taste Mariana's Oaxacan mole, prepared for a staff meal, and see her face light up at my suggestion that one day, she, too, could have her own restaurant.

I would hear Armando's hysterical laugh from the back as he danced to cumbia, while doing the day's inventory. Reem's is made up of all of my team members' rich experience and knowledge. Their talent and dedication are the real secrets behind our success; they are the very heart of Reem's. So, I knew I could not walk away from them; I had to stay and fight.

The pandemic of 2020 presented an opportunity for reinvention. It gave us a test kitchen to try out new models for a liberatory food system, one in which everyone's dreams are fed.

In the enterprise I envision, all workers' knowledge, experience, and cultures are assets, and each is equipped with the tools and confidence to build wealth. Together, we can heal and build the world we dream of, where each one of us can live a life with love, dignity, and self-determination.

If the pandemic has taught me anything, it's that we have the power to care for and protect one another. It turns out, we've had that power all along. By tapping into the wisdom of our ancestors and taking lessons from the land, we can build the resilience to thrive in even the hardest times. While change is inevitable, one thing remains true: no matter what happens next, Arab hospitality is not for sale.

Where I Go for Ingredients

AL'ARD

Al'Ard supports Palestinian farmers to find a market and a fair price. In addition to excellent extra-virgin olive oil, Al'Ard has grown to be a premium supplier of Palestinian-made products such as za'atar, freekeh, and tahini, all available in the online store.
www.alardproducts.com

BURLAP & BARREL

Burlap & Barrel is a single-origin spice company that partners directly with small farmers worldwide to provide the most equitably sourced and visually striking spices available to home cooks and professional chefs alike. You can find the spices on the Burlap & Barrel website; it's easy to get hooked on the selection. The company sources a significant number of spices from the Arab world and have many of the things you'll need in this book.
www.burlapandbarrel.com

CANAAN

Canaan is a network of thousands of artisan farms across Palestine with a mission to preserve generations of Palestinian foodways and the vibrant ecosystem of farming essential to Palestinian culture. Canaan products include olive oil, spices, grains, and fun tapenades. You can purchase directly on the website or find the products in select grocery stores in the United States.
www.canaanusa.com

CORTAS

Cortas is a Lebanese company that specializes in canned and bottled specialty goods, including but not limited to beans, pickles, essences, and preserves. This company is my go-to for rose and orange blossom water, pomegranate molasses, and fruit jams that are not as readily available in the United States, like quince jam. They also make ful madammas and tahini. Find the products at specialty and Arab grocers or purchase them online.
www.cortasfood.com

CORTO OLIVE OIL

Corto is a family-owned olive orchard in Lodi, California. What sets them apart is their harvest, which I joined for a day during a brief window in October.
www.corto-olive.com

DIASPORA CO.

This spice company is hands down the best place to get your turmeric, in addition to a whole array of single-origin spices directly from small farmers in

India leading the way in regenerative agriculture. Founded by third-generation Mumbai native Sana Javeri Kadri, this fierce woman-led business is on a mission to decolonize the spice trade. You can purchase directly from the website.
www.diasporaco.com

JUST DATE SYRUP

Just Date Syrup is a doctor- and women-led company in the Bay Area demystifying sugar and inspiring a future generation to live our healthiest lives while enjoying the natural sweetness of Mother Earth. This date syrup is a staple in my pantry, and I love swirling it into tahini to make a sweet dipping sauce for my bread. The company also added pomegranate molasses to its repertoire.
www.justdatesyrup.com

KAROUN DAIRIES

Karoun is located in San Fernando, California, and makes the specialty cheese and other dairy products that are essential to Eastern Mediterranean and Latin American cuisine. I rely on them for cheese that is hard to find, like Akkawi and Armenian string cheese (my favorite!). The company has an online platform that allows you to plug in your location to find the nearest source.
www.karouncheese.com/index/where-to-buy

KRONOS

After trying a lot of phyllo dough, I found that this brand makes the most consistent crispy golden baklava. This product used to be called Sinbad, so searching either name on your online engine will get you the ordering forms you need. You can buy it in bulk as it keeps in the freezer for many months.

OHANYAN'S

Ohanyan's is a family-run business in Fresno, California, specializing in specialty cured meats such as sujuk (a cured spiced sausage, similar to chorizo) and basturma (a cured, thinly sliced meat, similar to prosciutto). They are available at many Armenian and Arab grocery stores but can also be found online through a variety of Eastern Mediterranean marketplaces.
www.ohanyans.com

TARAZI

Today, more and more delicious small-batch artisanal tahini brands are making it to store shelves, but my go-to, for its consistent nutty taste and stir-ability, is a bigger brand called Tarazi. It's available at many Arab grocery stores and even some mainstream grocery store aisles. But you can also purchase it online.
www.tarazifoods.com

Giving Thanks

SHUKRAN! THANK YOU!

Words alone cannot capture my thanks. For that, I would need food. And justice. And love. To all the people who have stood by me, held space for me, and experienced joy with me, you have my infinite gratitude.

My mama, Iman, equally powerful against adversaries and generous beyond measure. You are my rock.

My baba, Naim, your knack for knowing when I need to be connected to my roots has fed me time and again.

My sisters, Dalyah and Manal, who fill my life with pleasure. You are the orange blossom syrup to my knafeh.

My aunts and uncles, near and far, your meals and laughter lift and inspire me.

My partner, J, whose motto, "Don't stop, don't quit," has pulled me through hard times. Your grace and ease safeguard me. Our beautiful son, Zain. Who knew the human heart could love like this? In the words of poet Ellen Bass, I've become one of the ". . . mothers, with their hearts beating outside their bodies."

My grandparents, Nabigha and Tahsin, you demonstrated that the meals we eat together can feed our souls along with our bodies.

My Uncle Eyad, whose homemade focaccia was the first, and best, I've ever tasted. Asker-of-hard questions, you helped crack open my defenses under the refuge of California's redwoods.

The Reem's team, past and present, I have learned from every one of you. Hai, my fairy god-mother, your administrative wizardry made space for the important things. Zaynah, my ride-or-die, who brings Reem's to life with me. You embody the truest spirit of Arab hospitality.

La Cocina staff and entrepreneurs. Caleb Zigas, you went out of your way to drum up support each time I reached the brink, and Emiliana Puyana and Blake Kutner, you taught me how to cook bold and refined dishes that defied my insecurities.

My guardian angel Ghassan Haddad, you drove your masonry and tools up from Southern California to build me the hearth from which a thousand loaves would rise.

All the entrepreneurship programs (there were a lot): ICA Fund Good Jobs, Food Systems 6, Centro Community Partners, Women's Initiative, you each had a hand in nurturing my inner entrepreneur.

My unofficial uncle Jess Ghannam, who provided support in just the way I needed it and doubled down when the going got tough. You believed in me even when my own belief faltered.

The fierce activists who continue to tell the truth about the Palestinian struggle. I am blessed to walk in your footsteps.

Rasmea Odeh, you remind me to find joy in the struggle, even when I'm afraid.

My organizing community, past and present, you encourage me to take a chance on food.

Arab Resource and Organizing Center—Lara Kiswani, Sami Kitmitto, Chris Lymbertos, Sharif Zakout, and the crew—you continue to be my political home. Center for Third World Organizing, East Bay Alliance for a Sustainable Economy, School for Unity and Liberation, Residents United for a Livable Emeryville, and SEIU, your trainings in ground-up organizing are part of everything I do.

My allies—Jewish Voices for Piece, International Jewish Anti-Zionist Network, Critical Resistance, ANSWER, Third World for Black Power—always ready with a flatbed truck and microphone to amplify our voices. Thank you for having my back against my harassers and fighting for a more liberatory abolitionist future.

Left Wing Fútbol Club, you build community while fighting imperialism. A special shout-out to mama Sita Kuratomi Bhaumik, you schemed menus with me for team dinners while we peeled thousands of chickpeas for my first pop-ups.

Alicia Garza, you summoned your own food origins in the foreword and inspire me to live my best life even in the hard work of transformation.

Palestinian women cookbook writers Laila El-Haddad, Joudie Kalla, Reem Kassis, and Rawia Bishara, you paved the way for our voices to be heard.

Bay Area chef community, you accepted me as one of your own, despite my unconventional path to food, and opened opportunities of which I could only have dreamed.

IMEU and Life and Thyme crew, you helped tell stories that I didn't even know I had. And all the food media writers and producers, you made space for my voice in the face of death threats and raging opposition.

My high school history teacher Bill Schechter, you taught me that we live our history and first helped me find the words to capture it.

All the kick-ass women who helped bring this book to life:

Michelle Minori, chef extraordinaire, you tested every recipe and added you own special flair to deepen flavors. I am thankful for your mentorship.

Alana Hale, Jillian Knox, and Fanny Pan, you rocked the photoshoots and brought laughter and dance into the mix. Cece Carpio, you captured the essence of my story in your beautiful illustrations.

My agent, Rica Allanic, you followed my work from across the country and kept after me until I finally agreed to write this book.

My editor Kelly Snowden and art director Betsy Stromberg, along with the rest of the Ten Speed Press crew. Your enthusiasm and eye for beauty provided the cracks that let the light in during the darkness of a pandemic.

Emily Timberlake, you came to my side when I was figuring out what this book would be and offered wit and wisdom as an editor and lover of food and justice.

And finally, my Aunt Emily. Yours was another kitchen that I grew up in. Thank you for excavating family stories with me, distilling meaning and rhyme from the way the world has shaped me. Thank you for believing in this project and taking a chance to help me bring it to life, with your heart wide open.

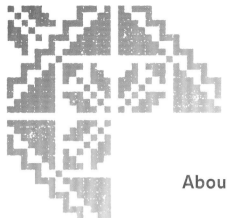

About the Author

REEM ASSIL IS a Palestinian-Syrian entrepreneur based in Oakland, California, and founder of Reem's California, a nationally acclaimed bakery and restaurant inspired by her passion for Arab street-corner bakeries and the vibrant communities they feed. Reem has garnered an array of top accolades in food, including as a back-to-back James Beard Semifinalist for Best Chef: West (2018/2019), StarChefs' 2019 San Francisco Rising Star Restaurateur, *San Francisco* magazine's 2018 Chef of the Year, and a *San Francisco Chronicle* 2017 Rising Stars Chef. Reem built her food career at esteemed worker cooperative Arizmendi Bakery & Pizzeria and is a graduate of the women's food business incubator program La Cocina, through which she had the privilege of learning from some of the Bay Area's most notable chefs.

Prior to her food career, Reem spent more than a decade organizing workers and residents in marginalized communities to have voices on the job and in their neighborhoods. Combining her lifelong experience fighting for justice and twenty years in the nonprofit and food industry, Reem's current work sits at the intersection of her three passions: Arab hospitality, community building, and social justice.

Reem chose to write this book with her aunt Emily Katz, who is Jewish. Emily works in nonprofit public interest communications and advocates for social justice. She grew up in rural Northern California, beyond Humboldt County's electric poles and phone lines, eating the vegetables that her family grew on its homestead and tending the goats and chickens that they raised beneath their cabin.

The process of book writing was new to them both, but the exercise of self-discovery and reflection was something Reem and Emily had been doing together for most of Reem's life.

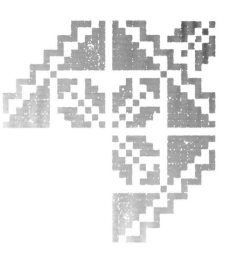

Index

To Arab women—future and present, with our many intersectionalities—this book is for you.

Library of Congress Cataloging-in-Publication Data
is on file with the publisher.

Hardcover ISBN: 978-1-9848-5907-5
eBook ISBN: 978-1-9848-5908-2

Printed in China

Editor: Kelly Snowden
Production editor: Kimmy Tejasindhu
Art director and designer: Betsy Stromberg
Production designers: Mari Gill and Mara Gendell
Typeface(s): Set Sail Studio's Avallon, Fontfont's
    FF Balance Pro, and FontSmith's FSAlbert Arabic
Production manager: Serena Sigona
Prepress color manager: Jane Chinn
Food stylist: Fanny Pan
Prop stylist: Jillian Knox
Photo retoucher: Chris Dirker
Copyeditor: Dolores York
Proofreader: Amy Bauman
Indexer: Amy Hall
Publicist: David Hawk
Marketer: Samantha Simon

10 9 8 7 6 5 4 3 2 1

First Edition